INDIAN DIASPORA IN THE ERA OF GLOBALISATION

INDIAN DIASPORA IN THE ERA OF GLOBALISATION

Editor

S.K. Jain

KALPAZ

Indian Diaspora in the Era of Globalisation

ISBN : 978-81-7835-923-6

Published in 2012 in India by
Kalpaz Publications
C-30, Satyawati Nagar,
Delhi - 110052
E-mail: kalpaz@hotmail.com
Ph.: 9212729499

Lasser Type Setting : Rajender Vashist, Delhi
Printed at : Chawla Offset Printers, Delhi

Dedication

Dedicated to **Prof. Imtiaz Ahmad**, a Teacher and a True Friend, Philosopher and Guide in my journey from a student/researcher to teacher from JNU to Delhi University.

Contents

PART C : REGIONAL DYNAMICS

Foreword

The study of the Indian Diaspora has become attractive subject for the social scientists. However this area continues to remain confused and ill-defined. If it has to achieve a level of maturity it must begin to start paying greater attention to theoretical and methodological dimensions.

What constitutes the Indian Diaspora? There is as yet no clarity on this question. The term continues to be applied to differing populations whose history varies widely. On a superficial view, I am able to identify four or five groups who would technically qualify to be characterized as the Indian Diaspora but differ as to the sources, motivations, compulsions and consequences for host societies as well as the migrating groups.

1. The groups of Indiana origin who migrated to the British colonies during the nineteenth century in response to the demand for cheap labour to work at the plantations that were being developed. These migrant groups were not necessarily migrating from an economically depressed area to an area of great economic prosperity. They were in the nature of forced labour and were covered into migrating on limited incentives that the colonial rulers might have offered.
2. The groups of Indian origin who either accompanied the colonial masters who repatriated to their home country when power was transferred to colonial hands or who followed later taking advantage of the citizenship rights. Early Indian settlers in England broadly belong to this category.
3. The groups of Indian origin living in Sri Lanka. These groups belong to two distinct categories: those descendants of the Tamils who went to Sri Lanka during the rule of the Hindu kings a from the sixth to the thirteenth centuries and are known as the Jaffna Tamils, and those who went during the nineteenth century as indentured labouers to work on tea plantations. Curiously enough these groups are not rèckoned as part of the India Diaspora.

4. The groups of Indian origin who migrated to West Asia and Gulf countries to provide services and work as labourers when those countries launched upon building infrastructure from the sixties onwards. These groups went to West Asia and the Gulf countries on short-term service contracts and could not be called permanent settlers as the citizenship laws of those countries did not permit groups of Indian origin to settle there, except in very special and limited cases. However, these groups are also often characterized as a part of the Indian Diaspora.
5. Those groups of Indian origin who took advantage of the unsettled political situation arising out of Sikh terrorism in the wake of the demand for Khalistan. Taking advantage of the refugee laws abroad. These groups sought political asylum in whichever country they felt they had a better chance for their applications to be accepted, but their ultimate destination was UK or US. If they succeed to camouflage their papers, they ultimately managed to land up in Canada and the US.
6. Those groups of Indian origin who self-consciously decided to move to the US, and subsequently Canada, in search of greener pastures. They were already well-off and highly qualified (most of them were engineers, doctors, lawyers, scientist and professionals of different kinds) and their principle motivation for migration came from the better opportunity available in an advanced countries like US. They are described as much touted NRIs or Pravasi Indians and enjoy overwhelming presence in the Indian Diaspora because of the economic clout that they are suppose to posses.

These are a far-too diverse set of communities to the included in a single category called the Indian Diaspora. It is time that a more discriminating approach is adapted to understand their varied historical experiences, the problems they faced at the time of their original migration, the responses of the host communities towards them, and their relative strengths and weaknesses in contemporary times. This kind of discriminating analysis is necessary to map out their differentiated performance in relation to the host communities as well as the category called the Indian Diaspora.

Dr. S.K. Jain has put together this collection of articles. Obviously, he has not been able to deal with these different dimensions, which is often difficult in a collective volume, but his book should act as a spur to subsequent researchers in this area.

New Delhi, **Prof. Imtiaz Ahmad (Retd.)**
30 January, 2012 **JNU**

Acknowledgements

The present work is the out come of the National seminar on "Indian Diaspora in the era of Globalization : Implications for India" organised jointly by Foundation for India Development Initiative (NGO) New Delhi and Saheed Bhagat Singh College (Evening) University of Delhi at New Delhi in February 2009. In the process of making this seminar successful I am thankful to several people.

First of all I am thankful to Indian council of Social Science Research (ICSSR) New Delhi for the financial grant to organise this seminar. I am also thankful to Saheed Bhagat Singh College (Evening) for partial financial assistance and particularly principal Dr. P.K. Khurana for his encouragement to enhance the academic activities of the college. I am thankful to Prof. Imtiaz Ahmad, Prof. Zoya Hasan, Prof. Kamal Chenoy, Prof. Narang, Prof. S.N. Malakar of JNU for their encouragement and participation in the seminar. I am also thankful to Prof. Md. Badrul Alam, Dr. Anisur Rahman of Jamia Milia Islamia University New Delhi for their participation and contribution of the papers. I am thankful to all the contributors of the seminar without which this would not have taken the present shape of book. I am thankful to all my friends, colleagues and students from JNU, DU and different walks of life to make seminar more lively and meaningful. I am also thankful to all my family members for their good wishes in this endeavor. Finally I am also thankful to Kalpaz Publications, form with minimum time unlike many publishing house. At last but not the least I would like to express my sense of gratitude to Dr. Amuj Mahapatra CEO Development Facilitator (NGO) for all the logistic needed to organise this kind of event Finally I would like to thank all those who could not figure here but certainly not forgotten for their direct or indirect contribution towards the completion of this work.

S.K. Jain

Introduction

The Indian Diaspora generally evokes a common heritage underpinned by a sense of longing for the mother country. In the era of globalisation, a new relationship has emerged between the motherland and the overseas nationals popularly called as diaspora. They have emerged as dynamic factors shaping the relations between the host and home societies.

Over 24 million Indians live outside their home country perhaps the largest ongoing migration in the world. What makes it so wonderful is the diversity of the flow. Manpower and brainpower, expertise and acumen form this global diaspora and makes it unique in history. There used to be a joke that the reason why Indians didn't play football was that if you give them a "corner" they would open a teashop. The humour of that sporting reference to Indian enterprise has lost none of its significance; on the contrary, it is the strength and bedrock of the many splendoured successes of the Indian wanderlust. Indians not only built teashop but created empires right across the globe. We should feel proud of this because no diaspora has come close to this kind of global spread and endured so much hardship, sacrifice and deprivation and yet maintained its customs and traditions through the centuries.

The choice of 9 January for the celebration of Pravasi Bhartiya Divas coincided with the day when Mahatma Gandhi returned to India form South Africa after experimenting his satyagrah for the first time by laying the foundation for the dismantling of apartheid. As Mahatma Gandhi changed the course of history in South Africa and India, the great Indian diaspora too can play a major role in the building of a glorious future for India and the world. Pandit Nehru once remarked that wherever there is an Indian, a bit of India goes with him. "Indian diaspora have truly taken Indian culture, society, tradition, not to mention films and Indian cuisine. Our common Indian culture and, our Bhartiyata is the bond that unites all of us who belong to Bhartvarsh, the great global Indian family, a global *jugalbandi* between the Bharatvasis and Bhartvanshis".

Now the responsibility has come on our part as a government and people of India to do our bit to help our brothers and sisters abroad to feel that we are concerned with their genuine problems. The Government of India has taken some policy decisions (Dual citizenship, investment etc.) and is serious on many more but as responsible citizens we should make them feel that we are one and we stand united by our Indianness. However, the great Indian diaspora must not forget what Mahatma Gandhi told the Indian community in November 1927 in Ceylon, "I would leave one or two thoughts with you before I leave Colombo. Since you are earning your bread in this country, I would ask you to live as sugar in milk which is full to the brim doesn't overflow when sugar is gently added to it, the sugar accommodating itself in the milk and enriching the taste, in the same way I would like you to live in the Island so as to enrich the life of the people in whose midst you are living."

The present volume is an outcome of a seminar on "Indian Diaspora in the era of Globalisation: Implications for India" jointly organised by Dr. S.K. Jain, Member Secretary of Foundation of India Development Convener Academic Affairs Committee, Shaheed Bhagat Singh (E) College, University of Delhi on 21st-22nd February 2009. Fourteen papers of the volume are divided in three broad categorizes : (1) Theoretical Perspectives, (2) Sub-national Identities and (3) Regional Dynamics.

First part of the book deals with various theoretical aspects of diaspora in general and particularly those concerned with Indian Diaspora. This part consists of 7 chapters written by renowned scholars, policy makers and activists. Chapters of this part address a range of theoretical issues.

With the strength of 24 million people spread all across the world, Indian Diaspora has attracted considerable attention of scholars of the diasporic studies. They have migrated in different periods and in different capacities. Today they are known not only for their economic prosperity but also political successes in some of the countries and remarkable contribution in enhancing socio-cultural linkages between their motherland and land of their destiny.

Dr. S.K. Jain in the chapter entitled 'Indian Diaspora-An Overview', categorizes migration pattern of Indians in colonial period and also analyses trends of migration in post independent period. The chapter begins with analysis of the broader definition of the term 'Diaspora' and significance of various issues pertaining to diasporic communities in increasingly becoming a part of the globalised world. In order to explain the concept of "Indian Diaspora"; he analyses various related terms such as "Overseas Indians"; Indian National Overseas or Non-Resident Indians (NRI); Persons of Indian Origin (PIOs) and Persons Resident in India (PRI). Further, he investigates that in 19th century forced migration occurred under either of the three systems viz. Indentured, Kangani and Maistry system of Contracts. On the other hand, the large scale Indian migration of the twentieth Century has been directed towards the industrially developed advanced societies of Europe, North America and West Asia. According to the author, contrary to the nineteenth century's migrants, the twentieth century migrants are free passages causing 'brain drain' to motherland. Nevertheless, he believes that economic potential of Indian Diaspora is of immense help to India and the periodic remittances and investment are largely helpful for India's economic development.

Mr. Shivam in his chapter entitled 'Diaspora: An Introduction', traces origin of the term 'Diaspora'. He argues that, though originally used in terms of Jews migration the term can be gainfully employed for the study of any migrant community having sense of identity with their motherland. He investigates common features of Diaspora as listed by Robin Cohen and discusses typology developed by Cohen, Vertovec and other scholars. He also examines process of social adjustment and identity issues of migrant communities.

In the era of globalisation, economic issues have occupied dominant position. In this context monetary transfer done by migrant communities to their motherland in the form of investment, private transfer to their family or in other invisible forms becomes crucial.

Dr. Rajneesh Kumar Gupta and Mr Rahul Nath Chaudhury in the chapter Migrant Communities and Remittances- Indian Experience, highlights importance of remittances. The authors analyses remittances sent by migrant communities at global scale and compare it with Indian experiences. They argue that, although, in the last few years India has emerged as the largest recipient of remittances, it is still below the potential They believe that development of a hassle free and friendly system is required to pull remittances up to the mark.

Citizenship of migrant communities has been an issue of great contention. Since this is directly linked with the nationality and loyalty of a person or community. Policy makers have been always in a dilemma whether migrant communities should be solely responsible to their host land or they should have a say way back in the affairs of the motherland. In this backdrop, decision of government of India to grant dual citizenship to Indian Diaspora evoked serious debate. Dr. Ruchi Tyagi in the chapter on Dual Citizenship and Indian Diaspora, examines this issue. In view of developing a comprehensive approach, she analyses various relevant themes viz. Nationality and citizenship, Nationality in International Law, Citizenship Issues in the Constituent Assembly, Citizenship in the Indian Constitution, Dual Nationality in Some Other Countries, The Citizenship (Amendment) Act, 1986 and Dual Citizenship to Indian Diaspora. A substantial part of the chapter is devoted in analyzing merits and demerits of dual citizenship.

Mahatma Gandhi the 'Father of the Nation' is often regarded as an exemplary example of planetary citizenship and a role model of 'diaspora'. Born and brought up in a small town of Gujarat state of India, he went to South Africa as a free passage. He faced brutal racial hostility and decided to raise his voice against such discrimination. Thus, South Africa could be considered as the birth place of 'Gandhian ideas'. Celebration of Pravasi Bhartiya Divas on 9th January- the day when Mahatma Gandhi came back to India-truly symbolizes Indian urge to similar contribution from all offsprings of mother India. In the chapter 'Gandhi and Indian Diaspora', S.N. Sahu acknowledges that our freedom struggle under the leadership of Mahatma Gandhi was an extension of his first Satyagaraha launched in South Africa on the strength of Indian settlers. He argues that Indian Diaspora more than being a brain bank' is a vast reservoir of talent, innovation and culture. It is a vibrant and lively source of our civilisational values. Ideals of Mahatma Gandhi and his vision based on care and compassion for the larger humanity could be usefully employed in refutation of the theory of clash of civilisations, dismantling terrorism and all form of discrimination and injustice. Potentials of a vibrant and widespread Indian Diaspora in this regard need to be utilized.

It is an inevitable truth that migrant people don't go alone; instead they carry distinct socio-cultural traditions as well. 'Art' is an important segment of such socio-cultural heritage. Arshiya Sethi in the chapter entitled 'Rhizome Roots: The Indian arts and the Indian Diaspora' highlights some of the important facets of Indian Art that has been popularised by Indian Diaspora and give a sense of Indian-ness to them. Using analogy of rhizome roots, the author poses three questions and provides answers to those in her analysis: (i) How they settle in foreign soils; (ii) How they adapt, integrate and mature under international influences, a study of identity and assimilation, and iii) How they return or reconnect to their mother culture. The author believes that in the past, the spread of Buddhism, and the eastward impact of Indian culture and religion, left a footprint in Far East Asia. In our generation, Indian performing arts such as Chutney music, Bhangara, Qawali and so on, have spread all across the world like rhizome roots. She concludes that pluralism of Indian art, better described as *"Ganga-Jamuna tehzeeb"* could help us to over come from negative forces of globalisation. In a similar way, Mr. Rakesh Kumar Patel in his chapter, Cinematic Representation of Indian Diaspora analyses representation of Indian Diaspora in the Bollywood cinema from its inception till date. He focuses on the expansion and accessibility of Bollywood films around the world from its emergence to present time, the chronologically. One could observe in the chapter that forms and content of films depicting Diaspora are being changed and its universe is also expanding around the globe. His work vividly explores about Bollywood's expansion and includes various facts to prove it. Further he explains impact of liberalisation and globalisation on Bollywood cinema.

In any pluralistic country many identities co-exist. This is quite evident in case of India and thus it is often said that India is a land of 'unity in diversity'. This phenomenon generates sub-national identities obtainable under the umbrella of a common national identity. In case of Indian Diaspora we see many of such kind of sub-national identities based on region, religion, language, and so on. Second part of the volume is dedicated to such sub-national identities. This part is a collection of two scholarly chapters contributed by academicians of Jawaharlal Nehru University (JNU), New Delhi.

Caste system and caste based hierarchy is a bitter truth of Indian society. Dalits have been harsh victims of this exploitative division. Indian Diaspora has been analysed through a variety of socio-cultural identities. However, there is scarcity of study on Dalit Diaspora. Dr. Vivek Kumar in the chapter 'Dalit Diaspora: Invisible Existence', takes up this issue. The author examines a variety of issues such as definition of the term 'Dalit', migration and formation of Dalit Diaspora, causes of migration of Dalit, old and new Dalit Diaspora, caste discrimination in Dalit Diaspora, Dalit Diaspora and their organisations, impact of globalisation on Dalit Diaspora, role of Dalit Diaspora in organizing international Dalit conferences and bringing up issue of self esteem. Author argues that presence of Dalit Diaspora has been often unnoticed and his work is an effort to bring this crucial dimension in focus of mainstream academia. He believes, though, this work is any way not an exhaustive study of Dalit Diaspora but this can be taken as a starting material for further researches.

The next chapter provides practical example of arguments of previous chapter. Tenepalli Hari in his chapter 'British Malay: the untold saga of Untouchable Plantation Coolies' analyses dehumanizing conditions of the untouchable plantation coolies in British Malay. Author believes that under the influence of false British promises, untouchable plantation coolies migrated to Malaya. Life in British Malaya plantation was sold as being a paradise on earth compared to the social conditions in India. However, it proved to be hell. The social system of the Indian village reappeared. The Brahminised non-brahmins perfectly fitted the interests of the British colonial forces and basic human rights were denied to the untouchable coolies.

Indian Diaspora is not a monolithic community. They left the motherland in different capacity and in different phases. Clear and contrast differences are visible in terms of their presence in various parts of the globe. In some countries they have made remarkable political achievements or being considered as an economically affluent community. On the other hand, in several places they have been harsh victims of racial hatred and struggling to secure even their human rights. Thus, regional dynamics of Indian Diaspora cannot be overlooked. Part C is dedicated to this vital aspect. Five chapters of this part represent four different regions-Gulf, the United States, East Africa and South Africa.

Prof. Mohammed Badrul Alam in his chapter entitled Beyond the 'Imagined Community': A Study of the Indian Diaspora in the United States observes the status of Indian Diaspora in the United States by a set of sociological parameters. He has used the terminology of Bendict Anderson- 'Imagined Community' to asses Indian-ness among Indian communities, especially among migrants of aftermath of the landmark 1965 immigration legislation *of USA. He believes that t*he Indians are an interesting group among the cluster of newly formed immigrant communities; their level of educational standard is particularly impressive; the rapidity of consolidation of economic indicators is remarkable; and the internal mobility of the Indian community is very much viable. However, in general they value Indian social institution in personal life and it is visible in public life through 'ethnic associations'. The author describes this trend with the *'Phir Bhi Dil Hai Hindustani'* syndrome.

In the eleventh chapter Prof. Prakash C. Jain explores linkages of Indian Diaspora in Canada their motherland. His work entitled 'Diaspora and Motherland: Explorations into the Role of Indo-Canadians in India's Welfare Programmes' provides sociological analysis of the role of the Indo-Canadian individuals/ NGOs which are active in the welfare activities in India in such areas as education, environment, health care and aging, community and infrastructural development. In pursuit of realizing research objectives he has used primary as well as secondary data in the greater Vancouver area, which hosts the oldest and the second largest Indo-Canadian community in Canada.

The Gulf is another important region where the Indian Diaspora lives in a significant number. Recent estimates indicate that there are about 5 million Indians who are resident in the region. Majority of them are first generation immigrants holding Indian passport and having their strong family ties in India. Thus, it is not surprising that India gets the largest value of remittances from this region. Dr. Anisur Rahman in his chapter entitled 'Gulf NRIs as a Factor in Strengthening Indo-Gulf Relations' recognizes importance of the Indian Diaspora in promotion of Indo-Gulf ties. He believes that presence of Indian Diaspora is mutually beneficial to India and Gulf region. They are the major source of remittances and foreign exchange to India. On the other hand, Gulf countries are benefited by the NRIs' vital contribution in their economies. The author concludes that the population mobility has had positive impact on India's employment, balance of payments, commodity export, business profits and government earnings. The inflow of the Gulf remittances is playing a major role in this direction. The Indian business and government have been benefited in many ways. It is thus fully realised that Gulf NRIs are assets to the host and home countries.

Dr. Rajneesh Kumar Gupta, in his chapter on Indian Diaspora in East Africa: Entrepreneurships and Philanthropy examines entrepreneurships among Indian Diaspora in East Africa. He argues that Indians have enjoyed a long association with the region and British colonialism has only boosted migration process. The hard work and courage of Indians introduced monetary system, railways and brought modernisation in East Africa. Majority of Indians migrated their as indenture labours but their entrepreneurship skills made them economically affluent community. He contends to the popular notion that Indians are acting as a 'middleman minority' engaged in exploiting indigenous people and argues that Indians have been sharing their economic prosperity for the well being of their fellow indigenous people through various means of philanthropy.

In a similar line, Ms. Ruchita Beri in her chapter entitled Indian South Africans: Political Affiliations in the Post Apartheid era, traces presence of Indians in South Africa as old as two thousands years ago. Now, roughly 1.2 million people of Indian origin constitute about 2.5 percent of the total South African population. Though, numerically a tiny minority, they have been torch bearers in the political awakening of South Africa. During the struggle against Apartheid, Indians generally sided with African National Congress (ANC). However, post-Apartheid period witnessed a remarkable shift. The author examines voting behaviour of 'Indian South Africans' as she prefer to be called the Indian Diaspora in South Africa. She drew the conclusion that in the first two elections, votes of Indian Diaspora were divided between the White and the Black parties and ANC could not secure much votes of Indian communities. Further, in a voting intention survey held in 2002 majority of Indians opted for "undecided" or "would not vote" category. It indicates alienation of Indians from South African politics, in general and particularly from ANC. The author carefully scrutinizes this trend with the existing socio-economic realities of South Africa.

PART A : THEORETICAL PERSPECTIVES

1

Indian Diaspora: An Overview

S.K. Jain

When we pronounce the word "Diaspora" we feel a sense of affection and affinity. This is also the case of India Diaspora. The concept of Diaspora has acquired a renewed importance in the modern era of globalisation. The advent of globalisation has affected a change in the way the diasporic community is viewed. In the modernizing and highly interdependent nations where economics and social barriers are disappearing fast and in the context of advanced communication network the role of Diaspora has assumed significance.

Meaning of Diaspora – Etymologically the term Diaspora is derived from the Greek "Dia" (through) and speiro (to scatter) literally meaning scattering or dispersion.[1]

The term "Diaspora" according to V.S. Seth denotes "scattering of people with a common origin, background and beliefs."[2] With the enhanced interdependence between states transnational relationship and contacts Diaspora have become significant.

According to the *Encyclopedia of Social Science* (1931) "Diaspora is a Greek term for a nation separated from its own state or territory and dispersed among other nations but preserving its national culture."[3] For the scholars, the term Diaspora combines various categories such as immigrants, guest workers, ethnic and racial minorities, refugees, expatriates and travellers. Diaspora may be created as a community, as a result of voluntary or forced migration, mass migration, mass exile, and by the emigration of economically depressed groups to other countries. Diaspora cultural origin can be traced to their motherland and not to the country in which they reside. Given the relationship between the Diasporic community and the motherland, their exists a possibility of their return from the country of their adoption. Thus, Diaspora have originated from migration. Now the concept has been generalised to refer to any population, which has migrated from its country of origin and settled in a foreign land. They selectively incorporate and synthesize themselves with the roots of their origin and senses of their past. The assessment of the Diaspora goes beyond the historical and cultural ties and extends itself to the wider economic role.

In a globalized, world, migration is a significant force of historical change when a Diasporic community assimilates, acculturates into its host society and tends to loose its host society, affinity and linkages with its land of origin. Thus, the role of Diaspora is important in formation of ethnic identity, shaping ethnic relations and the reconstruction of societies. They provide a broad way for understanding the dynamics of culture. By this way, it is gaining competence in the contemporary history.

Indian Diaspora: In order to define the concept of "Indian Diaspora" we have to analyses the concept such as "Overseas Indians"; Indian National Overseas or Non-Resident Indians (NRI); "Persons of Indian Origin" (PIOs); "Persons Resident in India (PRI)".

Overseas Indians

The concept of "overseas Indians" is the residue and leftover of the British colonial legacy. This concept has emerged during the 20th century when the plight of the Indian emigrants overseas kindled a strong political protest in India against the British Indian government's attitude towards them because India was then a part of the greater British empire and all Indians residing in India or elsewhere were the British subjects.[4] The term overseas Indians comprises of NRIs (Non-Resident Indians) and PIOs (People of Indian Origin). But there exists a huge variation between these two. It is in terms of their period of migration. The PIOs migrated in the colonial period, whereas the migration of the NRIs is a recent phenomenon. The patterns, process and nature of the migration of the two are different. Thus, Indian overseas include those people who migrated from India in the 19th century and they are PIOs and NRIs could be identified as a separate group who migrated after Independence. This is the brain behind the concept of Indian Diaspora.

Indian National Overseas

In India the term Indian National Overseas (INO) is referred to as the Non-Resident Indians (NRIs).[5] The NRIs are said to have emigrated from India since 1947 to various countries. The word NRI appeared for the first time in 1984 in the parliamentary debates.[6] According to the Foreign Exchange Management Act (FEMA) 1999, which came into effect from June 1 2000, Non-Resident Indian (NRI) is a person who is resident outside India but keeps his Indian passport. He is employed abroad or carries out business or vocation outside India for an uncertain period. Under the NRI regulations, the NRI are not allowed to remain in the country for longer than 182 days at a time in financial year.[7]

Persons Resident in India

There is another category called the "persons resident in India." If a person resides in India for more than 182 days, he/she is called person resident in India.[8] Indian citizens who proceed abroad for higher studies, short business visits, training, medical treatment, foreign tours etc. are regarded as persons resident in India even during their temporary absence from India.

Persons of Indian Origin

The Persons of Indian origin (PIOs) are another category of the overseas Indians who are mainly the descendents of the Indian emigrants of indentured labour (especially on plantations) sent by the British in the 19th and the early part of the 20th century. According to the Foreign Exchange Management Act, a PIO is a person who is deemed to be of Indian Origin if he or she holds an Indian passport or any of his/ her parents/ grandparents were citizen of India by virtue of the Constitution of India or Citizenship Act 1955 (Act 57 of 1955) or the person who is a spouse of a person of Indian origin.[9] If a person born outside of the Indian territory on or after the 26th January of 1950, he or she shall be considered as a citizen of India by descent if his father is a citizen of India at the time of his/her birth, the birth must have been registered in Indian consulate within one year of its occurrence or the commencement of Citizenship Act.[10] The provisions of clause (b) (ii) of Article 8 of the Constitution provided that any person living abroad, one of whose parents or grandparents was born in India could be granted Indian citizenship by registration.[11] Thus, the term PIO is applied to a foreign citizen of Indian origin or descent.

The modern emigration from India was wholly a British creation. It began in the first half of nineteenth century when the British abolished slavery. Large scale labour was needed to work on the plantation in the various British colonies. Without dependable supplies of labour, survival of plantation would have become extremely difficult. The colonies sought cheap labour. India provided such labour. This was the main Pull factor. The colonial influence and domination created severe economic disturbances among the peasantry and for many, the prospect of a paid job was the sole way out of difficult circumstances. This was the main Push factor.[12] The British empire had favoured and even encouraged the labour migration from India under the Indentured system. Indentured labour from India was seen as a reliable and cheap source of labour. Under this the overseas Indians began to migrate in large number.

Patterns of Migration

The three patterns of migration such as organized, assisted and unassisted and involuntary migration were associated with the 19th Century migration of the Indians. The organised and assisted migration was carried out through the Indentured (1839-1916), Kangani (1833-39) and Maistry (1876-1941) system of contracts.[13]

Through the Indenture System the Overseas Indians had migrated towards various countries like South Africa, Fiji, Mauritius, Guyana, Trinidad and Tobago. Under the Kangani

System of labour they went to Sri Lanka and Malaysia. However, with the help of Maistry system they went to Burma.

However, after that some of the Indians moved overseas to serve the already settled Indians and also the indigenous people. These Indians were paid for their passage and sailed to various regions of the world to pursue occupations ranging from commerce to agriculture. This was termed as the "Passage" or free emigration. The nature of this particular migration was voluntary in nature. Under this they migrated towards Sri Lanka, South East Asia, Europe, North America and Africa.

The nature of the emigrants were largely laboures and some of them were bankers, shopkeepers, teachers, artisans, businessmen and contractors. The government is also involved in the process of sponsoring the emigration. The Government of India (GOI) sends some of the Indian nationals abroad on short Contracts, which includes technicians, advisors and teachers and all are prominently seen in Africa and in the Himalyan States.[14]

Post Colonial migration of the 20th Century

The large scale Indian migration of the 20th Century have been directed towards the Industrially developed advanced societies of Europe, North America and West Asia.[15] Under this the NRIs began to migrate from India. The characteristics features of the migration has been voluntary in nature. The nature of the migrants is of highly educated professional and technicians. A new category of NRIs are the "brain drain" migrants composed of young doctors, scientists, lawyers and Computer professionals, knowledge workers who left India for U.S, Canada and Australia to lead a better life.[16] The brain drain emigrants are different from the previous migrant Indians in one fundamental way. Their migration was temporary in nature. They are different from the coolie migrants of the yesteryears because they were urban, educated and English speaking people. Knowledge workers constitute the intellectual, technocratic and managerial elite, who have been imparted sufficient training. The Indian knowledge workers such as Doctors, Engineers, Scientists, lawyers, Nurses and Social Scientists are in big demand in the developed Western Countries.

The NRI Community is changing its profile. During the 1960s and 1970s mainly labour emigrants had taken place, to the Middle-East and Gulf Countries such as UAE, Kuwait, Saudi Arabia, Oman and Iraq. The nature of work of these emigrants was unskilled, semi- skilled and skilled labour. These were also temporary immigrants.

From the pattern and process, the Indian Diasporic population has been dispersed to various locations. For instance, the labourer under the indentured system mostly went to Africa and the Caribbean region. The professional and the educated class went to the mostly advanced Western Countries and Semi-Skilled and skilled labour went to the oil exporting middle east countries.

In this chapter an attempt has been made to define the concept the Indian. Diaspora and various categories of migrant Indians such as Overseas Indians and the Non- Resident Indians. From the above discussion, we can conclude that the word Diaspora has inborn association with the migration. Ethnic identities have been created out of them in which overseas Indians and the Non Resident Indians (NRI) account for a distinct case. These two categories of migrant Indians are said to be collectively coming under the broader expression called the "Indian Diaspora". It is quite clear that the migration of both the colonial and post colonial period accounted for the large scale movement and spread of the Indians to various countries of the world. Through various means, today the population of the Indian Diaspora is said to be about 20 million, spreading over Africa, Asia, America, Australia, the Caribbean and Europe. Although the numerical strength of the Indian Diaspora population is smaller as compared to the Chinese and Jewish Diaspora. They however concentrated in about 138 countries.[17] The rise and settlement of the Indian Diaspora in different parts of the world is a distinctive feature of the modern age. Indian Diaspora population is not rootless. It is like a banyan tree, the traditional symbol of the Indian Diasporic way of life, spreading out its roots in several soils. The Indian diasporic population has several homes and has largely come to feel at home in the world. Thus, the Indian Diaspora is omnipresent. Though the Indian Diasporic community is heterogeneous, they are united. They are sentimentally united through India, because they are India's overseas children.

The Indian Diaspora has become more significant in view of its adaptable nature and dynamism and initiative. The transformation of the Diaspora population from the status of migrants in search of better economic well being, to significant players in their host states has been somewhat gradual. Forced to move out from their motherland due to both "Pull and Push" factors, the Indian immigrants have struggled, survived and succeeded in earning for themselves a niche in the countries of their settlement. They have come to possess a unique place of being heterogeneous; are far more widespread than any other Diaspora in the world.

The Indian diasporic populations economic potential will be of immense help to India and the periodic remittances and investment are largely helpful for India's economic development. Now the government of India (GOI) started looking upon its Diaspora reflected in its policy (2002-2003 Budget), giving huge concession to the Indian Diaspora like full convertibility of deposit schemes for the Non-Resident Indians (NRI). The NRI are now free to repatriate in foreign currency, their current earnings in India such as, rent, dividend, pension and interest. Hence, the increasing economic value of Indian Diaspora has developed a positive attitude for Indian government vis-à-vis the diasporic population.[18] The growing strength of civil-society has given the Indian community abroad a new confidence to play a high profile role in meeting the needs of its home country, whether in times of crisis or to meet economic challenges. However, Indian Diaspora has also been urging the Indian government to address a number of wide ranging issues, including labour problems and related aspects; political representation back home; (Dual citizenship; right to vote etc.) greater involvement in Indian economy and host of other issues.

The Indian Diaspora, while responding to the changing needs of the time seem to be ready to play a dynamic role in the development of its mother country and wish to be seen not just as a source of remittances, but to be more respectable community.

The political achievements of Indian Diaspora are

commendable and some of them have become leaders and ruled/ ruling in various parts of the world such as Mauritius, Trinidad and Tobago, Singapore and British Columbia, Guyana etc. However, in some parts of the world, they have suffered/ suffering from racial discrimination like, Fiji, South Africa, U.K., U.S.A and lately Australia, etc. In these countries, they are being attacked, and the indigenous population treat them as alien/ outsiders etc. The Indian Government was not able to help its overseas population directly because it can't interfere in the internal affairs of other countries. Second the government of India right from Jawaharlal Nehru regime till date has been adopting different approaches towards its diasporic population. There is no constant policy of the government of India towards its diasporic population and its responses have been according to its relations with the host countries.

The government of India since 2003 declared 9th January every year as Pravasi Bhartiya Divas (PBD), as a mark of Mahatma Gandhi's return to India from South Africa in 1915. In this meet of PBD, the representatives of Government of India and the delegates of Indian Diaspora exchange the views and several members of diasporic community are honoured for their contributions.

The Indian Diaspora are not only cultural ambassadors of India but their contributions and achievements have been of a high order. It is a matter of great pride that many Indians are now heading large banks, Airlines, consultancy firms and of course information technology companies abroad besides being the core professionals like doctors, engineers architects, and Academician/ Researchers etc.

Indian Diaspora besides linked economically is culturally, emotionally, sentimentally linked with India. The Indian Diaspora has also maintained its group identity in terms of social compartmentalisation along caste, community and religious lines. Though the Indian diasporic population are distant in geographic terms, the link of Indian Diaspora continues to remain strong with their homeland and certainly can contribute in more concrete ways than just economic one.

Notes

1. www.uohyd.ernet.in/njword/.htm.

2. V.S. Seth, "Dynamics of Indian Diaspora in East and South Africa". *Journal of Indian Ocean Studies* (New Delhi) Vol. 8, No. 3, Dec. 2000, p. 218.
3. *Encyclopedia of Social Sciences*, Vol. 5 (New York: The Macmillan Company, 1935), p. 126.
4. P. Sahadevan in *India and Overseas Indians: The case of Sri Lanka* (Delhi, Kalinga Publication, 1995), p. 3.
5. P. Sahadevan, N. 6, p. 3.
6. The Foreign Exchange Management Act (FEMA) 2000.
7. Systematic Approach to Income tax and Central Sales tax (New Delhi, Bharat Lau house Pvt. Ltd. 2001), p. 25.
8. FEMAM, n. 9, p. 6.
9. *Ibid,* No. 9, p. 174.
10. The Citizenship Act, No. 12, p. 309.
11. The Citizenship Act, No. 12, p. 309.
12. Ravindra K. Jain *Indian Communities Abroad: Themes and Literature,* (New Delhi-Manohar Publishers 1993) p. 4.
13. Indentured System-was a system of contract by which the emigrant agreed to work for a given employer for specific period and performing the tasks assigned to him/her for a specified wages.

    Kangani- The Kangani System of recruitment was used to supply south Indian labour to Malaya and Sri Lanka. Tradesman known as Kangani, recruited the migrants. Each Kangani recruited people belonging mainly to his own caste and kin group.

    Maistry System- Indian labour contractor involved in construction work moved from village to village exhorting labourers to migrate to Burma.
14. Srikant Dutt "India and the Overseas Indians" *India Quarterly* (New Delhi) Vol. 36, 3-4 July-Dec. 1980, p. 323.
15. P.C. Jain, "Emigration and Settlement of Indian Abroad" *Sociological Bulletin*, New Delhi, Vol. 31, pp.163-164, March 1989.
16. Binod Khadaria, *The migration of knowledge workers: Second generation effects of India's Brain-drain* (New Delhi, Sage Publication, 1999) p. 54.

17 Report of the High Level Committee on the Indian Diaspora (New Delhi: ICWA 2001), p. v.

18. *The Times of India*, 1st March 2002.

2

Diaspora : An Introduction

Shivam

Human beings have immigrated from one part of the world to another since time immemorial. Human beings leave their place of origin for a variety of reasons, e.g., environmental deterioration, political and religious persecution and economic hardship. Migration, i.e., movements across borders – geographically or otherwise can be willful or forced. 'Expatriates' and 'Immigrants' belong to the former category and 'Exiles' and 'Refugees' belong to the latter one.

"The term 'Diaspora' is derived from the Greek word "Diaspeirein" (Diaspeirein = dia+ speirein), 'dia' = across, 'sperein' = to scatter', originally refers to the dispersion of the Jews after the Babylonian exile in 586 BC and to the aggregate of Jews scattered in exile outside Palestine was originally applied to the Jews who were forced out of their homeland. However, after many avatars and mutations, the term now stands for relocation of groups of people or members of a community from one nation to another nation and not necessarily by force. In common language, the diaspora refers to "the movement of people from any nation away from their own country".

In the wake of globalisation and transnational movements, community travels from one place to another and constructs their identities and culture - based on memories that are diverse, selective and particular. So in the current scenario the term diaspora could not be understood as the past single meaning attached to it-exile from their home country. James Clifford (1997) has appropriately called diaspora as "a traveling term, in changing global conditions." Diaspora in earlier times described Jewish, Greek, and Armenian dispersion but now the term diaspora shares meaning with a large semantic domain that includes word like immigrants, expatriate, refugee, guest worker, exile community, overseas community and ethnic community.

Now here the question arises as to what are the forces behind the global migration? Many early theories about migration focused on 'push and pull factors'. 'Push factors' referred to dynamics within a country of origin which forced people to emigrate, such as war, famine, drought and political oppression or population pressures. 'Pull factors' by contrast, were those features of destination, countries which attracted immigrants such as prosperous labour markets, better overall living conditions and lower population density, etc. could pull immigrants from other regions.

Background

Indian diaspora is generally used to refer to migrants who originated in areas falling within the territorial boundaries of present day India (Parekh 1993). The study of Indian diaspora, can be divided into two phases of emigration: (1) 'overseas emigration in the 19th century and (2) 20th century migration to industrially developed countries for convenience, these could be termed as the colonial and the post-colonial phases of Indian diaspora. In colonial time, migration was dominantly in the form of labour migration to the British colony and in the Post-colonial period, migration occurred in the form professional elites to the industrially developed countries.

Immigration is not merely a physical crossing of borders but also cultural and 'psychological crossing' from one world to another world. An immigrant goes to an alien land temporarily in search of job and better opportunity and always keeps a 'myth of return'. Immigrants carry a predefined socio-cultural identity of host country and lands to a new world where certain questions haunt their mind. Who are they? Where are they? What are they? How they survive in the lives of two worlds, the "world of motherland" and the "world of dreamland". How do they identify themselves as the 'country of ancestral origin' or the 'country of host origin' or 'the country of hybrid origin'?

How do they assimilate and what kind of assimilation takes place either 'full assimilation' or 'partial assimilation' or 'segmented assimilation'?

Conceptualisation

Now the question comes here who can be called diasporic? Ashcroft, Griffiths and Tiffin argue that, the notion of power, social position plays a major role in creation of a diaspora. In other words "the issue here is not simply of ethnic affiliation and cultural movement but also of social position". Of the many different peoples who have been scattered and dispersed throughout the world, only some of them can be called diasporic. For instance, we can talk about Irish diaspora or an Indian diaspora or African diaspora but we rarely talk about English diaspora. The question is one of power. It seems inappropriate to talk about the spread of a powerful colonizing people around the world as 'an exile'. Nor can we describe as a diaspora that cultural group that attains global dominance. Diasporas have come to mean cultural minorities, in social power if not always in number (e.g. African diaspora in the Caribbean) and as such are always seen to be established their sense of identity and cultural affiliation, their sense of home, their sense of subject position, against the background of a majoritarian rule." (Ashcroft, Griffiths and Tiffin 1995 : 426)

The conditions and circumstances, under which a community becomes a diasporic community, play an important role in the image formation and treatment of diasporic community in host country. In this regard, Brah (1996) argues that 'notion of the heart of diaspora is the image of the journey. Yet not every journey can be understood as diaspora. Diasporas are clearly not the same as casual travel. Nor are they normatively referred to as temporary sojourns. Paradoxically, diasporic journey are essentially about settling down, about putting roots 'elsewhere'. These journeys must be historicised if the concept of diaspora is to serve as a useful heuristic device. The question is not about who travels but when, how and under what circumstances? What socio-economic, political and cultural conditions mark the trajectories of these journeys?

Diasporic situation involves relocation not in terms of geography alone. The most significant aspect of such movement is the socio-cultural and psychological relocation. Individuals as well as group of people belonging to a particular nation communities in diasporic situations oscillate between two identities, two culture values system and even two mind sets - one belonging to the nation and the community they are migrating from and the other the nation and the community they are migrating into. Often these are referred to as the donor and the recipient cultures. The ambience and milieu of the adopted nation co-mingles with historical and cultural conditions of homeland. Old symbiotic ties give way to the new attitudes as one changes location. A hybrid culture evolves, because of the synchronisation of the inherited culture and the adopted culture: the home culture and the alien culture.

Common Features of Diaspora

Cohen (2001:26) gives common features of diaspora. These are :

1. Dispersal from an original homeland, often traumatically, to two or more foreign regions;
2. Alternatively, the expansion from a homeland in search of work, in pursuit of trade or to further colonial ambitions;
3. A collective memory and myth about the homeland, including its location, history and achievement;
4. An idealisation of the putative ancestral home and a collective commitment to its maintenance, restoration, safety and prosperity, even to its creation;
5. The development of a return movement that gains collective approbation;
6. A strong ethnic group consciousness sustained over a long time and based on a sense of distinctiveness, a common history and the believe in a common fate;
7. A troubled relationship with the host societies, suggesting a lack of acceptance at the least or the possibility that another calamity might befall the group;
8. A sense of empathy and solidarity with co-ethnic members in other countries of settlement; and

9. The possibility of a distinctive creative, enriching life in host countries with a tolerance for pluralism.

Typology

Among the immigrants of diverse nationalities, overseas Indians constitute a sizeable segment. It is estimated that besides six million Indian citizens, there are over 20 million people of Indian origin all over the world (Government of India 2000:680). Vijay Mishra (1996) presents two types of diaspora that is "exclusive" and "border" and tries to differentiate between the older diaspora of colonies ('exclusive') and new diaspora to advance countries ('border'). The old diaspora of exclusivism have created a 'little Indias' by transplanted Indian icons of spirituality to the new land–a holy Ganges here, a lingam or a coiled serpent. However, the diaspora of the border kept in touch with India through family networks and marriage, generally supported by state apparatus that encouraged family reunion.

Cohen (2001) in "Global diasporas" presented a typology of diasporas such as victim, labour, trade, imperial and cultural diasporas is more unambiguous than the history and development of diasporas suggests. Some groups take dual or multiple forms; others change their character over time. Africans and Armenians are shown to be analogous victim diasporas. The British have been represented as imperial diasporas, the Indians as labour diasporas, while the trading diasporas have been typified by the Chinese and Lebanese. Finally, the people of the Caribbean abroad are usefully characterised by as a cultural diaspora. Further, he says that he is not suggesting a perfect match between a particular ethnic group and a specific type of diaspora.

Vertovec (1996) suggests four ways of approaching the idea of diaspora.

(1) **Social category**: The first and most literal, is that of social category: for example, referring exclusively to the experience of the Jews, who dispersed throughout the world over the centuries. This concept of diaspora often focused on a forced displacement and therefore, was centered on negative experiences in terms of alienation, loss and victimisation.

(2) The second way of thinking about diaspora, membership of a diasporic community implies a self-conscious attachment to the place of origin as well as a sense of being somewhere else; a sense that one can share with others whose roots are left behind in the same country. To that extent, the first generation immigrant may have a choice as to whether or not to become part of diaspora. There is less of a choice for daughters or sons when the parents have clung to their cultural and linguistic roots: these people and their offspring, if they retain that sense of identity, constitute a diaspora, but the term diaspora is sometimes applied rather loosely to cover all individuals who share a foreign heritage within the host culture (Vertovec 1996).

(3) The third way in which the term diaspora is used is a 'mode of cultural production': Cultural identity is fluid, produced and reproduced so that it often results in hybrid forms of expression. In British South Asian example, bhangra music or curry houses, neither of which could have come into existence without the interaction of different cultures; each marks the presence of the diasporic community within the majority culture and the way that each has influenced the shape of the other (Hall,1990; Vertovec, 1996). This cultural approach sees the diaspora as part(s) of the host culture(s) and vice-versa.

Finally, Vertovec suggests a fourth approach, (4) 'diaspora as a problem': Transnational communities may be, and often are seen as problems of threats to state security and the social order when seen from right-wing perspectives within the host countries (Vertovec 1996, p. 54). Here the individual's connection with the country of origin calls into question their loyalty to the host country. The existence of hybrid cultural forms and multiple identities are viewed as diluting or undermining the traditional norms of indigenous population.

The Process of Social Adjustment

Sharma (1989) provides a list of six categories to understand clearly the process and mode of adaptation. These are:

1. **Background conditions and characteristics of immigrants:** This category includes time and condition of emigration; motives behind emigration; sponsoring agencies and arrangements; racial, religious, caste, class

and community backgrounds of the emigrants, their level of education, occupational skills and professional status; and their command of the language of the country of immigration.

2. **Their demographic, generational and organisational status in the country of immigration:** This category includes number and proportion of the natives, Indian immigrants and other immigrant communities in the total population of the host country; majority/minority status of the Indian immigrants, their concentration and dispersion, their rural-urban distribution, their generational composition, their homogeneity and heterogeneity, their ethnic associations and religious organisation and their cultural exclusivism and inclusivism.

3. **Their economic performance and power position in the host country:** This includes proportion of immigrants in the various sector of the host economy; proportions of Indian immigrants therein, their employment status vis-à-vis natives, their economic performance, their income levels, their status as achiever or non-achiever, their class alliance, their contribution to the development of the host country as perceived by them and by the natives, their hold over the host economy; their involvement in the power sector, the degree and form of their participation in the domestic politics, their hold over the host polity, their proportion in the legislature, administration and judiciary; the threats that they pose to the natives in the fields of employment, professional attainment, income levels and power.

4. **Response of host community culture, and religion:** This set includes the generalised attitude of the natives towards immigrant in general and Indian immigrant in particular, their sense of cultural and racial superiority or inferiority, their perception of the immigrant culture, their openness to or tolerance of the immigrant culture, their perceived images of the immigrants along with stereotypes and stigmas attached to them, their ethnic prejudices and cultural hostility against the immigrants

and their attempts at religious conversion of the immigrant.

5. **Level of development and manpower needs of the host country:** The level of economic development of the host country and her manpower needs are the crucial factors.
6. **State policy in respect of immigrants:** This includes immigration law, civic status of immigrants, their rights and obligations, contract and agreements, decrees and disabilities, restrictions on their property rights and on access to positions of power; the cultural policy of the host state with the home state of immigrants; and the policy of the home state with respect to its people abroad.

Identity

Sharma (1989) argues that, the question of cultural identity of overseas Indians needs more scrutiny. It involves several issues for example how Indians abroad perceive their self-identity as Indians or as Punjabis, Guajarati, etc.? In other words, do they perceive themselves in terms of pan Indian identity or in terms of a parochial ethnic category? According to Fisher (1980), Indians have difficulty in organising as Indians. More often than not, they tend to identify themselves in terms of narrow ethnic categories. By and large, Fisher is right. However, we also see this context is also important and it determines their self-identity. While dealing with the non-Indians they tend to take on pan-Indian identity. However, when it comes to interact among them their regional, linguistic and religious identities take precedence. A second issue is that how others look upon Indians. Are they seeing them as Indians or as Asians? That depends on several issues such as their numerical strength in the host country. Wherever Indians form a substantial group, they are viewed as Indians having a distinctive identity. On the other hand, in other countries where their numbers is small and the ethnic groups of other nationalities are present they tend to be bracketed with the other Asians.

Sharma (1989) argues that it is wrong to speak of a uniform mode of adaptation so there may be at least three modes of adaptation: (a) assimilation, (b) cultural preservation with economic integration and (c) ethnic politicisation for power cultivation. These refer to three processes namely merger, adjustment, and striving for dominance. For the first mode of adaptation, namely assimilation, he gives example of Jamaica, Grenada.

The second mode of adaptation is widespread among Indian immigrants in Southeast Asia, in east Africa, in Britain, and in the U.S.A and Canada give ample evidence of it. Indian immigrants in U.S.A have the following observation that in the cultural domain Indians tend to preserve their identity while in the economic domain they are quick to integrate (Gordon 1964); that they remain Indian in their primary groups but act Americanised in their secondary group (Saran 1985)

Evidence of the third mode of adaptation comes from the country like Mauritius, Guyana, Trinidad, Fiji and Srilanka where Indians have carved out a place for themselves in the power politics of the place.

3

Migrant Communities and Remittances-Indian Experience

Rajneesh Kumar Gupta and
Rahul Nath Choudhury

It is a proved fact that the world distribution of opportunities is extremely unequal. This unequal distribution leads to a phenomenon of migration of human being in search of better livelihood. Migration of people across the political boundaries has been taking place since ages- either due to compulsion or by choice. However, the twentieth century has witnessed international migration fastest than ever. The *International Migration Report-2002* notes that today international migration is at an all-time high and about 175 million people are residing outside their country of birth. They constitute almost 3 per cent of the world population. Further, *Human Development Report-2009* recorded total number of international migrants approximately 200 million. Report states that every year about 5 million people cross international boundaries. However, there has been tendency of highlighting only negative aspects of international migration. People and governments of host countries look them with suspicion and fears that resources and opportunities exploited by those migrants would be much higher than their contributions. On the other hand, government and policy makers of the motherland of migrants consider it as a loss of human resources in the form of 'brain drain'. Here we will take up contribution of those migrant communities to their motherland in the form of remittances.

Remittances-Conceptual Framework

With the growing trends of liberalisation, privatisation and globalisation, monetary transfers from people of one country to another country commonly described as remittances has gained tremendous importance. Now, remittances are considered an important source of earnings for any economy. They impact both the foreign exchange of a country as well as its households. The roles of remittances in the development of an economy have increased manifolds in the recent times. Depending upon the nature of remittances and the economic conditions characterizing the remittance-receiving economics, remittances affect consumption and investment decisions in receiving economies. It influences private consumption too. Influence on consumption could also lead to economic growth as consumption creates investment demand through its multiplier effect.

It should be noted that in contemporary world order every country hosts some amount of foreign nationals as well as some of their own citizens overseas. Thus, remittances are of two types- inward remittances and outward remittances. Inward remittances are those which a nation gets from her overseas citizens and outward remittances are those which are sent by foreign nationals to their motherland, residing in political boundaries of a nation.

Thus, in case of India, according to RBI definition, remittances include two flows: inward remittances and local withdrawals from Non-Resident Indian (NRI) deposit accounts. The term NRI popularly refers to members of the Indian diaspora, including Indian citizens living abroad and people of Indian origin. Inward remittances are direct transfers of funds from one person abroad to another in India, typically through a bank or wire transfer agency. Such transfers are generally understood to provide family support. There are two main theoretical approaches to migrant remittances.

The first approach is known as "Migrant Syndrome" (Reichart, 1981), popularly called the "Dutch Disease". According to this approach the inward remittances resulting from migration can only partially compensate for the loss of human capital. It is contended that migration carries "Dutch disease" effect on the migration source economies, as there is competition for limited labour by the local production entities that may result in decline in the production of tradable goods. (Jadhav, 2003).

A different opinion on the migration and remittances is given by the developmental perspective rooted in the New Economics of Labour Migration (NELM) (Stark and Bloom, 1985). This approach refers to migration as an integral part of the household objective to raise income levels, investment potential and attain insurance against risk. It is argued that remittances can ease the production and investment constraints, setting in motion a development dynamics. A fundamental departure of the NELM migration model from that of the individual model (Todaro, 1969) is that under the NELM household model, decision-making is based on a larger context with collective decisions.

Macro-economic impact of Remittances-A Literary Survey

The remittances flow to an economy has a number of macro-economic impacts. It increases the foreign exchange reserve; modifies the Balance of Payment situation, develops the investment scenario in a country. Recently, the UNCTAD has made an extensive study of the different variables like investment, GDP, foreign exchange reserve and their linkages with remittances.

Remittances boost national foreign exchange reserves by encouraging further emigration and by reminding emigrants that they have a patriotic duty to invest their savings back home, often in specially designed government bonds and high-yielding savings accounts. Further, it enhance government revenue by taxing this income stream, if not directly, at least by setting inflated rates for the issue of passports and visas, departure taxes, international telephone calls, and so forth, all of which are facilities used disproportionately by migrant workers. Draw the excess funds into deposits in the formal banking system, thereby hugely improving its liquidity, because the volume of funds remitted in this way is often so large it cannot be soaked up in immediate expenditure by recipients (Hrushikesh Mallick, 2008).

Pant (2008) argues that, whether remittances are utilised for consumption or purchasing houses, or other investments, they produce positive impact on the economy by stimulating demand for other goods and services. Migrants provide different forms of capital that have developmental impact on their countries of origin. Faini (2002, 2003) finds a positive relationship between growth and remittances using cross-country data. Adelman and Taylor (1990) find that "every dollar that the Mexican migrants send back home or bring back with them increases Mexico's GNP from anywhere between $2.69 and $3.17, depending on which household income group received the remittances". Durand *et al.* (1996) suggest that for every $2 billion in remittances that entered Mexico, production in the economy increased by over a $6.5 billion. Ekanayake *et al.* (2008) examine the impact of foreign remittances and foreign direct investment on the economic growth of developing countries. Barajas *et al.* (2009) point out that for developing countries remittances are large relative to other financial flows. Bouhga and Hagbe (2004) explain the importance of remittances to Morocco as a source of foreign exchange that could be used positively for development.

Flow of Remittances

Now, let us focus on actual flow of remittances. According to World Bank sources there has been a continuous growth in the flow of remittances in the last one decade. Fig. 1, depicts the trend of inflow of remittances to major countries from 2000 to 2010. Philippines, Mexico, China, India and Bangladesh were top five remittance receiving countries during the period of 2000-2010. Table 1 investigates the data of top remittance recipient countries in the world in the year 2010. Here, India emerges as the top remittance receiving country in the World followed by China, Mexico, and others. The total remittance came to India in 2010 is 53.1 billion USD.

However, an in-depth scrutiny tells a different story. In the absolute term though India tops the list but when we compare the ratio of remittance to Indian emigrants with other major remittance recipient countries we find India is lagging far behind them (see table 2). Even a cursory glance of table 2 make it clear that even though India is getting higher amount of remittances but per head remittances transferred to India is lower than many others in the list. In case of ratio, the small African country Lebanon has performed the best and it is followed by Nigeria and China.

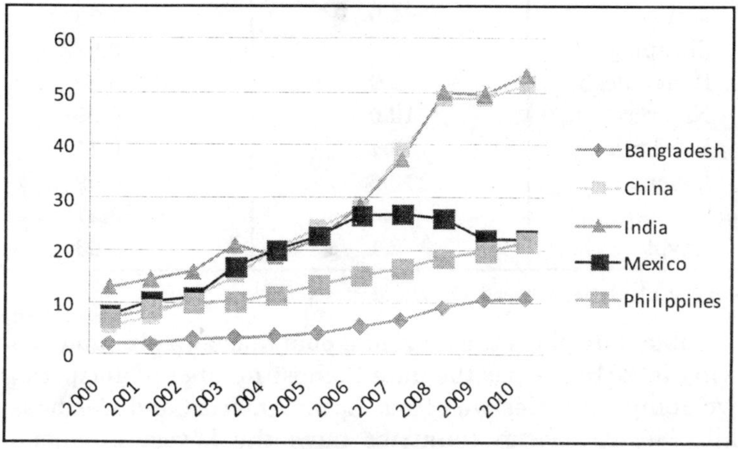

Fig 1: Inflow of Remittances in Top receiving countries (In billion US$)

Source: Constructed by authors from World Bank data.

Table 1 : Remittances Inflows in 2010

(In billion US$)

Country	*Remittances Inflows*	*Rank*
India	53.1	1
China	51.3	2
Mexico	22	3
Philippines	21.4	4
Bangladesh	10.8	5
Nigeria	10	6
Pakistan	9.7	7
Lebanon	8.4	8
Vietnam	8	9
Egypt	7.7	10

Source: Calculations based on World Bank data.

Table 2 : Remittances ratio of major recipients

(In US $)

Largest recipients	*Remittances Ratio to Emigrants*	*Remittances Ratio to Immigration*
India	4.7	0.21
China	6.1	1.22
Mexico	1.9	1.63
Philippines	5.0	0.98
Bangladesh	2.0	0.50
Nigeria	10.0	0.09
Pakistan	2.1	0.11
Lebanon	12.6	0.09
Vietnam	3.6	3.21
Egypt	2.1	1.53

Source: Calculations based on World Bank data.

Table 3 displays the data of global diaspora size and their saving in 2010. As per the data highest number of diaspora in developing countries was from Latin America and Caribbean while North African countries have the lowest number of diaspora in the world. Similar case can also be noticed in their saving level. In the year 2010, the total number of diaspora was 161.5 million in developing countries and their saving was estimated at around 400 billion USD.

Table 3 : Saving by Global Diaspora in 2010

	Diaspora size (millions)	*Estimated Diaspora Saving ($ billions)*
Developing countries	161.5	397.5
East Asia and Pacific	21.7	83.9
Europe and Central Asia	43	72.9
Latin America and Caribbean	30.2	116
Middle East	9.3	18.9
North Africa	8.7	22.3
Sub-Saharan Africa	21.8	30.4
South Asia	26.7	53.2

Source: Migration remittances Fact book 2011, World Bank.

Flow of Remittances in India and China- A Comparison

India and China are two emerging economies of the world, often competing with each other on various accounts. Both of the countries are heavily reliant on their Diaspora for remittances, investment, export promotion and other aspects of the economy. It is un-doubtful that in overall numbers Chinese Diaspora is much larger than of India. However, in terms of citizen living outside country, China lacks behind India. As there are about 7 million Chinese citizens living in different parts of the world. On the other hand, the total stock of Indian citizens residing outside the political boundaries of the nation is more than 8 million. These people are commonly known as NRI (non-resident Indians). The major countries with concentration of NRIs are UAE, USA, UK and Canada. On the other hand, Chinese nationals have mostly migrated to Japan, Thailand, Australia, Canada etc. (Migration Policy Institute 2010, Washington D.C.).

In recent years India has replaced China from top most remittance recipient destination of the world. In the year 2010, India received a total remittance of US$ 53.1 billion, little higher than of US$ 51.3 billion remittance received by China. But if we study it in terms of per capita remittances we still lag behind China. In case of China the per capita remittance is 6.1 thousand USD, while for India it is only 4.7 thousand USD. In case of outward remittances again a very high amount is going out of the country. More than 500 million USD have been transferred from India to different countries in the world in 2010. But only 70 million USD has been transferred from China in the same time period. It is pertinent to mention that less than 1 million outsiders are living in China while more than 5 million people from other nations are working in India.

Fig. 2 depicts the share of Indian migration by the destination. The data shows that highest amount (approx one third of the total migrated population) of Indian migration has happened to Asian continent only. fifteen percent of population has migrated to North America while 10 percent of population has migrated to Europe.

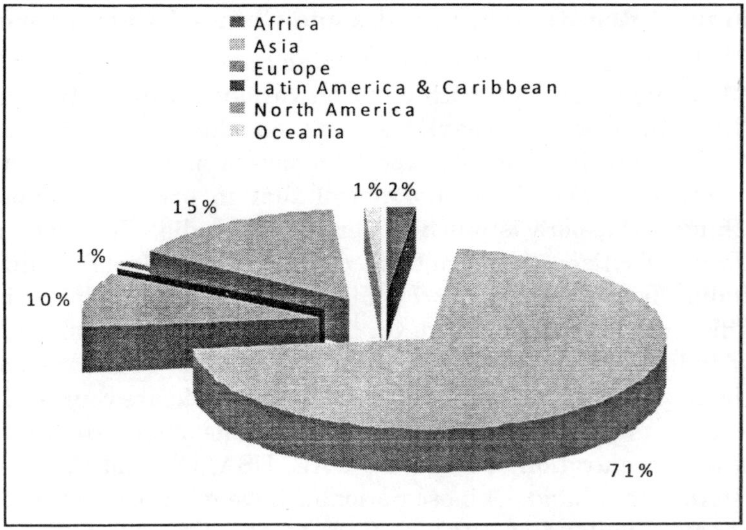

Fig. 2. Share of Indian Migration by Destination.

Source: Migration Policy Institute.

As per a study made by Migration Policy Institute, 58 percent of remittances are coming to India from Asia and the inflow is 27 percent from North America and 13 percent from European countries. The share of remittances in the GDP of India was 5.63 percent in 2008-2009 (RBI Handbook of Statistics on the Indian Economy, 2009-10).

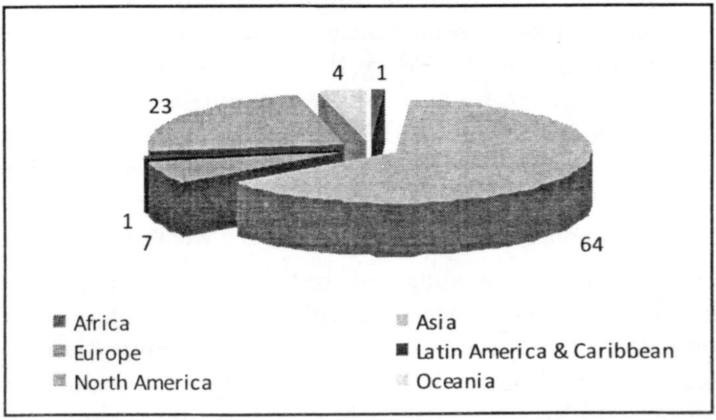

Fig. 3. Share of Chinese Migration by Destination.

Source: Migration Policy Institute.

In Fig. 3 the distribution of Chinese migrated population in the different destinations are given. The data reveals that 64 percent of Chinese have chosen Asia as their destination, while 23 percent have moved to North America. 7 percent Chinese have moved to Europe and only 1 percent has moved to both Africa and Latin America.

According to a study conducted by Migration Policy Institute, 62 percent of remittances transferred in China are coming from Asia, while the country is getting 27 percent of its remittances from North America. Remittances contributed 1 percent of Chinese GDP in the year 2010 (International Financial Statistics).

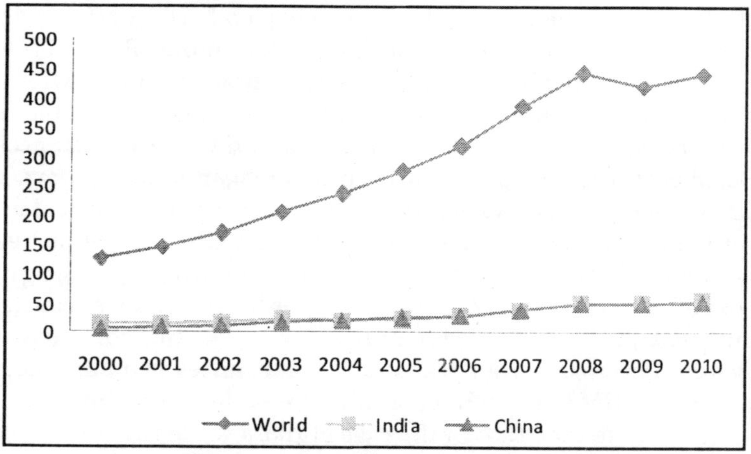

Fig. 4. Comparison of inflow of remittances.

Source: Calculated from World Bank Data.

The Fig. 4 compares the trend of inflow of remittances in the India, China, and World. It is clear from the figure that inflows of remittances in both India and in China are approx similar over the period of time. The growth of inflow was constant for both the economies. In case of world, a sharp increase can be seen up to 2008, but it decreased in 2009. However, again in 2010, the data recovered to a large extent. The share of India and China were 12.1 and 11.7 percent respectively in the latest available year. This is also to be noted that both the nations are maintaining their shares in the world for a long time.

The Channels of Remittance Flows to India

The channels of transferring fund are very important to understand the concept of remittance data in any country. In India, the major organisations engaged in the profession are the commercial banks. However, a number of other non-bank players have also entered in the area of money transfers with innovations in products and the recourse to new methods. They have close co-ordination and alliance with the international banks / exchange houses.

The network at the remitter's end comprises the local banks, building societies, money transfer operators (MTOs), Postal system and the overseas branches or associate offices of the Indian banks. At the receiving end, the entities are Indian banks, branches of foreign banks, Indian Post, MTOs, non-bank finance companies, travel companies and FMMCs. Presently, there are about 87 commercial banks designated as authorised dealers, which can receive and transfer remittances. Besides, there are 53 Money Transfer agents. The informal agents include unregistered entities such as hawala dealers, returning migrants, friends, relatives and trading companies. Designated post offices can only receive remittances. Globally, post offices are involved in the cross border remittance transfer business given their wider branch network. In India, postal system for cross border transfer of remittances is mainly used by the WUMT to deliver funds in wider locations. It is interesting to note that in the case of India while the traditional banking channel (i.e., wire transfer, drafts and cheques) accounts for bulk of the inward remittances, two other channels, viz., Money Transfer Service Scheme (MTSS) and Rupee Drawing Arrangements (RDA) that provide benefits of easier and speedier operations have assumed significance in expanding the delivery of remittances. (Bhupal Singh, 2006).

Conclusion

Migration is a natural phenomenon and in present circumstances it is bound to increase. We need to change our mindset in regard to this process. Migration has many positive consequences and contributes to the hostland as well as motherland in a number of ways. Remittances which are important constituents of any economy are a significant contribution of migrant communities. India is among those countries having large overseas population. In recent years, India has emerged as the largest recipient of remittances in the world. However, an in-depth analysis indicates that in terms of ratio this amount is lesser than not only China but many smaller nations of the world. There is substantial scope for enhancement of remittances. For this India needs to adopt hassle-free and friendly system.

References

——Human Development Report-2009, UNDP.

——International Migration Report-2002, UN.

——UNCTAD, (2011). "Impact of Remittances on Poverty in Developing Countries", UNCTAD, Geneva.

Adelman I. and Taylor Je (1990). "Is Structural Adjustment with a Human Face Possible? The Case of Mexico." *Journal of Development Studies*. 26(3): 387-407.

Akee R. and Devesh Kapur (2011). "Remittances and Rashomon Center for the Advanced Study of India", University of Pennsylvania. (Unpublished)

Bouhga-Hagbe J. (2004). "A theory of workers remittance with an application to Morocco." IMF Working Paper No. 04/194 (Washington D.C.).

Chami R., Barajas A., Cosimano T, Fullenkamp C., Gapen M. and Montiel P. (2008). "Macroeconomic Consequences of Remittances", IMF occasional Paper No. 259 (Washington: International Monetary Fund).

Chishti M. (2007). "Migration Information Source - The Rise in Remittances to India: A Closer Look", Migration Policy Institute, Washington D.C. USA.

Durand, Parrado A., and Massey D.S. (1996). "Migradollars and Development: A Reconsideration of the Mexican Case." *International Migration Review*, Vol. 30, No. 2, pp. 423-44.

Ekanayake E.M., Mihalis H. (2008). "Do remittances and foreign direct investment promote growth? Evidence from developing countries." *Journal of International Business and Economics*, Jan-1.

Faini R. (2002). "Development, Trade, and Migration," Revue d'Économie et du Development. Proceedings from the ABCD Europe Conference, 1-2, pp. 85-116.

Faini R. (2003). "The Brain Drain: An Unmitigated Blessing?" Centro Studi Luca d'Agliano Development Studies Working Paper No. 173.

Jadhav N. (2003). "Maximising Developmental Benefits of Migrant Remittances: The Indian Experience", Paper presented at the International Conference on Migrant Remittances jointly organised The Department for International Development and The World Bank (London, October 9-10, 2003).

Mallick H. (2008). "Do remittances impact the economy? Some empirical evidences from a developing economy", Working Paper No 407 Centre for Development Studies, Trivandrum, Kerala, India.

Pant B. (2008). "Mobilizing Remittances for Productive Use: A Policy-oriented Approach." Nepal Rastra Bank, working paper Serial Number: NRB/wP/4, Dec 2008.

Reichart, Joshua (1981): "The Migrant Syndrome: Seasonal U.S. Wage Labour and Rural Development in Central Mexico", *Human Organisation*, 40: 56-66.

Singh B. (2006). "Remittances Statistics: First Meeting of the Luxembourg Group". IMF Washington D.C. USA.

Stark, O. and D. Bloom (1985). "The New Economics of Labour Migration", *American Economic Review*, 75: 173-8.

Todaro, Michael (1969). "A Model of Migration and Urban Unemployment in Less-Developed 'Countries", *The American Economic Review*, 59: 138-4.

4

Dual Citizenship and Indian Diaspora

Ruchi Tyagi

Many waves of migration took Indians to different lands during different periods of history. Most of them who went before the advent of the East India Company have been assimilated in those countries. Those who went as indentured labour during the British rule have become citizens of the countries where they settled. Those countries have gained independence. Indians whose ancestors migrated to these countries are full-fledged citizens of those countries. In most countries, the overseas Indian communities have blossomed and have come into their own. Later waves of migration to the developed countries of the world account for the bulk of the Indian community in those countries. Most of them, except those who had gone to some of the Commonwealth countries as agriculturists or as passengers have also become citizens of those countries. For better expression, we call them Persons of Indian Origin. They are Indogenic people, the Bharatvanshis, who at different periods of history have taken the citizenship of the countries where they took their domicile. Of those who left India for further education or in search of better opportunities, many have taken the citizenship of foreign countries. Many of them, however, do continue to have Indian passports but they have rights of residence including the right to indefinite residence in those countries. Those who have taken citizenship of foreign countries are full-fledged citizens of those countries. Their legal status is defined by the law of the country of which they are citizens. Their status in the Indian law at present is that they acquired the citizenship of another country and renounced the citizenship of India.

Nowadays, there are broadly two distinct categories of overseas Indians:

(i) Persons of Indian Origin (PIOs) who have acquired the Citizenship of other countries;

(ii) Non Resident Indians (NRIs) who continue to hold Indian passports and are citizens of India.

Basically, all NRIs are PIOs, but all PIOs are not NRIs. We use the two expressions for the sake of convenience of reference. Non-Resident Indians (NRIs) do, of course, retain their Indian citizenship and Indian passports. Indian laws apply to them except in certain situations of conflict of laws under private international law and the laws of the countries in which they reside. Their stay in the countries of their domicile depends on the provisions of the laws of the country where they reside.

The first generation Indians are keen to be allowed to retain or regain their Indian nationality. Many of them voluntarily acquired foreign nationality due to the pressure of circumstances. Many of them have kept their Indian citizenship despite those pressures.

The demand of dual nationality stems from the practical convenience, such as:

- It may ensure advantages of the citizenship of the countries where they have made their homes.
- They can maintain strong linkages with their country of origin as well as their desire to forge emotional and cultural bonds of their future generations with India.
- Dual citizenship would also help to perpetuate and cement the links of the younger generation of the diaspora with India as they will be keen to keep in touch with their elders in India as well as relate to their roots. Their love for India and their pride in their Indian heritage propels their consistent demand for dual nationality.

- It is believed that this measure would also facilitate the contribution of the Diaspora to India's social, economic and technological transformation and national development.
- Persons of Indian origin settled in the economically more advanced countries of the world have skills and expertise in vital sectors including information technology, biotechnology, space, financial services, infrastructure, education and health care and management consultancy. Investments are induced principally by the logic of business considerations and the psychology of investment climate.
- Their citizenship of the western countries would make it easier for them to travel to different countries without the inconvenience of having to obtain innumerable visas on their Indian passports and at the same time their travels to and fro India.

Diaspora for dual citizenship, indeed, is sentimental and psychological; promotes investments in business ventures and fosters a greater sense of belonging. The diaspora in North America, Europe, Australia, New Zealand and Singapore yearns and longs for it. It will create a climate conducive to Diaspora's fuller participation in philanthropy, economic developments, technology transfer, cultural dissemination and overseas political advocacy on behalf of India.

India stands to benefit substantially by consolidating its bonds of solidarity with the diaspora by granting dual citizenship to those who were Indian citizens or those who were eligible for Indian citizenship at the commencement of the Constitution of India as well as their children and grandchildren who migrated to certain countries such as U.K., U.S.A., Canada, EU countries, Australia, New Zealand and Singapore.

Nationality and Citizenship

The two expressions 'citizenship' and 'nationality' are often used interchangeably in international law, though there exist certain shades of distinction between the two. Citizenship is acquired by birth or by naturalisation. Nationality, on the other hand, is more a description of cultural identity than a matter of political and personal rights. In some Latin-American countries, for example, the expression 'citizenship' is used to denote the sum total of political rights of which a person may be deprived, by way of punishment or otherwise without being divested of his or her nationality. A different kind of distinction between the two terms exists in the U.S.A. The States of the United States of America may grant citizenship to their residence in their respective territories after fulfilling certain conditions under their laws, whereas the Federal Government of U.S.A. confers American nationality. Moreover, persons belonging to territories and possessions which are not among the States forming the Union are described as 'nationals'. They owe allegiance to the United States and are United States nationals in the contemplation of international law but they do not possess full rights of citizenship in the United States. It is their nationality in the wider sense, not their citizenship, which is internationally relevant. In the Commonwealth, it is the citizenship of the individual states of the Commonwealth which is of primary importance for international law, while the concept of a 'British subject' or 'Commonwealth citizen' is relevant only as a matter of the internal law of the countries concerned.

Nationality in International Law

The term nationality is, however, often used in common parlance synonymously with citizenship. Oppenheim describes it as "the principal link between individuals and the benefits of the Law of Nations". Ordinarily matters connected with nationality fall within the ambit of the constitutional or public law of a State. The jurisdiction of a State to legislate or regulate on matters relating to nationality has, however, to be exercised in consonance with the prevailing norms of international law and practice so as to obviate or minimize conflicting situations which may arise in a number of ways. The question of nationality or citizenship of individuals, the conferment as well as the deprivation, is thus largely determined by the Sovereign States. Nationality laws must, however, take note of the laws of other countries as far as possible and should be consistent with international customs, usage and conventions. Such laws should also aim to avoid statelessness and other anomalies.

Dual or multiple nationality may often arise as a result of the operation of different national laws and the absence of global uniformity in respect of citizenship laws. It is noteworthy that after the Second World War, there has been a growing movement in the direction of recognising plural nationality or citizenship.

Nationality is acquired by birth or naturalisation as well as by operation of laws. Nationality at birth could be acquired in different ways, each of the ways showing proof of a connection between the national and his or her State. A person born within the territory or the State could acquire the nationality of that State by operation of law under the principle of *jus soli*. Nationality by birth underlines the territorial connection of the person with the land of his or her birth. It does not however apply to the children of diplomatic agents or of an alien in transit; or to those whose residence is due to their being in the service of a foreign country. On the other hand, the principle of *jus sanguinis* confers nationality by descent according to the nationality of one, or both, of the parents, usually of the father alone, but in some cases also of the mother. A patrilinear or matrilinear connection is, therefore, a part of the *jus sanguinis*. The principles of *jus soli* or *jus sanguinis* came to be generally accepted as forming the basis of national laws concerning nationality by the beginning of the 20th century. Both those principles were based on the evidence of a connection between the individual and the State of his nationality. Similarly, marriage has also been recognised as one of the involuntary modes of acquisition of dual nationality in many countries. For instance, the national laws of India, Indonesia and the Philippines allow a woman marrying a foreign national to continue to retain her original nationality even when she acquires automatically the nationality of her husband by virtue of marriage according to the law of her husband's country. In the Indian legal system, there is no automatic acquisition of nationality by marriage, but marriage to an Indian national is regarded as a good ground for the purpose of naturalisation. It appears that most countries do not object to dual nationality arising from involuntary modes of acquisition or conferment of nationality. The problem is somewhat more complex in cases of relinquishment or renunciation of one's nationality and the voluntary acquisition of another nationality by naturalisation and registration.

Nationality may be acquired by naturalisation or by procedures of registration. A period of residence in the country of naturalisation is often required by the legislation as a condition of naturalisation. In many countries, the period can be reduced substantially for those seeking naturalisation if they belong to specified categories: e.g. those who are married to a national or have their ancestral connection with the country upto a specified number of generations or possess particular educational qualifications or have rendered service to the State in which naturalisation is sought. In some countries, the ability to read and write the language of that country is also stipulated as a condition for naturalisation. In certain cases, a certificate of naturalisation was held to be invalid on account of the non-compliance with the legal requirement of the required period of residence. In many cases, naturalisation is preceded or accompanied by a declaration of renunciation or relinquishment of the original nationality.

While the procedures of naturalisation and registration are voluntary modes of acquisition of nationality, the other two principles – *jus soli* and *jus sanguinis* – are not. By virtue of the operation of those principles governing nationality, dual or plural nationality arises in several cases even if dual nationality is not expressly recognised by a State. For instance, India recognizes both *jus soli* and *jus sanguinis* principles. A person born in the U.S.A. to an Indian father would become an Indian citizen automatically by descent under the principle of *jus sanguinis*. (Section 4 of the Indian Citizenship Act, 1956). At the same time, he acquires the American nationality by virtue of his birth in that country (*jus soli*). Similarly, if a person was born to American parents in India on or after the 26th day of January, 1950 and before the commencement of the Citizenship (Amendment) Act 1986, he or she became an Indian citizen by birth. A person born after the commencement of the Amendment Act, 1986, if either of his or her parents was a citizen of India at the time of his or her birth would also be an Indian citizen. (Section 3 of the Act as amended).

Citizenship Issues in the Constituent Assembly

The Constituent Assembly received numerous memoranda on behalf of the people of Indian origin from different parts of the world but the question of dual nationality as such was not discussed in detail in the Constituent Assembly. The idea was neither accepted nor negated. Loss of Indian citizenship, as a result of the voluntary acquisition of foreign nationality, was expressly contemplated in Article 9 which seemed to have a wider application, although that was mainly with a view to avoid the confusion with regard to citizenship at the time of partition and its consequences. The *travoux preparatoire*, the draft articles and the debate in the Constituent Assembly reflect that at the commencement of the Constitution, the question of citizenship was the main focus of attention.

When draft Articles 5 and 6 of the original draft came up for discussion on 10 August, 1949, the President of the Constituent Assembly, Dr. Rajendra Prasad observed that "there was a veritable jungle of amendments, something 130 or 140 amendments", to those two articles. However, Dr. Ambedkar made it clear repeatedly that "it is not the object of this particular article to lay down a permanent law of citizenship for this country. The business of laying down a permanent law of citizenship has been left to Parliament, and as Members ....to determine by any law that it may deem fit." The premise of the constitutional provisions as contained in Part II of the Constitution was that they were only for the purpose of conferring citizenship on the date of the commencement of the Constitution. With the partition of the country, it was necessary to define citizenship as on the date of the commencement of the Constitution, and to exclude those who had chosen to opt for Pakistan from the citizenship of India. The rest was left to Parliament. Thus, the entire law of citizenship could not be incorporated in the Constitution itself. The articles in the Constitution relating to citizenship were entirely provisional and that the question of citizenship laws was left to legislation by Parliament.

Prof. K.T. Shah moved an amendment under which "the nationality by birth of any citizen of India shall not be affected in any other country whose Municipal law permits the local citizenship of that country being acquired without prejudice to the nationality by birth of any of the citizens .... and where under the Municipal law no citizen is compelled either to renounce his nationality by birth before acquiring the citizenship of that country or where under the Municipal law nationality by birth of any citizen does not cease automatically on the acquisition of the citizenship of that country." Prof. K.T. Shah's amendment would have had the effect of preserving the nationality of those who had or were entitled to have Indian citizenship by virtue of their birth at the commencement of the Constitution. He was keen to make citizenship not only a birthright, but also an inheritance and wanted to confer it on individuals whose grandparents were born in India. He intended that such person would acquire the privilege of being an Indian citizen automatically. Interestingly, Prof. Shah went on to address the question of "those who by settlement in other lands for business connection or by a formal act of acquisition of another citizenship, under the naturalisation laws of that country, become citizens of that country, we would be right in providing that, if they desire to acquire the citizenship of India, their path should be simplified." He wanted that option to be made available subject to the condition that they really intended to reside in India, be part and parcel of India, and were prepared to share all the duties and obligations of the country's citizenship. Prof. Shah also referred to the countries of South Asia "where large numbers of Indians have settled and where, under the new upsurge of local nationalism, their treatment is not all that can be desired." Referring to Africa as the most glaring, the most poignant case of invidious discrimination against Indians, Prof. Shah wanted India to retaliate against nations which did not mete out equal treatment to people of Indian origin and did not protect their dignity and honour. He criticised the inequalities and indignities faced by Indian citizens within the Commonwealth.

Both Pandit Thakur Das Bhargava and Shri R.K. Sidhwa were opposed to the draft provision which enabled the return of those who had migrated to Pakistan and the deeming provision which made them Indian citizens. Shri R.K. Sidhwa wanted the doors of Indian citizenship to be kept open to Parsis outside India. Shri B.P. Jhunjhunwala moved an amendment to the effect, *inter alia*, that "a person who on account of civil disturbances or the fear of such disturbances, having the domicile of India, as defined in the Government of India Act, 1937, and being resident in India before the partition, has decided to reside permanently in India, or has migrated to the territory of India from the territory now included in Pakistan, shall be deemed to be a citizen of India at the date of the commencement of this Constitution.

Sardar Bhupinder Singh Mann stoutly opposed the deeming provision which enabled those who had migrated to Pakistan and had then returned to India to be recognised as Indian citizens. Shri Mahboob Ali Baig Sahib supported the deeming provision.

In a significant intervention, Pandit Jawaharlal Nehru pointed out that the articles relating to citizenship "have probably received far more thought and consideration during the last few months than any other article contained in this Constitution." He referred to two factors which had given rise to the difficulties relating to the provisions on citizenship. He said, "One was of course the partition of the country. The other was the presence of a large number of Indians abroad, and it was difficult to decide about these Indians whether they should be considered as our citizens or not, and ultimately these articles were drafted with a view to providing for these two difficulties... Inevitably no provision could be made, which provided for every possibility and provided for every case with justice and without any error being committed. We have millions of people in foreign parts and other countries. Some of those may be taken to be foreign nationals, although they are Indians in origin. Others still consider themselves to some extent as Indians and yet they have also got some kind of local nationality too, like for instance, in Malaya, Singapore, Fiji and Mauritius. If you deprive them of their local nationality, they become aliens there. So, all these difficulties arise and you will see that in this resolution we have tried to provide for them for the time being, leaving the choice to them and also leaving it to our Consuls Generals there to register their names. It is not automatic. Our representatives can, if they know the applicants to be qualified for Indian citizenship, register their names."

Pandit Jawaharlal Nehru, however, devoted the greater part of his speech to the question of those who had migrated to Pakistan and had returned to India under permits issued under the authority of the Government of India. The number of such persons was quite small, but the debate was heavily preoccupied with the issue.

Shri Alladi Krishnaswami Ayyar, an eminent lawyer and a Member of the Drafting Committee, explained that the object of the draft articles on citizenship was not to place before the House anything like a code of nationality law and that no State had tried to lay down its laws of citizenship at the time of ushering in of its Constitution. He said, ".... Therefore there is no use of our attempting in any Constitution and much less in the present Constitution which is now making a tentative proposal in regard to citizenship to deal with the problem of double citizenship or double nationality." Pandit Hirday Nath Kunzru concentrated mainly on the provision giving citizenship to those who had migrated to Pakistan but had then returned to India. Shri N. Gopalaswami Ayyangar justified the proposal.

Replying to the debate, Dr. B.R. Ambedkar devoted much of his time to the question relating to immigrants from Pakistan to India and to those who had returned from Pakistan to India. He reiterated out that it was for the Parliament to enact a comprehensive legislation on citizenship in due course.

The Constituent Assembly Debates on citizenship show that the main concern of the Constituent Assembly was:

- to provide for citizenship at the commencement of the Constitution;
- to exclude those who had migrated from India and had acquired the nationality of other countries (mainly Pakistan); and
- to treat those who having migrated to Pakistan had returned to India as Indian citizens.
- Other questions relating to nationality including the larger question of dual nationality were left largely to the Parliament, although the issue of dual nationality was marginally touched upon by some of the members of the Constituent Assembly, notably Prof. K.T. Shah and Pandit Jawaharlal Nehru and was kept open.

Citizenship in the Indian Constitution

The Constitutional provisions relating to citizenship are embodied in Part-II of the Constitution in a fasciculus of seven articles from Article 5 to Article 11 inclusive. Those provisions were meant mainly to delineate the framework of citizenship at the commencement of the Constitution by inclusions, exclusions, and deeming provisions. More importantly, the Constitution left it to the Parliament to enact a comprehensive legislation on citizenship.

Article 5 makes it clear that the purpose of the Constitution was only to provide for citizenship at the commencement of the Constitution and is in the following terms: "citizenship at the commencement of the Constitution: At the commencement of this Constitution, every person who has his domicile in the territory of India and –

(a) who was born in the territory of India; or (b) either of whose parents was born in the territory of India; or (c) who has been ordinarily resident in the territory of India for not less than five years immediately preceding such commencement, shall be a citizen of India."

Article 6 was formulated specifically in respect of the rights of citizenship of certain persons who migrated to India from Pakistan. It was necessary to make that provision so that those who had migrated to the territory of India from the territory then included in Pakistan may be deemed to be citizens of India at the commencement of the Constitution. Accordingly, Article 6 reads as follows: "Rights of citizenship of certain persons who have migrated to India from Pakistan – Notwithstanding anything in Article 5, a person who has migrated to the territory of India from the territory now included in Pakistan shall be deemed to be a citizen of India at the commencement of this Constitution if –

(a) he or either of his parents or any of his grandparents was born in India as defined in the Government of India Act, 1935 (as originally enacted); and

(b) (i) in the case where such person has so migrated before the nineteenth day of July, 1948, he has been ordinarily resident in the territory of India since the date of his migration, or (ii) in the case where such person has so migrated on or after the nineteenth day of July 1948, he has been registered as a citizen of India by an officer appointed in that behalf by the Government of the Dominion of India on an application made by him therefore to such officer before the commencement of this Constitution in the form and manner prescribed by that Government: Provided that no person shall be so registered unless he has been resident in the territory of India for at least six months immediately preceding the date of his application."

Article 7 expressly provides that "notwithstanding anything in articles 5 and 6, a person who has after the first day of March, 1947, migrated from the territory of India to the territory now included in Pakistan shall not be deemed to be a citizen of India." This provision was, however, subject to a proviso to accommodate those who after having migrated to Pakistan, returned to the territory of India under a permit for resettlement or permanent return issued by or under the authority of any law and every such person for the purpose of article 6(b) was deemed to have migrated to the territory of India after the nineteenth day of July, 1948.

Article 8 provided for the rights of citizenship of certain persons of Indian origin residing outside India and was based on the principle of *jus sanguinis*. Article 8 reads as follows: "Rights of citizenship of certain persons of Indian origin residing outside India – Notwithstanding anything in article 5, any person who or either of whose parents or any of whose grandparents was born in India as defined in the Government of India Act, 1935 (as originally enacted), and who is ordinarily residing in any country outside India as so defined shall be deemed to be a citizen of India if he has been registered as a citizen of India by the diplomatic or consular representative of India in the country where he is for the time being residing on an application made by him therefore to such diplomatic or consular representative, whether before or after the commencement of this Constitution, in the form and manner prescribed by the Government of the Dominion of India or the Government of India."

Article 9 of the Constitution refers to persons who had

voluntarily acquired citizenship of a foreign State and declared that such person shall not be citizens of India by virtue of Article 5 or deemed to be citizens of India by virtue of Article 6 and Article 8 if he or she had voluntarily acquired the citizenship of any foreign State. Article 9 was meant to apply principally to those who had migrated to Pakistan and to demarcate clearly the exclusive zone of Indian citizenship at the time of the commencement of the Constitution.

Article 10 provides for continuance of the rights of citizenship and lays down that "every person who is or is deemed to be a citizen of India under any of the foregoing provisions of Part II of the Constitution shall, subject to the provisions of any law that may be made by Parliament, continue to be such citizen."

Article 11 constitutes an overriding exception to the other provisions of Part II of the Constitution. It provides unequivocally and unreservedly that "none of the provisions in Part II of the Constitution shall derogate from the power of Parliament to make any provisions with respect to the acquisition or termination of the citizenship and all other matters relating to the citizenship." Article 11, thus, confers a flexible and plenary power on the Parliament to enact any law or provision with respect to acquisition or termination of the citizenship and all other matters relating to citizenship.

Clearly, the power of the Parliament is unfettered by the formulations embodied in Articles 5 to 10 of Part II of the Constitution. It follows that the question of dual citizenship is open for the consideration of Indian Parliament as a question of policy without any particular constitutional impediment or constraint. No constitutional amendment would be required if Parliament wished to provide for dual nationality through appropriate provisions in the Citizenship Act, 1955 or by a separate Act of Parliament.

Dual Nationality in Some Other Countries

Since the enactment of the Indian Constitution and the Citizenship Act, 1955, there has been a sea change in terms of the growing acceptance of Dual Nationality. More than 70 countries have permitted dual nationality. They allow their citizens to retain or regain citizenship or nationality after being naturalised in another country. Many more are in the process of considering similar changes in their laws.

To illustrate, until 1976, **Canada's Citizenship** Act provided that Canadian citizens could lose their status by voluntarily acquiring citizenship in another country. Under the 1976 Citizenship Act of Canada, a Canadian citizen loses citizenship only when he or she applies for permission to renounce and a citizenship judge grants such permission.

The acquisition and loss of British nationality is now governed by the British Nationality Act, 1981 and the special provisions made in the British Nationality (Falkland Islands) Act, 1983, the British (Hong Kong) Act, 1990, the Hong Kong (War Wives and Widows) Act, 1996 and the British Nationality (Hong Kong) Act, 1997. The 1981 Act replaced the provisions of the British Nationality Acts from 1948 to 1965 and repealed those Acts with the exception of a few sections. The 1981 Act replaced citizenship of the United Kingdom and Colonies with three separate citizenships, namely, (i) British citizenship, (ii) British Dependent Territory citizenship, and (iii) British Overseas Citizenship. The 1981 Act makes general provision, inter alia, for reducing statelessness; for registration and naturalisation; for the classes of persons who have the status of the Commonwealth citizens or the British protected persons; for depriving a person of British citizenship; and also for legitimated and posthumous children. Section 1 provides for acquisition of British citizenship by birth or adoption. Section 2 provides for acquisition by descent. Section 6 provides for acquisition of British citizenship by naturalisation. Section 8 provides for registration as a British citizenship by virtue of marriage. Section 9 deals with the right to registration as a British citizenship by virtue of father's citizenship, etc. Section 10 incorporates the provisions of the British Nationality Act 1964 (Resumption of Citizenship) and applies also to cases in which a person may have ceased to be a citizen of the United Kingdom and Colonies as a result of declaration of renunciation. Section 13 deals with resumption of British citizenship and provides that a person who has ceased to be a British citizen as a result of a declaration of renunciation shall be entitled, on an application for registration as a British citizen, to be registered as such a citizen if (a) he is of full age and capacity;

and (b) his renunciation of British citizenship was necessary to enable him to retain or acquire some other citizenship or nationality. These two provisions are of particular relevance to the question of dual citizenship for persons of Indian origin who may have renounced their Indian citizenship to enable them to retain or acquire the citizenship or nationality of a country in which they had settled. The law in the United Kingdom no longer visits voluntary acquisition of another nationality or citizenship with the loss of local status. The present law of the United Kingdom may be said to favour rather than discourage plural nationality. It recognizes the concept of primary or master- nationality, that is to say the nationality of the habitual residence of the person concerned with which he or she is in fact most closely connected. It is in the country of one's primary nationality alone that military service upon a double national may be imposed, "although deprivation of his alternative status may be made the price of his exemption for service in the state of that status." A plural national who is entitled to renounce or decline the nationality of a State is exempt under the law from service of that State during minority.

The French amended the Civil Code in 1973 to liberalise the citizenship laws to permit dual nationality and to prevent the automatic loss of nationality on acquisition of another nationality.

A **Swiss citizen** does not lose his citizenship by voluntarily acquiring a second nationality.

It appears that **the German law** on nationality grants citizenship at birth to children born in Germany to parents legally resident for at least eight years, but such children who have dual nationality, by the time they reach the age of 23, have to renounce the other nationality or lose their German citizenship.

Citizenship laws in Europe are, however, in a state of flux. One may assume that the nationality laws in Europe would undergo further significant and far-reaching changes in the near future. Dual or multiple nationality is likely to be increasingly acceptable in Europe.

After over a century of forbidding dual nationality, **Mexico** amended its Constitution in 1998, and also its statutes, to permit Mexicans to simultaneously hold foreign citizenship and Mexican nationality. Under these amendments, Mexican dual nationals are able to preserve their Mexican-owned property, protect family inheritances, and avoid the restrictions on business and stock ownership placed on foreigners in Mexico.

In 1990, **the US** State Department adopted a policy statement under which a US citizen naturalised in another country is presumed to have the intent to retain US citizenship, although the presumption may be overcome by the person's express declaration to renounce US citizenship. In a 1995 opinion circulated to all US diplomatic posts, the Department of State observed that "it is no longer possible to terminate an American's citizenship without the citizen's cooperation". Thus, it is the US citizen's express intent that governs the loss of citizenship, if any. Even where the foreign state's naturalisation process includes an oath explicitly renouncing all but the foreign state's citizenship, the US State Department treats such oaths as "routine" and hence not resulting in expatriation unless the individual specifically insists on the renunciation of US citizenship. Conversely, the US oath of naturalisation requires renunciation of other allegiances. US government officials routinely and increasingly advise prospective citizens that even this oath will not result in loss of their earlier citizenship. The rationale is that most other countries under their own laws will not recognise the loss of citizenship based solely on the US oath, as the US does not consider its citizen to lose his/her citizenship by taking a similar oath in another country. It appears that the oath of renunciation is also not uniformly and invariably insisted upon. Nor does it have the consequence of automatic loss of citizenship. Voluntary acquisition of the nationality or citizenship is, thus, no longer an operative ground on U.S. practice to deny or deprive any person of his other nationality.

In States like **Singapore, Taiwan, the Republic of Korea and Japan**, the renunciation of one's own nationality is not a condition precedent for acquiring nationality by naturalisation or registration. For instance, in Singapore, there is no prohibition for naturalisation of a foreign national who is allowed to retain his nationality. Under the laws of the

Republic of Korea, an alien can retain his foreign nationality up to six months even after acquiring Korean nationality by naturalisation. The nationals of the Republic of Korea can voluntarily acquire foreign nationality without losing their Korean nationality. To renounce their Korean nationality, they are required to seek express permission of the Korean Government by submitting an application for the purpose to the Ministry of Justice together with documents establishing their dual nationality. Under the laws of Taiwan, the individual acquiring foreign nationality may at his option renounce his Chinese (Taiwanese) nationality; but this is with the permission of the Minister of Interior. Thus, in the situations described above, if the individuals concerned do not choose to renounce their nationality, or the governments concerned refuse permission for such renunciations, it would result in dual nationality.

Countries like Bangladesh are conferring their nationality on foreign nationals with a view to attract foreign investment and skills. Bangladeshis residing abroad are permitted to retain their Bangladesh nationality, even if they acquire the nationality of a foreign country of their domicile, provided that they make regular or periodical remittances of foreign exchange to Bangladesh. Any foreign national willing to invest in large-scale development projects in Bangladesh may also acquire Bangladesh citizenship without giving up his original nationality. The only requirement in these cases of dual nationality is that the security and intelligence agencies of Bangladesh have to give clearance. It is pointed out by an author that the system in Bangladesh is based largely on "administrative practice devoid of any legal basis and is being pursued 'as a matter of policy involving vital economic interests".

Some countries have accorded certain rights and privileges to dual nationals. In Japan, there is no discrimination between the dual nationals and the citizens. The dual nationals can also exercise, *inter alia*, the right of franchise, right to hold property and engage in other economic activities, right to education and the right to return. The dual nationals, however, are not entitled to hold any post in the Foreign Public Services of Japan. In 1960 and 1964, the Philippines had enacted laws to confer on the dual nationals the right to vote and the right to be appointed to public offices. These privileges are, however, confined to those Filipino nationals possessing simultaneously the nationality of any of the Iberian or friendly Ibero-American countries or of the United Kingdom. In Taiwan, the Chinese nationals holding the nationality of any other country are entitled to be nominated to certain public bodies, though they are otherwise ineligible to hold any public office.

Dual Nationality is a growing phenomenon in the world. The conditions, on which dual nationality operates and the rights and responsibilities of dual citizenship are determined, are worked out by each State. The incidence of dual nationality arises by virtue of operation of domestic laws of various States embodying the well-recognised principles of *jus soli* and *jus sanguinis*. It is allowed under the national laws of some countries despite deliberate and voluntary procedures of acquisition of nationality, namely naturalisation and registration.

Citizenship under the Citizenship Act of 1955

When the Citizenship Act, 1955 (Act 57 of 1955) was brought forth, the question of dual nationality had not acquired either the character of a public demand nor an issue of wider public concern. Migrants from India to the developed world did not add up substantially in numbers, affluence or influence. Indeed, they were making headway as nationals of an independent India. The Citizenship Act, 1955 did not and was not called upon to deal with the question of dual nationality in-depth. The Act merely took its cue from some of the provisional and tentative formulations contained in Part II of the Constitution. Nor had the new aspects of the dual nationality laws in different countries emerged clearly in the evolutionary process by 1950.

The Statement of Objects and Reasons appended to the citizenship legislation invoked Article 11 of the Constitution and stated that the Constitution as originally enacted did not make any provision with respect to the acquisition of citizenship after its commencement or the termination of citizenship or other matters relating to citizenship. The Act provides for the acquisition of citizenship after the commencement of the Constitution, by birth, descent, registration, naturalisation and incorporation of territory. It also makes necessary provisions for the termination and deprivation of citizenship under certain circumstances. The Act permits the Central Government to extend on reciprocal basis such rights of an Indian citizen as may be agreed upon to the citizens of other Commonwealth countries and the Republic of Ireland. The Act was amended in 1957, 1985 and 1986. Among the cognate Acts related to the Citizenship Act 1955 are the registration of Foreigners Act, 1939 (Act 16 of 1939), Foreigners Act, 1948 (Act 31 of 1948) and Passport Act, 1967 (Act 15 of 1967).

The Citizenship (Amendment) Act, 1986

The Citizenship Act of 1955 as amended does not provide for dual nationality or citizenship. **Section 3** recognizes citizenship by birth. Every person born in India on or after the 26th day of January, 1950 but before the commencement of the Citizenship (Amendment) Act, 1986 shall be a citizen of India by birth. Every person born in India on or after the commencement of the Citizenship (Amendment) Act, 1986 one of whose parents is a citizen of India at the time of his birth shall be a citizen of India by birth. Sub-section 2 of Section 3 provides for the exceptions to the rule of *jus soli* contained in Section 3(1). Sub-Section 2 of Section 3 provides that a person shall not be a citizen of India by birth if at the time of his birth his father possesses such immunities from suits and legal process as is accorded to an envoy of a foreign sovereign power accredited to the President of India and is not a citizen of India; or if his father is an enemy alien and the birth occurs in a place then under the occupation by the enemy. **Section 4** provides for citizenship by descent on the principle of *jus sanguinis*. A person born outside India on or after the 26 January, 1950 shall be a citizen of India by descent if his father is a citizen of India at the time of his birth. There is a proviso to Section 4(1) which lays down certain exceptions and conditions to citizenship by descent. Section 5 provides for citizenship by registration. **Section 6** deals with citizenship by naturalisation. A person to whom a certificate of naturalisation is granted is required to take an oath of allegiance in the prescribed form. **Section 7** provides for the Indian citizenship of persons by reasons of their connection with any territory which becomes a part of India. **Section 8** deals with renunciation of citizenship and provides that if any citizen of India of full age and capacity, who is also a citizen or national of another country, makes in the prescribed manner a declaration of renunciation of his Indian citizenship, the declaration shall be registered by the prescribed authority, and upon such registration that person shall cease to be a citizen of India. It appears that many of the Indian citizens who became citizens or nationals of another country may not have formally renounced their Indian citizenship or their declaration of renunciation may not have been registered by the prescribed authority. **Section 9** deals with termination of citizenship and provides that any citizen of India who by naturalisation, registration or otherwise voluntarily acquires or has, at any time between the 26 day of January, 1950 and the commencement of the Act of 1955, voluntarily acquired the citizenship of another country shall, upon such acquisition or, as the case may be, such commencement, ceases to be a citizen of India. Whereas Section 8 deals with renunciation of Indian citizenship by a citizen of India of full age and capacity, Section 9 provides for the automatic termination of Indian citizenship in the case of any person who subsequently and voluntarily acquires citizenship of another country. Section 9 is similar to Article 9 of the Constitution but somewhat wider in scope.

Section 12 of the Act contemplates within its orbit the concept of dual citizenship. It contains the seeds of dual nationality and provides an indicative model on the basis of which a specific concept of dual nationality can be elaborated. Section 12 reads as follows: "Power to confer rights of Indian citizen on citizens of certain countries :

(1) The Central Government may, by order notified in the Official Gazette, make provisions on a basis of reciprocity for the conferment of all or any of the rights of a citizen of India on the citizens of any country specified in the First Schedule.

(2) Any order made under sub-section (1) shall have effect

notwithstanding anything inconsistent therewith contained in any law other than the Constitution of India or this Act."

It is clear that Section 12 empowers the Central Government to make provisions for the conferment of all or any of the rights of a citizen of India on the citizens of any country specified in the First Schedule. Such conferment of all or any of the rights of a citizen of India on the citizens of any other country is tantamount to the recognition of the principle of dual citizenship. The countries specified in the First Schedule under Section 12 are primarily the Commonwealth countries and the Republic of Ireland. With regard to the conferment of all or any of the rights of a citizen of India on the citizens of any country specified in the First Schedule, the Central Government may make a provision but only on the basis of reciprocity. If a provision for dual nationality is to be made in respect of some of the Commonwealth countries and countries like the U.S.A., Canada, the U.K., members of the European Union, Australia, New Zealand, Singapore and such other countries as the Government may consider appropriate, an additional provision which may be Section 12A may have to be added in the Citizenship Act, but without the condition of reciprocity as is stipulated in Section 12. The names of the Commonwealth countries which are specified in the First Schedule and which may then be included in the Schedule under the new Section 12A would have to be deleted from the First Schedule. An indication would also have to be given in the new Section 12A with regard to the non-conferment of electoral rights and the right to apply for and serve in the armed forces and other such rights. Section 12 provides a pattern and a building block which commends itself to the Committee of appropriate adaptation in respect of dual nationality. It can also be clarified that the conferment of all or any of the rights of a citizen of India on the citizens of other countries specified in the Schedule to the Act would be confined to those who were or were entitled to be citizens of India at the time of the commencement of the Constitution as well as children and grandchildren of those persons.

It is noteworthy that Section 12(2) provides for the effect of an order granting dual nationality under Section 12 to override anything inconsistent therewith contained in any law other than the Constitution of India or the Act of 1955. Section 12 clearly contains the seeds of dual nationality. It provides an indicative model on the basis of which the concept of dual nationality can be unfolded and elaborated. Dual nationality should also be granted to the children and grandchildren of those who apply and obtain dual citizenship under the amended provisions of the Citizenship Act.

Issue of Dual Citizenship

The Merits of the Proposal

The demand for dual citizenship deserves to be considered in a positive and forward-looking spirit and without the conventional and stereotyped blinkers which have often obfuscated an objective consideration of the issue on the merits of the proposal.

The expression 'NRI' which is used in common parlance as a synonym for the Diaspora consisting both of those who have retained Indian passports and those who have taken foreign nationality, are no longer to be regarded as the 'Not Required Indians". Instead, the 'NRI' may be described as the 'National Reserve of India' and also as the 'National Resource of India'. Dual citizenship has become a rallying point for the Indian Diaspora's solidarity with Mother India and that dual citizenship is an idea whose time has come. The demand for dual citizenship has an emotional resonance particularly for the first generation Indians who have made their homes in Europe, North America, Australia, New Zealand, Singapore, and Thailand. Many of them have taken the nationality of the countries of their domicile but look upon their passports with nostalgia. Many of them must have had to renounce their Indian citizenship by making a declaration to that effect but that did not weaken their emotional bonds with India. Dual Nationality is regarded by them as a badge of belonging. They feel unhappy when they have to apply for their Indian visas "to go to their own country."

Generally, the question is asked about the keenness for dual nationality when the PIO Card Scheme did offer practically all the benefits of dual nationality. Their answer has been twofold: firstly, it is argued that if the Government had already offered practically all the benefits of dual nationality under the Scheme of PIO Cards to the entire Indian Diaspora, it should have no difficulty in providing for dual nationality for citizens of a few specified countries by legislation; and secondly, a legislative provision of dual nationality has been considered a higher form of the acknowledgement of their linkage with Mother India.

Arguments against Dual Citizenship

The most frequent and forceful argument against dual citizenship is the argument of security implications of dual nationality. Whenever the question of grant of dual nationality is considered, apprehensions have been expressed that the entry and exit of persons to whom dual citizenship may be granted would become impossible to regulate under the Foreigners Act and may jeopardize the sensitive internal security scenario in the country. It is also erroneously assumed that the induction of persons having dual citizenship in sensitive organisations and armed and paramilitary forces is implicit in the concept of dual citizenship. It is sometimes feared that the grant of dual citizenship would lead to the creation of another privileged class, which would result in a further sharpening of the existing social divide in the country.

Even though the regulation of the entry and exit of any person under the dual citizenship is questioned; the entry and exit of persons into India even at present is insufficiently regulated and according to media reports, there are millions of illegal entrants in India especially from neighbouring countries, some of whom might even be security risks and the existing legislation including the Foreigners Act and the Illegal Migrants' (Determination by Tribunal) Act etc., has not been able to deal with the problem effectively. Whereas under the dual citizenship, a person of Indian origin living in the countries would be specified and to whom a proper document of dual citizenship would be granted, would be subject to more effective regulation than the lakhs of visitors who enter India without any let or hindrance and make India their home without any visa or work permit.

It is not possible to understand why the entry or exit of a person to whom the document of dual citizenship is granted after full scrutiny is any more difficult to regulate and monitor than the entry and exit of any foreign national or an Indian citizen. If the existing procedures are inadequate, they can be altered; if the will and vigilance is lacking, remedial measures can and ought to be taken.

A person traveling on a document of dual nationality would be like any other visitor or a PIO cardholder or an Indian national returning to India. The Government of India may, if it so desires, prescribe the period of one year at a time for the dual citizen's stay in India except when permission for a longer or indefinite period is granted as in the case of senior citizens. A dual citizen may also be covered by the Passport Act of 1920 and the Passports Act of 1967. In the alternative, he or she may be covered by the Foreigners Act by means of a limited deeming provision. Special forms may be prescribed for holders of dual citizenship both for entry and exit and those may also be deemed as registration of dual citizens on their entry. Security implications are minimal in case of dual citizens of Indian origin because those who desire to have dual citizenship would have to make an application in the first place; they would have to make a full and faithful disclosure; they would be subject to scrutiny before dual citizenship is granted to them; they would fill prescribed forms when they enter and exit; subject to appropriate exceptions in case of students and senior citizens, they would be able to stay only for a period of one year at a time; their dual citizenship passports would be stamped on entry and exit.

Wherever necessary, provisions of the Passport (Entry Into India) Act, 1920 and those of the Passports Act, 1967 are made applicable to dual nationals *mutatis mutandis*, the authorities would be armed with sufficient control mechanisms. In the alternative, certain provisions of the Foreigners Act, 1947 may be made applicable to those to whom dual citizenship is granted, and this could be done by means of a deeming provision, particularly because those persons would continue to have their foreign passports. Care should, however, be taken to simplify rather than multiply procedures and to make their application and implementation effective without making them cumbersome or onerous.

Keeping in mind serious security implications, persons under dual citizenship shall not, as a rule, be entitled to be inducted in the civil services of the States or the Union. They shall also not be entitled to be inducted in any sensitive organisations or in armed and paramilitary forces. Further, their entry document should be deemed to be their registration and the period of continuous stay for them should be one year. An exception should also be made in case of senior citizens who may be granted permission to stay indefinitely; Diaspora students who have dual citizenship under Indian law should be granted permission upto a maximum of two years at a time.

The introduction of dual nationality cannot make any difference to the so-called existing social divide in the country. The PIO Card Scheme attracted a mere 1200 applicants. Even if there were a hundred times more number of applicants for dual citizenship, it could hardly make any difference whatsoever to the "existing social divide" in the country.

As a matter of policy, the Government of India welcomes and encourages ethnic tourism which has come to constitute a significant proportion of tourists who visit India. The demand and expectation of dual nationality deserves to be considered in a positive and constructive spirit taking into account the goodwill it would generate among the PIOs.

The scheme of dual nationality can be worked into our legislation acquired by following an appropriate procedure as may be laid down in the Parliamentary legislation and the rules framed there under with appropriate safeguards.

- The document of dual nationality or citizenship should clearly specify, wherever applicable, the details of the previous documents of Indian nationality or proof thereof as well as full details of the foreign nationality or citizenship of the person concerned.

- It should also be a requirement of the entry and departure procedures to stamp the document of dual nationality as well as the document of the individual's other nationality, which ought to be regarded as the primary nationality.
- The nationals of the countries in respect of which we have security apprehensions may not be included under the scheme;
- A few countries may be specified, the nationals of which, if they are members of the Indian Diaspora and if they were or were entitled to be citizens of India at the commencement of the Constitution, may be granted dual nationality and the provision may be extended to their children and grandchildren;
- The principle of *jus sanguinis* may be appropriately applied to verify and monitor the Indian linkage;
- The requirement of complete disclosure on an affidavit and the provision for careful scrutiny by the Missions as well as a nodal agency comprising of representatives of Ministry of External Affairs and Ministry of Home Affairs would safeguard the security interests of the country;
- Procedures should be simple and swift and should be insulated from red tape and corruption;
- In the wake of a series of terrorist attacks, to accord paramount priority to security concern is a national imperative. Dual citizenship and national security are not mutually exclusive: indeed linkages of love and loyalty represented by dual citizenship and all-round vigilance safeguarded by procedures of scrutiny to be embodied in the forms and the Rules would prove to be the bastion of India's national security and worldwide economic, cultural and political interests;
- Moreover, it will not be practicable to grant any electoral rights or right to contest elections to elective bodies in India or the right to hold any elective office in India to persons to whom dual citizenship is granted, particularly if those rights have to be operationally exercised outside

India. Postal arrangements are tardy, impracticable, and often infructious;

- If a person of full capacity who has ceased to be an Indian citizen as a result of a declaration of renunciation (for whatever reason made) and has acquired the citizenship of any of the countries specified in the Second Schedule makes an application for his registration as a dual citizen of India, the Central Government may, if it thinks fit, cause him to be registered as such a citizen

Dual Citizenship had been a long-standing demand of the Indian Diaspora. The principal rationale of the demand, however, is sentimental and psychological. Desire of People of Indian Origin (PIO) to forge emotional and cultural bonds with their country of origin is quite evident in the scale of philanthropic activities done by them in India. Dual citizenship will strengthen this bond and facilitate Diaspora's contribution in India's social development. In contrast to economic rights where the Diaspora should be treated at par with other foreign investors, on the matter of social, civil and cultural rights it should be treated on par with other Indian citizens.

Dual Citizenship to Indian Diaspora

Dual citizenship has, thus, been an old demand of Indian Diaspora and it was first voiced when the then Prime Minister Narasimha Rao visited the United States in 1994. Then Indian ambassador, Siddhartha Shankar Ray had worked out a scheme that would have met the demand without any hiccups. The Ray scheme never saw the light of the day as successive government tied themselves in legal wrangles. Vajpayee government tried to overcome the hurdle by offering an Identity card for Persons of Indian Origin (PIO) that would have given all the benefits of Indian citizens except voting right.

During the First Pravasi Bharatiya Divas, held on 9-11 January 2003, the Hon'ble Prime Minister of India announced the policy of Dual Citizenship for the PIO. Subsequently, the draft bill was introduced in the Rajya Sabha on 9th May, 2003 for amending the Citizenship Act 1955, to give effect to this policy announcement. In December 2003, Parliament passed the Bill (the Citizenship (Amendment) Bill 2003 to grant dual citizenship to the PIOs belonging to 16 countries, and on January 7, 2004 the President gave his assent. The 16 countries are: USA, Canada, United Kingdom, Netherlands, Italy, Ireland, Portugal, Switzerland, Greece, Cyprus, Israel, Australia, New Zealand, France, Sweden, Finland. The consequent changes in the Citizenship Rules 1956 have to be effected by the Ministry of Home Affairs. After notification, the Rules have to be laid on the table of both Houses of Parliament before they come into force and the Rules would be laid on the table of both the Houses of Parliament in the session beginning in August 2004.

The consequent changes in the Citizenship Rules 1956 have been effected by the Ministry of Home Affairs and guidelines have been circulated to our Missions for implementation of the above.

Dual citizenship became a reality in December 2005 for the Indian Diaspora in 71 countries including the US, UK, Australia, Sri Lanka and Italy that allow dual citizenship under their local laws in some form or the other. The Overseas Citizenship of India (OCI) status was granted to persons of Indian origin (PIOs) of all nationalities, except Pakistan and Bangladesh. There are about 25 million people of Indian origin staying overseas, but OCI status has been granted only to PIOs — or their descendants — who have migrated after January 26, 1950. OCIs are entitled to benefits such as multiple entry, multi-purpose life long visa to visit India, exemption from reporting to police authorities for any length of stay in India, and, parity with NRIs in financial, economic and educational fields except in the acquisition of agricultural or plantation properties. They, however, do not have voting rights, equal opportunity in matters of public employment or be able to hold any constitutional position.

While the NDA regime had initiated moves on dual citizenship, Prime Minister Manmohan Singh had during Pravasi Bhartiya Divas 2005 announced the extending of OCI to PIOs. This required an amendment to the Citizenship Act, 1955 as the Indian Constitution did not provide for dual citizenship. The formal launching of the scheme was done by

Dr Singh at Pravasi Bhartiya Divas on January 7, 2006.

You can take the person out of India, but you can't take India out of the person. An Indian will always remain an Indian no matter where they go. The cultural ties are just too strong for first generation immigrants to lose the connection with their parents, relatives and the way they have been bought up. It's very difficult to forget your roots even though you live in a foreign country and follow a different culture. The Indian government now offers a partial subsidy called Overseas Citizens of India that allows quite a few privileges of being an Indian citizen. But if a large section of the Indian diaspora chooses to retain their Indian citizenship, its good for India. A reverse brain drain attracting talented doctors, scientists, etc will definitely make India a better place to live in and a force to reckon with!

5

Mahatma Gandhi and Indian Diaspora

S.N. Sahu

An exemplary Indian and planetary citizen Mahatma Gandhi stands out in history as an exceptional Pravasi Bharatiya. He made pioneering contributions in understanding the challenges faced by people of Indian origin in different parts of the globe and outlining their immense talent and caliber in diverse areas of human endeavour. His arrival in Mumbai from South Africa on 9th January 1915 is being commemorated as Pravasi Bharatiya Divas in India.

His unprecedented non-violent struggle for the restoration of rights of Indians in South Africa constitutes an epoch making event in history. He explained that Indians there, mostly consisting of coolies and labourers, were discriminated due to their ability to compete with the white settlers in the field of business. He wrote in numerous articles on trade jealousy against Indians which prompted the British authorities in South Africa to take measures to impair their capacity to pursue any trade and commercial activities.

His first Satyagraha was therefore a Satyagraha to restore the inherent right of Indians to engage themselves in business. Indians in South Africa with hardly any access to education and political power could display their business intelligence and garnered better profits than white settlers. Mahatma Gandhi mingled with them and elicited their opinion to draft petitions in defence of their rights. He insightfully observed that brain splitting was as much the right of the educated and awakened as it was of those who are immersed in deprivation and exploitation. Such an approach in the context of colonial policy of excluding Indians assumes significance in putting an end to all discriminations and proclaiming the principle and practice of inclusion.

In 1897 in an interview to the Natal Advertiser he insightfully observed that the "The policy of exclusion is obsolete". He stressed on repealing all the exclusivist policies to establish harmony among different parts of the British Empire.

That observation of Mahatma Gandhi that the policy of exclusion had become obsolete is of paramount significance in the globalised world of twenty first century, the architecture of which is inevitably going to be based on inclusion and understanding.

He boldly declared in South Africa that Indians were born traders and therefore the colonial policy of denying them the right to pursue business was a denial of a right which was inherent to them. Today India is a major centre of trade and commerce in the world. If Indian settlers in South Africa were succeeding in adverse circumstances in displaying their business intelligence against the British settlers, Indians, in twenty first century with favourable indices of human development index and residing in almost all parts of the world are bound to register unprecedented success in the domain of business. We need to underline these insights of Mahatma Gandhi while discussing Indian Diaspora in the era of globalisation.

The late President of India, Shri K.R. Narayanan while serving as India's Ambassador to America during 1980-84 had described in his book *India and America* that Indians in that country constituted a brain bank. It is fascinating to note that in 1924 Mahatma Gandhi expressed the opinion that Indians going out of the country did not result in draining our resources. He was responding to a remark that "every Indian worker going out of India was so much economic waste". He categorically asserted that "My residence in South Africa was not an economic waste of power". Today the Indian Diaspora has emerged as a vast reservoir of talent, innovation and culture. It is more than brain bank. It is a vibrant and lively source of our civilisational values.

In the globalised world of twenty first century proponents of the dangerous theory of clash of civilisation are becoming more strident. It is interesting to note that in nineteenth century similar theories were cited to discriminate Indians and deny them their rights. Mahatma Gandhi quoted two observations one from General Smuts and the other from Lord Selborne. Both of them said that east and west could never meet. General Smuts went to the extent of writing that there would be explosion if people of eastern civilisation came in contact with people of western civilisation. Stating that worldviews of these two civilisations were different he elaborated that the western civilisation believed in multiplying wants and desires and the eastern civilisation stressed on simplicity and moderation in life. He, therefore, said that people with such differing outlook and approach could not have same set of rights. Mahatma Gandhi however underlined the commonalities of civilisations and stressed on their essential unity. That larger vision of unity and understanding informed all his actions which aimed at addressing thc challenges faced by the Indian Diaspora. India is a standing refutation of the theory of clash of civilisations. Indians anywhere in the world stand testimony to our long cherished values which spring from the confluence of civilisations. When Indian Diaspora is more vibrant and widespread we need to rediscover these ideas of Mahatma Gandhi and recapture his vision based on care and compassion for the larger humanity.

As early in 1908 Mahatma Gandhi wrote that if Indians intended to settle in diverse regions of the world and prosper they should follow their faith scrupulously, establish unity among Hindus and Muslims and acquire right kind of education.

These seminal observations of Gandhiji are of critical relevance for the world often facing mayhem and violence from terrorists. Such an approach will dispel the notion that one particular religion promotes terrorism. His emphasis on Hindu-Muslim unity and interfaith harmony as a precondition for the settlement and prosperity of Indians in diverse regions of the world are indispensable factors for peace and security of the Indian Diaspora.

Mahatma Gandhi reflected on Indian settlers in Canada and other parts of the world. When he was informed that Indians faced discrimination in Canada, he cited the example of Japanese who confronted the same challenge. While he admired the courage of Japanese in fighting against discriminatory polices he regretted that Indians confined themselves to home in face of the threat to their livelihood. Eventually he attributed the fiercely independent spirit of Japanese to the freedom enjoyed by their home country which never came under colonial rule.

Our freedom struggle under the leadership of Mahatma Gandhi was an extension of his first Satyagaraha launched in South Africa on the strength of Indian settlers. When he was being given a farewell in South Africa he saw a news item which informed him of a legislative measure which withdrew franchise rights of Indians. The Indian settlers were not aware of the magnitudes of the deprivation and discrimination arising out of that legislative measure. It was Mahatma Gandhi who made them aware of its crippling effect on their ability to lead a dignified life. He was thus instrumental in sensitizing them about the value of right to vote and its role in making informed choices. They were reading newspapers only to find out the price of commodities and were ever ready, in the words of Mahatma Gandhi, "to pocket insult and pocket profit" He brought about a change in their thinking and mobilised them to successfully participate in the first ever non-violent struggle for freedom and independence.

Even as he was doing that, he was also educating them about the values of cleanliness, sanitation and hygiene which they lacked.

In fact, Gandhiji not only educated the members of the Indian Diaspora but also educated Indians to appreciate their plight. During his stay in South Africa he authored a green pamphlet and gave reasons for writing it.

The object of publishing it was to place the entire facts regarding the position of Indians in South Africa before the Indian public. The people have belief that India does not know exactly how many Indians were outside the country, and what their status was, and the object was to draw their attentions to the subject, and it was with that view that the pamphlet was published.

He thought that independence of India from British rule would eventually enable India to effectively address the challenges faced by the Indian Diaspora. When he and his wife arrived in Mumbai from South Africa they were given a rousing welcome. On that occasion he had said that "I can only hope that by our future conduct we shall have deserved this welcome". He did excel in world history by his exemplary conduct. The Indian Diaspora and Indians need to replicate his example to carry forward his vision. It is important to study and analyze the thoughts of the Mahatma Gandhi vis-à-vis Indian Diaspora and creatively understand their relevance for our own time.

6

Rhizome Roots: The Indian arts and the Indian Diaspora

Arshiya Sethi

I would like to begin by thanking Dr. S. K. Jain, Member Secretary of the "Foundation for Indian Development Initiative" New Delhi and the management of the Saheed Bhagat Singh College (evening) University of Delhi for inviting me to participate in this seminar on "Indian Diaspora in the Era of Globalisation: Implications for India. I am privileged to have as Chair of this session, my former teacher Prof. Imtiaz Ahmed. It is after a long break and a circuitous journey that I am returning to Academics, so in advance itself I will apologise for any aberration of Academic "maryada" that I may indulge in.

I believe that this topic is a very important one because living in today's age and not factoring the impact of globalisation is like choosing the way of the dinosaur. I am also glad that Dr. Jain has included some elements of the arts in this multi faceted discussion of the Diaspora. For, frankly the arts are the core of the Indian-ness of India. Though the arts are very culture specific they grow like Rhizome Roots, and it is interesting to see-three things:

(i) How they settle in foreign soils

(ii) How they adapt, integrate and mature under international influences, a study of identity and assimilation, and

(iii) How they return or reconnect to their mother culture.

In India, the power of culture since ancient times is well known. We have the distinction of a cultural impact without political and economic colonisation. I refer to the spread of Buddhism, and the eastward impact of Indian culture and religion, that has left a footprint in Far East Asia.

What has happened to Indian performing arts overseas, in the hands of the people of Indian origin, over the last two centuries is an interesting study. A quick overview would establish the start of this story to the early 19th century. Concurrent with the end of slavery, this story began with the French Reunion Island and then other parts of the Caribbean followed. The "Chutney" music from the Caribbean is how the world sees the adaptation of Indian religious and folk songs that the labourers carried with them. Today's "Chutney" music stars include filmi songs as inspiration- a tribute to Indian cinema- Hindi and Bhojpuri that knows no barriers!

Another success story from music is in the cultural impact of Bhangara. Today it is being interpreted in the space where Asian – UK, and hip-hop cultures meet. In a New York Time story titled "Bhangra's Ambassador: Keeping the Party Spinning", D.J. Rekha expressed her cultural accountability to her music that is being accessed, assessed and consumed by other cultures. Today Bhangara music is in an international setting, no longer stashed in the exotic "world music" category. It was UK that took the lead, spurred on by the large Indian market created by immigrants and the easy travel afforded by the size of the country. Bhangara is also used effectively to pace physical exercises and workouts. Bhangara got the boost in the arm when US rappers picked it up. This hyphenated Bhangara helps second generation immigrants to juxtapose both identities- the identity of origin and the identity of the current living space.

I would like to take the next example of Indian dance in UK and USA. Here if we apply the three pronged model referred to earlier, we find that in the US, because of its acceptance of being a multi cultural society there is some degree of funding available for Indian Dance in its "as is where is from". The strong network of regional (Andhra Association)/ language (Telgu Association)/ sociological groups (Rajput Association of North India) and religios associations like the Federeation of Jain Associations of North America (JAINAS) also help in supporting the arts in a diasporic setting. There are two manifestations here.

- the opportunity to local artists/ practitioners of Indian arts.
- The support extended tours by eminent dancers and teachers from India.

The interface thus afforded upholds higher standards of authenticities by diasporic artists. The potential of expanded funding possibilities often lead towards fusion work, but in the US Indian arts in a fusion setting is mostly at an experimental level. No stars have been born. However, in the UK- given London's effort at portraying itself as a "World City" have possibily been behind the support received by dancers like Akram Khan(Bangladesh origin Kathak dancer) Shobhan Jaysinghe (is of Sri Lankan origin and is trained in Bharatanatyam). Their work is truly contemporary and has only a token connect with the original arts both have practiced.

In the rest of the Europe the performing arts scene of the diaspora is not as robust. There is however high receptivity to esoteric South Asian forms. I would like to make a special reference to the fact that for several decades, almost consistently Dhrupadiyas have enjoyed support from Europe, where they find a more enthusiastic response to their art than they do back home in India which is "dumbing down its appreciation for high art". The popularisation of Qawali Singer Nusrat Fateh Ali Khan dates back to his recordings and broadcasts from radio France. South Asia recognised his genius post this. His sound track in "Dead Man Walking" was a watershed – albeit it has been beaten by A R Rahman's winning run with "Slumdog Millionaire".

In contrast is the case of Sattriya. Sattriya, hailing from Assam is the recently declared classical dance of India- actually the words of the 15th November, 2000, notification explicitly says "A major dance tradition of India, at par with other major dance traditions of India, like Bharatnatyam and Kathak"- has a negligible diasporic presence since the people from Assam by and large are insular and not very daring to travel out. While in the US Sattriya remains a negligible presence, in UK and Europe the form has more visibility - not necessarily because of a diasporic presence but because the form itself has a rare USP. It is a manifestation of a 500 years old living tradition and is steeped in devotion. The sincerity of its practitioners, many of whom are who "perform it for God and not money", and I quote the young master Phabanand Barbayan, wins the hearts of a materialistic west that is appreciating alternative ways of living life. Celibate monks, who have for centuries been custodians of the art, make it an exotic art that finds a perfect fit in to the performance programmers of museums. For the same reason it finds a natural fit in the slew of sacred music festivals around the world. Menka P.P. Bora a young woman practitioner of Sattriya presently located in UK and working on the dance and Museum project there recognizes the deep link her dance affords her with her life and identity. "Dance is my oxygen but there comes a social responsibility when you are presenting a traditional classical art form from a country like India. This responsibility is of presenting correctly".

In the way the art returns to its country of origin, I would like to mention, that there is no standard way, but what is common is the deep rooted desire to perform in the country of origin, for this performance serves as a validation, an endorsement and a certification. Sometimes it also results in a spurt of new work, new collaborations and new aesthetics entering the art scene in the mother country. This is a positive development testifying to the dynamism of the tradition. However, the example of the Madras music season where NRI dancers, buy prime slots for themselves more on the power of the dollar than on capacity and capability, dilutes the standards of the arts and is not a healthy practice.

How can we ensure the highest standards of the core of the art being available, practiced and retained in the diaspora? One possible solution is to open more and more centres of Indian arts in countries with a strong diaspora presence. Secondly, formal forums for presentation of the arts practiced in a diasporic setting should be created. Thirdly, subsidies for the study of Indian subjects by diaspora students should be encouraged and enhanced. On going programmes could have a special element to increase this. For example, many who come from USA to India, under the Fulbright programme are of Indian origin and they come here to study some aspect of India. This should be strengthened. The Government could look at creating more India study chairs where there is a strong diaspora presence to meet the needs of curiosity, roots and identity.

The writing on the wall is clear- India is destined to be a global soft power. If not in these ways then through the unstoppable route of Bollywood that has given us a globally popular music form and a globally irresistible dance form. Just as Hollywood spread American culture world wide, Bollywood could be the vehicle for the spread of Indian culture world wide. NFDC could see a creative role for itself here. If Yash Chopra and Karan Johar have made their fortunes from films that are in the Des-Pardes- Swades mould, then this is certainly a route to explore. The abundant popularity of Bollywood, is testified to by the Star tours, that are eagerly awaited.

If in the National interest of India there is a recognition of the fact that the soft power is as important as the hard power, as China has done, and so its efforts at promoting culture have gone hand in hand with promoting industry and markets, then there is need to see the potential of the diaspora differently. It would require a mild re-engineering of priorities so that key ministries could mainstream the potential of People to People contact with the diaspora, in their plans and schemes. I refer particularly to the Ministry of External Affairs, Culture, Tourism, and Education (Human Resource Development). All this will help promote brand India better, in the world.

In a globalised context its all about pairing things to a common vocabulary of shared concerns. In a terror stricken, polarized (me and them) stressed out world India could use the immense strengths of her arts and a vibrant diaspora preserving, performing, practicing and presenting her arts to a world that needs to be reminded that India is a land that has successfully practiced pluralism where the "Clash of Civilisations" has been avoided by a shared " Ganga-Jamuna" *tehzeeb*, and where the sacred forms a strong central core and helps us deal with the negative forces of globalisation.

7

Cinematic Representation of Indian Diaspora

Rakesh Kumar Patel

Human beings have natural tendency to migrate from one place to another because of different reasons. This migration may be seasonal, temporary, and permanent, within the country and outside the country as well. Jayram argues that "in human migration... migration does not mean the mere physical movement of people. Migrants carry with them socio-cultural baggage which among other things consists of (a) pre defined social identity (b) a set of religious beliefs and practices (c) a framework of norms and values governing family and kinship organisation, and food habits and (d) language" (Jayram 2004:16). Further according to him, "the phenomenon surrounding such human migration is best conceptualised under the rubric Diaspora" (*ibid*).

The Greek word 'Diaspora' was specifically used to indicate the experience of the Jews exiled to Babylon after defeat of Jerusalem in 587 B.C. Regarding their migration Cohen (1997) explained that, "for Jews Africans, Palestinians and Armenians, Diaspora signifies a collective trauma where one dreams of home while living in exiles. For Tololyan, the editor of *Diaspora*, a journal of transnational studies, the concept of Diaspora is related to, "the entire semantic domain that includes words like immigrant, expatriate, refugees, guest workers, exile community, overseas community, ethnic community" (Tololyan 1991:4). William Safran (1991:83) has attempted a kind of an 'ideal type' definition of Diaspora. According to his analysis

Diaspora means, "Expatriate minority communities, dispersed from an original 'centre' to at least two 'peripheral' places. They maintain a memory or myth about their original homeland; they believe they are not and perhaps cannot be fully accepted by their host country, and they see the ancestral home as a place of eventual return and a place to maintain or restore". Thus, academicians, scholars, intellectuals, leaders or activists from various disciplines use the word Diaspora for those communities who live outside their homeland. Actually Diaspora is that community, which in one way or another has a history of migration. The Diaspora community now 'serves as the exemplary communities of the transnational moment', where the Diaspora culture goes beyond and challenges the national boundaries.

Before exploring the interrelationship between cinema and Indian Diaspora we would like to define cinema. Actually, Cinema is unique confluence of literature and art. As we know literature always is the cumulative image of the temper of people. Those who bestow with 'creative imagination talent' will be able to depict the social realities in literature. According to Nicholas, "the films are a living mirror of a nation's life, even if one did not understand everything that the mirror showed, it would surely repay a few hours of study (Nicholas, 1946:95). Thus, the films are like important text from which we make meaning and could understand history of a nation's life. On the other hand cinema is a very effective medium of communication and due to advance technologies its accessibility to the audiences all over the world from the place of production itself has increased tremendously. One of the most important reasons for its span and popularity is that it is the main source of entertainment to the masses wherever they reside. Films on Diaspora contain facts about everyday life of people in Diaspora and hence give knowledge about them.

India has the third largest Diasporic community after China and Britain, numbering about 25 million people across 110 countries. Overseas Indians have distinguished themselves in the host society, contributing immensely to local economies and cultures and at the same time adding to India's development as well. With the onset of the process of globalisation there has been an information revolution with internet, DVDs, CDs, cable TV, dish TV, etc. Also the privatisation of the airways has increased number of flights which have compressed both time and space. In this context films from Bollywood industry can easily reach to any part of the world where Indian Diaspora live. Thus, films from Bollywood work as resource of Indianness and provide cultural feedback to the Indian Diaspora. This trend has picked up after globalisation that is why films based on the lives of Indian Diaspora have become more visible after the emergence of the process of globalisation. However, a careful observation reveals that most of these films narrate the story of Indian Diasporic communities residing either in USA or UK, who belongs to the affluent sections of the Indian society. They rarely depict those Indians who are settled in Malaysia, Sri Lanka, Africa, Mauritius, Trinidad, Fiji etc., to name just a few countries; it is interesting to note that these are the countries where Indians were taken as indenture labourers. It is co-incident that most of these indentured labourers were from lower caste-class strata of Indian society. Hence this study is a humble effort to investigate and analysed the myth and reality about the Indian Diaspora and its cinematic representation. We have tried to analyze the contents of films which are based on the lives of Indian Diaspora in UK and USA. In doing so we have selected films made by both Bollywood filmmakers as well as films produced and directed by people in Indian Diaspora.

Conceptual Explanation

Before we come to the core issue of our study, let us define certain concepts which have been used in this chapter. In the light of these conceptual clarifications we would carry out our findings.

Diaspora are those human groups who have history and experiences of migration and the attendant anxiety of displacement, homelessness and a wish to return to homeland (Singh 2003:3). Etymologically the term Diaspora is derived from the Greek composite verb 'dia' (through) and 'speirein' (infinitive) literally meaning, 'to scatter', 'to spread' or 'to disperse', (Jayram 2004 : 16).

Bollywood: It is the biggest film industry in the world, situated in Mumbai, India. Film production activity has been given the status of industry very recently (1998) by government of India. Bollywood films are very popular in audiences throughout the world, in Diasporas and local Indians as well. Bollywood, the name of Indian film industry emerged as an imitation to Hollywood, the film industry of USA. Nicholas (1946) in his book 'Verdict on India' called it *Hindu Hollywood.* According to Dudrah (2006) "the naming and popular usage of the Mumbai film industry as Bollywood not only reveals on a literal level an obvious reworking of the appellation of the cinema of Hollywood, but, on a more significant level that Bollywood is able to serve alternative cultural and social representations away from dominant white ethnocentric audio-visual possibilities"(Dudrah, 2006:35).

Globalisation : According to *Blackwell Dictionary of Sociology* (1955) "Globalisation is that process which affects the socio-political and economic aspects of the different societies. It has also brought changes in the area of music, dress and mass media at the international level with high speed". Giddens (1990) defines globalisation in the following words "increasing interdependence or mutuality among different people and different territories of the world is globalisation. This mutuality exists in social and economic relations. It compresses time and space". And in this compression of time and space media products like films play vital role.

Indian Diaspora, Bollywood and Globalisation

It is a well known fact that 'The success of Indian movies at the global level since the late 1990s has attracted much scholarly attention (Desai 2004, Kaur 2002, and Rajadhyaksha 2003). For Indian immigrants living across the globe, movies from India are an essential part of their popular culture. Bollywood films are a resource for Indian Diasporas to restore the memory of homeland and provide them cultural and emotional feedback. According to Mehta, "For the Diasporas the only connection with India is Hindi film and Hindi film is India for them" (Mehta 2004: 64). Scholars have argued that Indian popular movies are one of the most significant and visible components of Indian popular culture both at home and in Diaspora (Desai, 2004; Prasad, 1998). Indian movies epitomize what Hannerz (1997) has described as the cultural 'flow' of images across the globe, a characterizing feature of globalisation, albeit in a direction counter to the normative west to east media flows. "Globalisation as a process compresses time and space. It has hastened as the result of new information technology and economic liberalisation and in consequences, is radically restructuring, the traditional relationship between culture and economy as well as hastening a consciousness of being in the Diaspora" (Singh, 2003:5).

"It can be argued that the people of Indian origin in the Diaspora, living in different countries, share similarity of experiences while watching Indian movies, which thus contribute to the construction of a global 'public culture' (Appadurai 1989:58). The similarities of experiences exist among Indian Diaspora because of their common Indian origin, history of migration and their nostalgia to homeland. Thus, the structure of the cinema must be such that the individual finds himself to be a part of the larger whole which constitutes his surroundings. And Hindi popular cinema represents the Indian social realities in such a way, that people like to see their societal images in the mirror called 'cinema', a sort of art and literature. Here, it must be noted that the Diaspora shares this similarity of experiences also with the Indians in the homeland, as these movies are primarily made for home audiences. "The similarity of experiences is rooted both in their Diasporic identity and ethnic Indian identity free from territorial confines of the national boundaries. Indian movies and movies in general have, traditionally played a crucial role in constructing national identity by combining features from diverse multicultural and ethnic-linguistic identities that constitute the Indian nation-state (Chakravarty 2003, Nandy 1998).

When we see the impact of globalisation in India, on public culture and Indian Diaspora, we find that world today is connected in an unprecedented way. Due to large scale advances in transportation, media technologies, and flow of capital among other things have made it possible for persistent interaction and exchange across distance and time. In this sequence international·co-production of films, exchanges of stars and distribution of Indian movies across the globe are constructing a global Indian identity, and negotiation occurs between national identity and the Diasporic identity in the film texts, thus helping to construct hybrid identities. To understand the above phenomenon, Bollywood movies must be situated within the context of globalisation and its new emerging features. Bollywood movies can be seen as a counter-flow of media products from a developing country to the more developed west. In the same vein Dudrah (2002) highlights the interconnection of Indians through the cultural flows and public culture. He argues that, "And even though this counter-flow of media products (news, movies, T.V. shows etc.) from the homeland to the Diasporas sustains itself using the same systemic structures of globalisation that operate in cultural flow from the west to a developing country, and functions through the principles of free market economy and technology diffusion. Bollywood movies constitute an element of 'public culture' for the Indian Diaspora and to some extent by the Diaspora from the Indian sub-continent (Dudrah, 2002b). An aspect of this inter-connectedness is a growing realisation that the connections do not necessarily have a unilinear direction, making dichotomies such as centre-periphery, global-local, modern-tradition and other related, once problematic, if not redundant. Appadurai goes as far as to argue that the new global organisation of culture cannot be understood in terms of existing centre-periphery models, even those which allow for multiple centre and peripheries (Appadurai, 1996:6). Hannerz (1996) likes to capture the multi-centrality of connections with the metaphor of flow". The emergence of global satellite television channels from the countries outside the west is constructing global communities of Indians. Thus, the homeland media organisations reach out to the Diasporas flips the phenomenon of globalisation and the global/local dialectic. It has reversed the dialectic of the binary global/local to local would become the dominant ideology and the global becomes the resisting ideology.

Though the above perspectives are helpful, but do not help us to understand the reverse flows of the Bollywood phenomenon. Now media products made in home countries (local) and are consumed by the Diaspora (global). In this case the dominant ideology is a local (nation-state) one that faces resistance from the global (post-national). This flow of local ideology to global, create and establish transnational connections. 'The related term Trans-nationalism is said to capture a condition in which despite great distances and notwithstanding the presence of international borders (and all the laws, regulations and national narratives they represent) certain kinds of relationships have been globally intensified and now take place paradoxically in a planet-spanning, yet common-however virtual-arena of activity" (Vertovec, 1999:448).

Expansion of Bollywood Movies around the World

Scholars of film study and filmmakers agree on this point that audiences of Bollywood films are present in every corner of the world. "Indian commercial cinema has been a transnational phenomenon almost throughout its history, whether this be a matter of its appropriating and adapting foreign elements, techniques and narratives, or of Indian films being shown in Africa, the Middle East, Greece, Turkey, China, South East Asia, Russia and Eastern Europe since the 1940s and 1950s" (Jain, 2005:71). Following facts mentioned by Bose (2006:26) reveal the vastness of Bollywood, "Every year the Indian film Industry produces more than a thousand feature films, every day Fourteen million see a movie in the country, a billion more people a year buy tickets to Indian movies, and these numbers are growing" (Bose, 2006:28).

The above discussion reveals that Indian movies were accessible and very popular in many countries of the world and audiences belong not only from Indian Diasporas but local people as well. Now we would like to discuss the contribution of Indian filmmakers, whose efforts made Bollywood very popular throughout the world. Along with this we would also focus on joint ventures of filmmaking and beginning of representations of Indian Diasporas in Indian cinema. Simultaneously we would mention the films produced by Indian Diaspora filmmakers. Applying comparative method, we would try to enlarge our knowledge about Indian Diaspora communities residing in different national locales.

Indian Movies: Hybridized Cultural Products

Let us see how Bollywood movies have traditionally practiced hybridisation in a multicultural and ethnic linguistic society. Bollywood is a best example of "melting pot" where people come from different backgrounds (cultural and ethnic) and play a significant role in constructing Indian national identity, co-habiting with many sub-national identities in the Indian nation-state (many of them have their own well developed cinema) (Chakravarty, 1993,Vasudevan, 2000). Blackledge (2002) argues that in multilingual and heterogeneous societies, dominant language ideology is constructed and reconstructed at all levels of the media. In case of India, Hindi is Lingua-franka and prevalent language of movies made in Bollywood, but as film makers are sensitive to the cultural angularities of multilingual India they have over the years constructed and reconstructed the language of Bollywood movies as 'Hindustani' (it is similar to a hybridisation seen in the news media, in the form and content of 'Hinglish' a combination of English, Hindi, Urdu, Punjabi and other Indian dialects). Therefore, one of the most significant aspects of the cultural hybridity in the Bollywood movies is language which is also known as Hindustani.

Chatterjee (1995) argues that, Indian popular movies made in Bollywood have traditionally constructed hybrid identities in their narrative and characterisation as well. In most cases it is difficult to identify the protagonist with one ethnic identity. Indian filmmakers belong to diverse ethnic and cultural background and were conscious of the fact that they were making movies for audiences spread across in different ethnic, linguistic and religious-cultural settings. Bollywood movies are also referred to as *masala* (hotchpotch) movies because they always have something for everyone, and now globalisation has helped open up new markets all over the world wherever Indian Diaspora lives. And it is reasonable that Bollywood filmmakers are sensitive to the cultural hybridity of their Diasporic audiences. Thus, the long established hybridity in Bollywood films has to be reworked in new ways to accommodate and appeal to Diaspora audiences and a context of globalisation and global network capitalism.

Diasporic Film Making and Bollywood Cinema

We have discussed about co-production, Joint ventures and expansion of Bollywood films around the world in previous pages. We have also discussed briefly how and when Bollywood film makers began depiction of foreign locale and Diasporic Indians. A film 'Dr. Kotnis Ki Amar Kahani' directed by V. Shantaram (1946) is a story of dedicated and humanitarian doctor who went to China to serve victims of war and sacrificed his life there. However, this film was the first ever such film which depicted a foreign locale with a story of Indian and it was exception because after that, there was a drought of films with such plot. In the decade of 1960s Bollywood produced films with such composition and plot and established new tradition and genre, for instance, Sangam (1964), Love in Tokyo (1966), 'An Evening in Paris' (1967), 'Around the World in Eight Dollars (1967), 'Purab aur Paschim' (1970) 'Des Pardes' (1978), and Naam (1986) to name just a few were such films, which depicted Indian Diaspora. The decade of 1990s brought a new dawn of diasporic films. Few milestone products of this stream are Dilwale Dulhania Le Jayenge or DDLJ (1995), Pardes (1997), Jeans (1997), Aa Ab Laut Chalein (1998), Proud to Be an Indian (2001), Yeh Hai Jalwa (2001), Kabhi Khushi Kabhi Gam or K3G (2001), Leela (2002), Kal Ho Naa Ho (2003), Lajja (2003), Salaam Namstey (2005), Namstey London (2006), Tara Ram Pam (2007) Bombay to Bangkok (2008) and many more.

This list is very large. However, suffice to prove the point that number of NRI- Genre movies are growing day by day. This list also indicates that Bollywood has become global and number of its audience is growing instantly. The audience is not only comprised by members of Indian Diasporic community but also members of host countries. There are many producers and directors belonging to Indian Diaspora community who are making films based on the everyday life of Indian Diaspora. For instance, Mira Nair, Deepa Mehta, Nagesh Kukunoor, Gurinder Chadha, Jagmohan Mundhra, and Kajad Gustag to name just a few, are prominent producers and directors who have produced films on Indian Diaspora. Thus, depicting Indian Diaspora has become a well established stream of film making.

The impact of this phenomenon is that "the Diasporic grouping of Indians has come to gain a positive visibility within Indian politics and the discourses of nationality formation. Correspondingly, there is emphasis on the NRIs in Mumbai cinema in the so called NRI-genre in the 1990s. The producers have been also attracted to NRIs because of Valorisation of the Indian Diaspora by successive governments as a key provider of economics flows and cultural capital, having a genuine interest in the development of their home country. It is a fact that due to many governmental efforts like 'Pravasi Bhartiya Divas' and double citizenship status, Indians abroad have been increasingly investing in real estate development rural infrastructure and education" (Brosius and Yazgi, 2007: 357). In this manner we can see Bollywood has become global in nature. There are numbers of players with foreign connections. The joint ventures and plots of the films with Diaspora in the centre, it has explained its boundaries. With the Indian Diaspora jumping in the production of such films it has gained new direction.

Understanding Diaspora through Films

After brief discussion about films based on Indian communities abroad, produced by both Bollywood and people in Indian Diaspora, we would explore the content of few selected Bollywood movies which represents the life stories of Indian Diaspora. Films are considered to be strong and stupendous medium of communication, art entertainment and literature. It has rightly argued that art and literature imitates life and we can consider movies as literary creations. Bollywood film makers have made many films depicting Indian Diasporas and overseas location from the decade of 1960s onwards, for instance Sangam (1964) Love in Tokyo (1966), An Evening in Paris (1967) and Purab aur Paschim (1970) as well. That trend is being more visible after the Bollywood films targeting Indian Diasporic audiences provide them memory of homeland as well as cultural and emotional feedback. These early film shows the fervour of nationalism and establish supremacy of Indian culture over western culture. Hindi movie Purab aur Paschim is the best example of this category.

Purab Aur Paschim (dir. Manoj Kumar, 1970)

The film 'Purab aur Paschim' as its name suggests is based on the dialectic between the East and the West, tradition and modernity. Deriving from Mumbai cinema's role in highlighting the power of Indian culture and tradition, the film affirms the moral superiority of the East over the west. The film suggests that the duty of modern hero of India lies not only in helping his country in becoming a developed nation but also in conveying to westerners and westernised Indians about the superiority of Indian spiritual values to mere materialistic interests. During the decade of 1970 (post- colonial) many young Indian men left the country to study abroad funded by European development programme for third world countries. After completing their study scholars were expected to return to their homeland. While some returned, other tried to stay on finding employment.

In the above mentioned film protagonist Bharat's host G.P. Sharma portrayed as stereotypical unpatriotic- modern NRI of 1970s who feels shame at India's status as an under developed nation and has distanced himself by cutting all ties with his homeland. He stays in England after completing his studies and chose to marry a British-born Indian girl. Bharat as a living emblem of nationalism, patriot and proud ambassador of Indian's spiritual heritage convinces other NRIs of England to be associated with our culture and nation. His mission also has to extend to converting Indians living abroad who have hitherto been untouched by patriotic love and so he responds to all westernised and confused British-Indians by a patriotic devotional song which explore exclusive and unique characteristics of mother India.

"G.P. Sharma's offspring Preeti and Shankar, though born to an Indian father, are hilariously ignorant of India. Bharat tells them about the 'real India'. Sharma asks Bharat to marry Preeti, Bharat agrees on the condition that he goes back to India with Preeti but she reluctantly agrees. Bharat believes that Preeti will fall in love with India once she goes there. And at the climax we find that Preeti sheds her 'western' ways her cigarettes, alcohol and short skirts and stays on in India with Bhart as an ideal wife wearing a red saree, singing a bhajan (devotional song) in village temple. Preeti's change of heart and emergence of love for India reiterated the supremacy of Indian values and traditions. These include the sanctity of the family and the traditional idealised role of women within it" (Gangoli, 2005: 152).

Dilwale Dulhania Le Jayenge (dir. Aditya Chopra, 1995)

While 'Purab aur Paschim' portrayed locality and love for homeland and 'the idea of sacrifice for the nation' etc. By the 1990s all these elements disappeared from the films which included depiction of Diaspora. A new cosmopolitan middle class has emerged who believe in Trans-nationalism. They remained Indian and practice Indianness without any contradiction wherever they reside throughout the world. Between the late 1970s and 1990s overseas Indian does not seem to have features centrally in mainstream Bollywood cinema, without any appropriate reason. In this context it has been rightly argued that, "the early 1990s films presented the need for renegotiating the modernity-tradition impasse. This juncture saw a spate of 'clean' family films in which the figure of the overseas Indian made a comeback, now presented as the successful wanderer between confidents and cultures, and between modernity and tradition" (Brosius and Yazgi, 2007: 369).

'Dilwale Dulhania Le Jayenge' theamatizes the problems of transnational location in respect of courtship and marriage. It proposes that Indian family values are portable assets. This proves the point discussed earlier in this chapter about Diaspora that when people migrate they do so with their socio-cultural baggage as well not only with their physical bodies. "DDLJ is a love story portraying Indians settled abroad, which define Indianness with reference to specificities of family life, the institutions of courtship and marriage in particular (Uberoi, 1998: 305). The primary aim of DDLJ to director Chopra was, "to make a very honest love story ... which can show the international audience that India is not a country of snake-charmers. I wanted to tell them how we Indians love, think and react today. I was also trying to articulate that if your love is strong enough your parents will be convinced about it ultimately. I also want to comment that position of girls in Indian household has remained unchanged and they can't take any important decision of their life still today" (interviewed by Mohamed 1996).

DDLJ is a typical Bollywood film with love, romance, dance and songs sequence. Raj (Shahrukh Khan) and Simran (Kajol) both are off-springs of successful NRI business men settled in London. Both of them go on a holiday tour co-incidentally and fall in love. Simran's father Baldev Singh Chaudhari (Amrishpuri) is a conservative and authoritarian patriarch who fixed arranged marriage of Simran with Kuljit (Parmeet Sethi) son of his old friend of Punjab. After the tour Simran's family leaves immediately for the Punjab for her wedding. Raj also visits Punjab to pursue Simran. Raj and Simran meet in the golden mustard fields but Raj refuses to consider elopement. Raj indulges in preparations of marriage and resides in Simran's home but her mother comes to know of Raj's true identity, and urges the two to elope away, but Raj insists that he would marry Simran ...with her father's approval. But Baldev Singh refuses to do so. After a lot of ups and downs at the climax Baldev Singh acknowledges the sincerity of Raj's love and his willingness to sacrifice love for the wider interests of the family, so he lets go of his daughter with Raj.

DDLJ is a film beginning with a monologue of Baldev Chaudhari in which he remembers his motherland with very nostalgic ways. He has been residing in London for the last 22 years but feels himself alien to that land. Feeding the pigeons he compares himself with them, because pigeons do not have a country; they go to the place where they get food. And he always thinks that one day he definitely will return to India his own mother land. He also remembers the flavors of Punjab-*Makke-di-roti* and *Sarson-da-sag*! When Baldev received, his friends' letter from Punjab as a proposal of Simran's marriage. He asks Simran's mother about her opinion towards the proposal. Simran runs her room pretending to be shy. The filmmaker wants to show the impact of Indian culture, even today a daughter feels shy in front of her father while parents are talking about her marriage. I have not failed; I have kept India alive here in the heart of London, he says. Not only has Baldev wanted to see Indianness in his family but in the families of other Indians who reside in London.

Chastity and virginity of unmarried Indian girl is expected and desirable even today. One scene of this film explores it vividly; let us see this during the tour of Europe, incidentally Simran and Raj are forced to spend the night together in a small hotel. Simran oppose Raj for daring to drink rum in front of an Indian girl. Late night as snowfalls through the roofs and she shivers with cold and hunger, she drinks the rum and starts singing and dancing. In the morning she wants to know what happened last night. After sometime a joking and teasing Raj declares that, he is after all a Hindustani and is well aware of what an Indian girl's honor means to him. Then she concludes with relief that she has not lost her virginity.

All the characters in this film are nationalist and proud of being Indian. "My Country, my land ever is available there but not this culture... Everywhere I go I have India in my heart." film shows tyranny of tradition on many occasions. For instance an Indian girl's desires are of little account when it comes to arranging her marriage. In this regard monologue of Simran's mother reveals the real status of Indian woman as she laments, "when I was a little girl my grandfather told me that there is no difference between man and woman. But when I grew up I understood that it was not true. My education was stopped so that my brother's education could be continued because their education was more important than mine. I sacrified my life first as a daughter and then as a daughter-in-law. I don't want that the same thing happens with my daughter, she should live her own life without any sacrifice". But the happy ending of the film resolve all the conflicts with the parental endorsement of a relationship between Raj and Simran.

Swades (dir. Asutosh Govarikar, 2004)

Swades is a story about the new concept of re-brain drain as professional NRIs come back to India to complete the nation building project. These NRIs argue, this country, we call India, is our own country. Further relation between India and Indians is the relation of Mother-son/daughters respectively. It is another kind of Hindi cinema whichshowcased the foreign educated hero returning to India usually as an engineer, doctor or business manager to direct the nation-building project in some locality. It means NRI off springs of mother India contribute their motherland to alleviate the situation and enrich it. In Swades a NASA scientist Mohan Bhargav (Shahrukh Khan) returns to his village, in India to contribute and spend his dollars with a feeling of duties. Deshpande (2007:99) argues

"Mohan as an external agent of modernisation and humanism, returns to the village to spend his dollars on welfare measures like electricity generation, Destroy caste based division and discrimination, convey importance of education to the villagers". Set in modern day village India 'Swadesh' is a film which tackles the issues facing the citizens of this nation at grass roots level. More than 50 years have passed since independence; however, this country is grappling with problems that development throws. The India of 'Swades' is colorful, heterogeneous and complex, with people of diverse cultures and attitudes. And NRI scientist Mohan Bhargav who is working as a project manager in 'NASA' returns to on a quest to find his childhood friend. He tries to pursue Kaveri Amma (Kishori Ballal) the symbol of Motherland and family to him ' to return to America with him, so that he can serve her well. In this sequence he gets drawn into the life of a village called Charanpur and finds himself searching for answers to question of progress and development that the village was facing. Simultaneously he compares Indian and American conditions at the various dimensions of progress. Heroine of the film Geeta (Gaytri Joshi) an admirable and ideal young woman teaching in the village primary school. She chooses to live there despite many problems like casteism, prejudice and a lack of basic amenities. Geeta is proud of her profession, and she feels that it is her duty to contribute to her nation at grass roots because that is due of the ways to contribute to the process of nation building.

There are many differences between Mohan and Geeta about the national policy, governmental plan and development in India. Mohan criticizes Indian situations. But Geeta believes in governmental development processes and emphasizes the point that Indian citizens should also take up similar responsibilities for the welfare of the country. On a point Mohan and Geeta feel their aim is same but attitudes are little bit different. Although both of them develop affection for each other, Mohan goes back to USA alone with a promise to return. In USA he feels too much alienation and nostalgia to the people of India and their problems, especially for Geeta, Kaveri Amma and his village Charanpur. This dutiful response and commitment to the motherland arise new hopes from our

NRIs to solve various problems of our country as in 21st century India, the process of re-brain drain is happening.

Kal Ho Na Ho (Dir. Karan Johar 2003)

This film was shot in New York City and depicted the life of an immigrant Indian- American family living in New York. These geographic and demographic spaces are part of a deliberate attempt by the Diasporic audiences. 'Karan Johar' the producer of 'Kal Ho Na Ho' was reported as saying that "we have to cater to Indian Yuppie in New York and the man in rural Bihar, both at the same time" (Kabir, 2004:7).

As we know a film includes the cultural, religious and 'material practices' and 'everyday life' of a nation or of the communities. In this reference Bollywood cinema is creating a 'Diasporic fiction' a social construction, by making choice in its representation of 'material practices' and 'everyday life' of the Diaspora and 'Kal Ho Na Ho' is a good example of such movies. It is a typical Bollywood movie; which is a mix of romance, comedy and pathos. The story is autobiographical, and is told by female protagonist of the film, that is Naina Catherina Kapoor (Preity Zinta). Naina is a young woman who is pursuing MBA and living with her family that comprises her mother, paternal grandmother and two siblings. The grandmother and her mother don't have good relationship and are shown constantly squabbling. As the family restaurant business is not doing well there is family scarcity and also they are defaulting on a bank loan. The mother Catherine Kapoor reassures the children that God will send an angel to solve their problems. "And that angel is Aman Mathur (Shahrukh Khan) a visitor from India comes to neighborhood who is too optimistic and energetic in nature" (Kher, 2003). This angel brings sunshine in the otherwise gloomy environment. He helps Naina's family to come out of the financial mess, gets Naina and Rohit (her classmate and friend) married and resolves the differences between the in-laws. But the 'Angel' himself has a 'fatal heart problem' and he has come to New York for a treatment.

The plot of the story says "New York" one of the world's biggest cities...the business capital of the world, every breath of the city, every heartbeat is defined by pace, people are always in a hurry, in a hurry to leave home ...in a hurry to reach office, to be a step or two ahead of life. There is no place for anyone, who cannot cope with its pace. Miles away from India, the city is crowded with Indians. With this monologue the film situates itself in a globalised environment, with New York City as center of the new global economy.

America, its global culture and non-Indo American characters are brought into the movie to construct the background and with the use of signs. People from different colors and regions like, white, blacks, Asians etc. are shown dancing with huge American flag in the background in the very first song of the movie, which deliberately reveals the loyalty of immigrants to the adopted land. The language of the film is Hinglish, a mixture of English, Hindi, Punjabi and Gujrati with the words cool, sexy, babe, and dog, is regularly used by different characters of the film.

If we analyse Kal Ho Na Ho a little bit deeper the film articulates that life is not easy in the west. Naina's family is struggling to make two ends meet as their restaurant is not doing well. From Diasporic perspective it is depiction of reality which number of Indians are not aware of. They are only lured by the rosy picture of pomp and show of the West. The global city of New York represents success of the west and its modernity that is very attractive; however Indian traditions values and structure like joint family and respect for elderly persons is valued. This is eloquently portrayed by the continuous scenes in which despite many difficulties and quarrelsome relationship between her mother and grandmother, Naina convinced that older parents are the responsibility of the children. Aman 'the Angel' teaches her to love herself and her family members and try to resolve existing problems.

The fixation to homeland is also depicted in the film in different scenes. For instance Naina's grandmother desires that her native Punjab becomes a part of New York. In this sequence Aman recommends Jennifer to re-model her restaurant, from a regular American restaurant to an ethnic Indian restaurant. His long dialogue is testimony to the above fact According to him "we must get Hindustan to New York; we have to get Hindustan here, bring it to the streets, spread it in all directions". And finally re-modeled restaurant is named "New Delhi Restaurant" because New Delhi being capital of India beccmes representation of India constructing Indian identity as well. After marriage 'Naina Catherina Kapur' turns to adopt a new name-"Naina Catherina Kapur Patel. "She is now Hindu, Christian, Punjabi and Gujarati a mix of regional and religious identity representing Hindustani identity. She has "Arranged cum love marriage" in Indian style also is an important event which portrays importance of marriage as an institution in Indian Diasporas.

Diaspora Filmmakers and Depiction of Diaspora Communities

The world market for Bollywood cinema expanding continuously and in this expansion NRI film makers are also playing a vital role. Besides Yashraj films and Mukta Arts other production companies have less impact and space in world market. Hindi films produced in India have 12-15 percent accessibility in world market, rest 85 percent market is covered by the NRI film makers of USA, U.K., France, Germany, Japan, China and South Africa (Jha, 2007). These films have become quite popular and have drawn attention of many however these films still draw a lot from Bollywood cinema. Some of such films are 'Bhaji' on the Beach (dir. Gurinder Chadha 1993), Bend it like Beckham (2002), Bride and Prejudice (2004) (dir. Gurinder Chadha 1993) East is East (dir. Demino Donaell, 1999), Hyderabad Blues, and Bollywood Calling (dir. Nagesh Kukunoor 2001), Mansoon Wedding (dir. Mira Nair, 2002), Bollywood/Hollywood (dir. Deepa Mehta, 2002) and Provoked (dir. Jagmohan Mundhra).

The success of recent films by Deepa Mehta (Fire, Earth, Water) Gurinder Chadha and Mira Nair in particular have been discussed as attempt to present a feminist reckoning of South Asian Diasporic cultural production and politics. For instance Gurinder Chadha, has often been quoted in interviews as using her films as well as her film making practices as an expression of her angst towards an ethnocentric world view (Bhattacharya and Gabriel, 1994). Some other filmmakers in Diaspora are also doing well and are depicting experiences of their life realities in their movies. They are Bala Rajsekhurani,

Dr. Nikhil Kaushik, Kalpna Singh, Karansher Singh, Angad Paul, Anand Singh, Suresh Seth, Bipin Patel and Tarlok Malik and others. Bala's first film 'Green card fever' unfolds the deceptive face of NRI husband. Her second movie 'Black water' attacks on existing racism and malfunctions of politics in USA. Dr. Nikhil supports Bala's view about NRI husband in his film 'Future'. Kalpna Singh has made- 'Girl with an Ascent', 'Double Nentives', 'Anima', 'Cuban Missile Crisis' and 'God Bless America'. And now continuing her splendid carrier Kalpana is making a film on the Premchand's story 'Kafan' (Jha, 2007, Kaur, 2005). Now we would attempt to consider the cultural and social possibilities which, films like Provoked, Bride and Prejudice, Name Sake and 'ABCD' have been included with their plot.

Provoked (Dir. Jagmohan Mundhra, 2005)

This film is based on the autobiography (circle of the light) of an NRI woman Kiranjit Ahluwalia. Kiranjit killed her abusive husband Deepak Ahluwalia in 1989 in England. But that was neither first nor last incident of harassment of Indian girls by their NRI husbands. It is continuing even today in different forms and extent. Aishwarya Rai's (in the role of Kiranjit) poignant performance as oppressed wife reveals the panic situation Kiranjit faced in England. It's common expectation that a husband will provide complete protection, respect and affection to his wife and spouses will live together whole life. But married life brought only oppression, atrocities, insult for Kiranjit and she did bear all abuses against her continuous ten years, and one night she burnt her husband Deepak who was a drunkard and womanizer and also suspicious of Kiranjit's character. Consequently the court sentenced her to life-term jail as a murder accused. Jail is never a dreamed place for anyone but Kiranjit perception is totally different as she says, "I am feeling relaxed here after ten years of tortured life". Using flash back technique, director very vividly highlights the comparison between 'home' and 'jail'.

A woman organisation 'South hall Black Sisters' takes Kiranjit's case to high court and provides needful help and support, eventually, Kiranjit wins the case and restarts her life with her two children. The case of Kiranjit reminds all those parents who feel very fortunate to find out a NRIs groom for their daughters and blindly marry them without proper enquiry. Kiran Bedi, whose NGO 'Navjyoti' is fighting many such case comments, "It is the same story, even well-to-do families based in Delhi feel that getting their daughters married abroad will ensure a golden future for the girls. They don't even wait to check the antecedents". Thus, such illusion of bright future creates many problems for the Indian girls overseas, where they can't easily oppose their subjugation by in-laws. In the end of the movie 'Provoked' Kiranjit makes a valuable statement before media- "women should not bear any violence and oppression practiced against them. It is the duty of each mother to implant good habits in their children so that they learn to respect and love the women, not violence and hate." Thus, the film ends with a great message to all of us and specifically for those parents who are used to marrying of their daughters abroad without verifying the characters and habits of NRI grooms.

Bride and Prejudice (dir. Gurinder Chadha, 2004)

In the era of globalisation and transnationalism, marital relation between two people with different nationalities, cultures and religion does not restrict individuals to become partners and marry each other. This is the theme which Gurinder Chadha explores in her film 'Bride and Prejudice'. This film is based on the story of Jane Austen's novel 'Pride and Prejudice'. This film tells that 'East meets west.... And it's a perfect match. A classic romance not just retold, but reinvented in a new globally connected world. 'Bride and Prejudice' puts an entirely different spin on Jane Austen's Story of spirited Courtship Bollywood style, music, dance merge with love, vanity and social pressures as the original gets adopted into a comic tale of a young woman trying to find a suitable husband in a cross-cultural setting that spans 21st century India, London and America. Gurinder Chadha reveals in an interview around the launch of the film in October 2004, about the theme of this film, "It was three different worlds coming together... that are also why I was to do it now; because I felt Bollywood was being hijacked in a particular way. People were focusing on the really kitsch side of it. Yes there is a lot of Kitsch and it is formula, but at the same time there is a wonderful purity of emotion and a lot about it that is brilliant. I wanted to do something that paid homage to some of the films that were very much part of who I was as a film-maker" (Dudrah, 2006:163).

The Bollywood aesthetics are central to this movie in terms of its camera work, song and dance routines, dialogues, melodrama, and grand colorful sets and lavish outdoor location shots from Amritsar, Goa, London and Los Angeles. The story begins in Amritsar where the determined Mrs. Bakshi set out to find marriage for her four beautiful daughters, while there is a lavish wedding party in town. Right away, the beautiful Lalita Bakshi (Aishwarya Rai) announces she will only marry for love, giving her mother nightmares. Incidentally Lalita meets the wealthy American William Darcy and sparks immediately fly. A sequence of love and hate also take place between the two. Darcy comes across to Lalita as an arrogant Californian snob. Lalita looks to Darcy like a small-town Indian beauty who knows nothing of the world. Alternately enchanted by the suspicions of one another Lalita and Darcy nearly fall prey to assumptions, gossip and a comedy of errors... until pride is humbled and prejudice overcomes so that love can triumph.

One important comparative reading of a particular scene has done by R.K. Dudrah. He describes that "At the climax of the film Lalita and Darcy have to rescue Lalita's youngest sister Lucky who has been lured away by Wickham in order for him to seduce her. They follow and chase them... and catch up with them in a cinema hall that is showing a classic seventy Bollywood film 'Purab aur Paschim' which is essentially a conservative tale advocating the need to not forget one's Indian cultural identity. Darcy and Wickham explode on to the stage in front of screen and start fighting with one another. This is precisely at the moment when on-screen in the cinema, the film's lead Manoj Kumar is rescuing the heroine, Saira Bano, from being raped by the villain played by Prem Chopra and they also start fighting. Both the heroes overcome their villains and rescue the girl. In 'Bride and Prejudice' Lucky ends her liaison with Wickham by slapping him and thus emphasizes film's feminist message whilst using aesthetics of Bollywood from 'Purab aur Paschim' to be taken up a step further" (Dudrah, 2006:164).

In her analysis of film 'Bride and Prejudice', Parminder Bhachu has identified Gurinder Chadha, as image maker of the Diaspora. In her well explored article she writes. "I refer to Gurinder's socialisation in a realised multiple migrant communities in the Punjabi capital of England, South Hall, from which she accesses the source codes of her highly politicised and translatable images. Her interpretations emerge from the grounded cultural aesthetics of this Diaspora community, which she uses potently to subvert mainstream image economies and create new image landscapes. Her own eye-catching, 'culturally messy,' hybrid style is strongly played out on celluloid, the distinctive culturally infected interpretations of an organic and community oriented filmmaker. She astutely captures the fractured landscapes of migrants and their second generation progeny, their multiple identities and dynamic popular cultural forms that are products of movement and displacement, and settlement is new context. She is a high profile pioneering hybridizer. Her Diasporic base was already very hybrid and she is a second generation British Asian herself who articulates this and hybridises further in her medium of celluloid" (Bhachu 2005: 53).

Name Sake (dir. Mira Nair, 2006)

This film 'Name sake' directed by Mira Nair is based on the story of the Novel Name-Sake' written by Jhumpha Lahiri'. It raises a relevant question for Diasporic family that is what does it mean to be an American family? It has been film between the equally colorful and vibrant cities of Calcutta and New York. It is a family drama, about the Gangulis, who come to USA from India in order to experience a world of limitless opportunities. For a change the Indians in this movies are not Punjabi but from Bengali family.

On the heels of their arrange marriage Ashoke (Irfan Khan) and Ashima (Tabu) Jett of from sweltering Calcutta to a wintry New York where they begin their new life together. There Ashima gives birth to a son-Gogol. But life is not easy for Gogol. As a first generation American teenager Gogol (Kal

Penn) must learn to search a razor-thin line between his Bengali roots and his American birth rights in order to find his own identity. Gogol was a Russian writer, who wrote novel 'The Overcoat' and Ashoke was impressed by his writing, consequently he named his son Gogol'. But when Gogol attempts to forge his identity - rejecting his given name, his parents cling to their Bengali traditions. But their paths keep crossing with both comic and painfully revelatory consequence...until Gogol begins to see the links between the world his parents left behind and the new world that lies in front of him. Gogol a confused American desi boy tries to find out his real identity in this film and in search of truth and compatibility with two different worlds.

ABCD (Dir. K. Patel, 2001)

'American Born Confused Desi' is a derogatory label for Indians born in the USA who appear to have conflicting identities. According to Brosius and Yazgi (2007:375) "NRIs based in North America are now successful professional entrepreneur belonging to a transnational and cosmopolitan Indian ethnic upper middle class. In the 1990s this desi (literally translated it will mean indigenous people) community in North America emerged as new agent and producer film and musical cultural commodities within what has been wined as transal-Asia (to refer to an arena of cultural flows with shifting geographical, linguistic and imaginary grounds). In this film K. Patel has clearly addressed the notion of Indianness in ways that are more concerned with making a living in the host country. "ABCD is a reflective investigation into the desi self-experience that counters common stereotypes through a portrayal of the experience of growing up and a more subtle depiction of character. In an interview the director revealed the importance of their own migrant experiences as a major source of inspiration" (Chhabra, 2001). 'ABCD' tells the story of two siblings, Raj and Nina, who were born in India, but brought up in the USA. Nina is temperamental young woman who wants to marry Sam and is wholly averse to her widowed mother to find a suitable Indian boy as a match for her. Raj seems more stable at personal and professional level and is engaged to marry Tejal, a traditionally-brought up Indian girl, whom he doesn't like really. He faces racial discrimination over a long-awaited and well-deserved promotion. While Nina has to cope with a temporary break-up with her rich white boyfriend, Sam, because his family responds dubiously to their being together at the same time Nina's mother tries to set her up with Ashok a childhood friend, who has recently come from India. Witty and engaging Ashok is able to overcome Nina's resistance to spending time with Indian men when Ashok finally asks Nina to marry him, she is shocked and withdraws. Raj and Nina's mother, Anju dies suddenly, leaving the sibling to confront their options in USA, a less known world for them Raj leaves Tejal and quits his job; Nina marries Sam.

Previously Raj and Nina, both preferred white American ways rather than Indianness or hybrid identity. However, Raj was always very uneasy whenever a white colleague got a promotion even though he deserved. Raj used to identify that act as racial discrimination against him. Both Nina and Raj echo the image of the NRI residing in North America, bright, professionally dedicated and successful but struggling for mainstream exposure and recognition. After their mother Anju's death Nina tells Raj that she is dating Sam again and they intend to get married soon; Raj tells her about his break-up with Tejal. Raj is trapped between feeling both guilt and anger at his inability to be honest to both Tejal and his mother. However they imagine that they will give a greater control over their choices of partners and their individual destinies, and will cause them to turn away from choices dictated by a cultural order tied to their ethnic background. Though they feel absence of their mother but this event provides them release also. Raj and Nina assert their individuality, even their future remains uncertain and they do not aspire to being fully American. Though she do not like Indianness, but Nina asks Raj to 'give her away' as a bride, a gesture that would recall the Hindu ritual of 'Kanyadan' even though the marriage will take place in church. As they stand outside the church porch, Nina draws Raj's attention to the Indian custom of strengthening the brother-sister bond through 'Raksha-Bandhan'. "Whereas previously both had rejected such traditions, now they embrace this one ritual voluntarily, suggesting that the relation between the siblings can be salvaged for the future" (Brousias and Yazgi, 2007: 382).

This film ABCD is representation of the quest of Indo-American youth for a distinctive American identity. This underlies differences from Mumbai cinema's representations of NRIs. Bollywood's definition of NRIs as dutiful children, patriotic/modern Indian shows the nation's anxieties about being bled of its best talent and losing out on the investment potential of affluent sections of the Diasporic Indian community. This film tells that young NRIs/Indo-Americans are not much intuitive to their notion-state's home calling "Yet this is an issue that requires more research insofar as transnational nationalism also finds strong support among Diasporic youth by means of orthodox and militant networks that engage in the construction of cultural identities, in the case of, 'Yankee Hindutva' with alliance that affect universities, businesses and socio-cultural activities" (Mathew and Prasad, 2000). Construction of identity in the film ABCD is depicted as an individual quest, not necessarily synonymous with territorial borders; and home is that where they are residing right now, so home land and return is not a big deal for young NRIs.

The above discussed films have been made by Diasporic Indians. They have incorporated in these films their self experienced life realities, their suffering and discrimination they have faced in the alien land as an insider's view. That is why the depiction in films looks more real and authentic.

Conclusion

This chapter has dealt with the representation of Indian Diaspora in Bollywood cinema from its inception till date. It also focuses about the expansion and accessibility of Bollywood films around the world from its emergence to present time chronologically. One could observe in the chapter that forms and content of films depicting Diaspora are being changed and its universe is also expanding around the globe. Veteran film makers like Shyam Benegal and Govind Nihalani observe, that in the expansion of Bollywood, South Asian population outside of its own nation, play a vital role as this population welcomes Bollywood films for their entertainment.

The chapter vividly explores about Bollywood's expansion and includes various facts to prove it. Further we have explained here about post liberalisation era and its impact on

Bollywood cinema. For instance in May 1998, Bollywood got the status of an industry, which opened various sources for funding of films for instance Banks, Corporate sector, International media production houses, etc. With these developments, Indian film industry has become a successful market at the International level where Bollywood films will compete with Hollywood. Today many joint ventures and co-production are taking place which have been mentioned earlier in the chapter. In such scenario, films depict Indian Diaspora, their settlement, arrival and everyday life and connecting them with Indian culture and society. This whole development has extended horizons of Indians to understand Indian Diaspora through films in a better way.

Next part of the chapter analyzes the content of some selected movies which help us to develop a better understanding about Indian Diasporas. We have selected both types of movies made by Bollywood filmmakers and also made by filmmakers living in Diaspora. It is a significant issue that most of the films with diasporic content are based on the stories of UK and USA based Indians. If we observe carefully, Bollywood movies emphasize or impose patriotism, nationalism, homeland return, and overall supremacy of Indian culture over western society and culture. This attitude continues from first classical movies of this stream 'Purab aur Paschim' (1970) till latest release films on Diaspora. Arranged marriage in same caste-class, religion and with Indians only according to parental approval are also visible. In this context we have seen that parents visit India in search of appropriate bride or groom for their sons and daughters, which shows their nostalgia and conservatism towards their motherland and anxiety to maintain Indianness in new generation.

Dance and songs are inevitable part of Indian movies. In this chapter we have explored that each film with Diasporic content has a song which reveals feelings of patriotism, nostalgia, orientation and belongingness of Diaspora to their motherland India. For instance, the national pride is writ large in the following film songs:

- Bharat ka rahnewala hu Bharat ki bat batata hu (1 belong to India and tell u, about Indian in Purab aur Paschim)

- Watan se Chithi Aayi Hai (letter has come from motherland calling you in Naam)
- Ghar Aaja Pardesi tera desh bulaye re (come back dear your country is calling in DDLJ).
- Aa ab laut chalein (let us go back to our motherland in film Aa ab laut chalein)
- Indian national anthem in Kabhi Khushi Kabhi Gum
- Main Jahan bhi Rahun, Main Kahin bhi hun teri yad saath hain (whenever I go, I have your memory with me in Namste London)
- I love my India in Pardes
- Yeh Jo Desh hai tera, Swadesh hai tera, Tujhe hai pukara, yeh jo bandhan hai, kabhi tut nahi sakata (in Swadesh), and so on.

We have also included in our analysis that an Indian name, dress, feeling, strong family tie means acceptance of Indianness at all levels is major issue in Bollywood Diasporic movies. Bollywood has successfully explored this aspect of Indianness by portraying minutest details.

When we go beyond Bollywood movies and turn to movies made by Indian Diasporas like Mira Nair, Gurinder Chadha and Jagmohan Mundhra to name just a few in the chapter we find little difference in their perceptions about Indian Diasporic communities. Though, these filmmakers use Bollywood aesthetics in their movies, yet they have different experiences due to their locality, socialisation in a multiple migrant communities, their real feeling of being in Diaspora differentiates them with Indian filmmakers. They have adapted hybrid style and identity, multiculturalism and transnationalism. These entire elements they represent in their movies. Inter-racial, inter-religious marriages and hybrid cultural identity are not problematic for filmmakers belonging to Diasporic community. Homeland return and nostalgia to their original homeland are not big deal for them. They remain Indian with adapting their society of settlement.

We have also evaluated similarities and differences in depiction of Indians by the two types of filmmakers i.e.

filmmakers hailing from India and second hailing from the Diasporas. Both types of filmmakers tell the stories of Diaspora with positive and negative aspects of their life. They also depict co-existence and difficulties faced by Indian Diaspora in the society of settlement and their connections with Indianness. However, there are many differences between the two. For instance homeland return is big concern for Bollywood filmmakers but it is not important for filmmakers hailing from Indian Diaspora. Similarly Bollywood filmmakers show that the first generations of migrants felt more affection to their motherland and try to maintain Indianness in them and imbibe Indianness in their next generations. But the Diaspora filmmakers show that new generations which never grew up in India, Indianness and imposition of Indian culture is not accepted and welcomed. They try to adapt well with their contemporary social milieu that is not India, though they develop compatibility between two. Portraying supremacy of Indian culture and tradition used to be central theme, in the Bollywood films of 1960s which did not appeal to second or third generation Indian Diaspora. That is why today transnationalism, compatibility between two localities has become the main issues. Though Indian Diaspora faces many problems like racial discrimination and ethnic conflicts, however filmmakers hardly depict such realities of day to day life.

Another important fact which we have analysed in this chapter is that most of the Diasporic films are on UK and USA based Indians. Implicit reason for that is filmmaking at professional level is available in both these countries. Well educated, skilled and affluent sections of Indian Diasporas reside in these countries, which can relate these films better. Democratic government and environment provide equal space to immigrant communities where they can acquire better education and job opportunities and any profession of their choices. Ethnic clashes and marginalisation of immigrants are less or totally absent. In such environment they join filmmaking and portray their experiences by strong medium of communication. Bollywood filmmakers also found easy to shoot their films in these countries due to available facilities for that purpose. For instance, British cultural department provides information and accessibility to best locations of their countries.

Another associated reason why Bollywood filmmakers are including life of Indian Diaspora in UK and USA is that Bollywood film industry is capitalistic in nature which tells the stories of only upper strata of the society and ignores poor, Dalits, minorities and rural India. Moreover, Bollywood today is completely busy in competition with Hollywood and to acquire global standards, hence it has minimum space for the common Indians.

This chapter explores the recent shift in focus of popular Hindi (Bollywood) films from domestic characters encountering social issues, to members of the South Asian Diaspora (primarily in the West) negotiating their ethnic identities. Further it also offers insights into the evolution of the Bollywood narrative where identities are being renegotiated and connections with traditional Indian culture are being challenged. Acknowledging the economic liberalisation of India as catalyst, we examine the representation of the Diaspora and their connectedness with the diasporic reality in which they live. The representation is discussed in terms of the impact that religion, gender, sexuality, and regional/national politics have on the creation of a hybridized ethnic identity. Moreover, recent diaspora-centric films are openly utilizing the diasporic characters as a safer experimental platform to negotiate these complex issues. Thus, cinematic depiction of Indian Diaspora is an effort of Bollywoodizing Diasporas and reconnecting them to their original homeland, India.

References

Anderson, B. (1991), *Imagined Communities: Reflection on the Origin and Spread of Nationalism*, Verso Publication London, New York.

Appadurai A. (1996), *Modernity at Large: Culture Dimensions of Globalisation*, University of Minnesota Press, Minneapolis.

Bose, Mihir (2006), *Bollywood: A History*, Roli Books, New Delhi.

Bhabha, Homi K. (1994), *The Location of Culture*, Routledge, London.

Bhachu, P. (1985), *Twice Migrants: East African Sikh Settlers in Britain*, Tavistock Press, London.

Chopra, Anupma (2003), *Dilwale Dulhaniya Le Jayenge*, The Bravehearted will Take the Bride, B.F.I. Publishing London.

Chakravarty, Sumita S. (1993), *National Identity in Indian Popular Cinema*, 1947-1978', University of Texas Press, Austin.

Chatterjee, Gayatri (2002), Mother India, BFL, London.

Desai, J. (2004), Beyond Bollywood: The Cultural Politics of South Asian Diasporic Film,' Routledge New York, London.

Dubey, Ajay (2003), *Indian Diaspora*, Global Identity Publication, Delhi.

Dudrah, Rajinder K. (2006), *Sociology Goes to the Movies*, Sage Publication: New Delhi.

Desai Jigna (2004), *Hollywood: the Cultural politics of South Asian Diasporic Film*, Routledge New York.

Jain, R.K. (1970), *South Indians on the Plantation Frontier in Malaya*, Yale University Press, London and New Heaven.

Jain, R.K. (1998), *Indian Communities Abroad: Themes and Literature*, Manohar Books, New Delhi.

Kabir, Nasreen M. (2001), *Bollywood: The Indian: Cinema Story*; Channel 4 Books, London.

Kaur, Raminder and Sinha, Ajay, J. (2005), *Bollyworld: Popular Indian Cinema through a Transnational Lens*, Sage Publications, New Delhi, London.

Mehta, S. (2004), *The Maximum City: Bombay Lost and Found*, Vintage Books, New York.

Nandy, Ashis (1998), *The Secret Politics of our Desires: Innocent Culpability and Indian Popular Cinema*, Zed Books London.

Parekh, B. Singh and G. and Vertovec S. (2003), *Culture and Economy in the India Diaspora*, Routledge London.

Rajadhyaksha, Ashish and Paul Willemen (1995), *Encyclopaedia of Indian Cinema*, OUP, Delhi.

Rushdie, Salman (1991), *Imaginery Home Lands: Essays and Criticism*, 1981-91, Granta Books.

Vasudevan, Ravi S. (2000), *Making Meaning in Indian Cinema*, Oxford University Press, New Delhi.

Vertovec, S. (2000), *The Hindi Diaspora: Comparative Patterns*, Routledge, London.

Periodical and News Paper

Agrawal, B. (2001), Indian Diaspora, *World Focus* 22 (3): 3-5.

Appadurai, Aryan (1990), 'Disjuncuture and Difference in the Global Cultural Economy', *Public Culture*, 2(2): 295-310.

Bhachu, Parminder (2002), Film Director Gurinder Chadha: Image Maker of the Diaspora, *International Journal of Punjab Studies*, 9 (2): 253-273.

Brosius Christiane and Yazgi Nicolas (2007), Is there no place like home? Contesting Cinematographic Constructions of Indian Diasporic experiences, *Contributions to Indian Sociology* 41 (3): 355-386.

Deshpande, Anirudh (2007), Indian Cinema and the Bourgeois Nation State, *EPW* 95-103.

Dudrah, Rajinder K. (2002), Vilayati Bollywood: Popular Hindi Cimema-going and diasporic South Asian Identity in Birmingham (UK) in Javnost: *Journal of the European Institute for Culture and Communication*, 9(1): 9-36.

Jain, R.K (1998a), Reality and Representation: Aspects of the Electronic Media in Contemporary Indian Society and Diaspora, *Sociological Bulletin*, 47(2): 167-184.

Jain, R.K (1998b), Indian Diaspora, Globalisation and multiculturalism: A cultural Analysis' *Contributions to Indian Sociology* 32(2): 337-358.

Kumar Vivek (2004), Understanding Dalit Diasopora, *EPW* 39(1): 114-116.

Kakar, Sudhir (1981), The Ties that Bind: Family Relationships in the Mythology of Hindi Cinema, *India International Centre Quarterly* 8(1):11-21.

Nand Kumar, R. (1992), The Star System: A Note Towards its Sociology', *Deep Focus* 4(2): 44-45.

Prasad, M.M. (1993), Cinema and the Desire for Modernity, *Journals of Arts and Ideas*, pp. 25-26.

Rajadhyaksha, Ashish (2003), The 'Bollywoodisation' of the Indian Cinema: Cultural Nationalism in a Global arena'. *Inter-Asia Cultural Studies*, 4(1): 25-39.

Sahoo, Ajay (2006), Dalit Diaspora: An Emancipatory Agenda, Seminar (2005), 127-135.

Tololyan, K. (1996), Rethinking Diaspora (s): Stateless Power in the Transnational Moment, Diaspora, S. (1): 3-36.

Uberoi, Patricia (1998), The Diaspora Comes Home: Disciplining Desire in DDLJ, *Contributions to Indian Sociology*, 32(2): 305-336.

Vasudevan, Ravi (1998), The Melodramatic Mode and Indian Commercial Cinema, *Screen*, 30(3).

PART B : SUB-NATIONAL IDENTITIES

8

Dalit Diaspora: Invisible Existence

Vivek Kumar

Although there is a tendency to project Indian diaspora as a monolithic whole, it is a fact that Indian diaspora is internally differentiated on regional, religious, linguistic and caste lines. This internal differentiation can be proved from the fact that any rumbling and crises in India is reflected in the country where Diaspora is present in substantial number. For instance, Sikh Diaspora in UK and Canada made lot of hue and cry during the extremism in Punjab. The same was true for the South Indian Diaspora during the Gulf war. The contributions made by Gujarati Diaspora at the time of earthquake depicts the intensity of relationship between the Diaspora and community of people of origin. It is in this context that the presence of Dalit Diaspora which is raising the issue of violation of Dalit rights at the international level also assumes importance and needs further research.

More specifically, Indian Diaspora has been analysed through religious perspective like Hindu diaspora, Sikh diaspora, through regional perspective like-Tamil diaspora, Gujrati diaspora, etc., or on the economic basis of brain drain. There have also been studies which depict overseas Indians living in specific countries of the world like-Indians in UK, USA, Canada, South Africa, East Africa, Fiji, Malaysia etc., to name just a few. These studies have also depicted that Indian diaspora has dispersed all over the world along with number of socio-structural and cultural elements of Indian society.

However, with few exceptions like-Schwartz (ed. 1967) the Indian diaspora has been very rarely studied through caste perspective. Hence it remains an enigma whether caste and caste based relationship like exclusion and discrimination exists or not among Indian Diaspora residing in different parts of the world. Therefore this chapter is a humble effort to explore the existence of caste and with that Dalit castes giving birth to Dalit diaspora in the wider rubric of Indian Diaspora. More specifically the paper highlights the invisibility of the Dalit Diaspora. In doing so we will probe the efforts made by the Dalit Diaspora in establishing solidarity among them and self esteem for the community. This chapter is any way not an exhaustive study of Dalit Diaspora. Hence this can be taken as a starting material for further researches.

Defining Diaspora

Etymologically, the term diaspora is derived from the Greek composite verb dia- and speirein, literally meaning 'to scatter', 'to spread' or 'to disperse'. It was originally used to refer to the dispersion of Jews after the Babylonian exile in 586 B.C. and to the aggregate of Jews or Jewish communities living in exile outside Palestine (Jayram, 2004: 16). In the context of Jews the uses and the connotations of the term diaspora gets associated with forced displacement, victimisation, alienation and loss. Along with this there existed a dream of returning to the homeland. However, according to (Saffron, 1991), today "diaspora" and more specifically "diasporic community" is increasingly being used as metaphoric designations for several categories of people like expatriates, expellers, political refugees, alien residents, immigrants, ethnic and racial minorities in much the same way that "ghetto" has come to designate all kinds of crowded constricted, and dis-privileged urban environments and "holocaust" has come to be applied to all kinds of mass murder.

In this context Shukla (2003: 13-14) argues that, "Many have argued reserving the term diaspora itself for the sense of forced dispersion that is recalled in modern notions of Jewishness or Blackness, or for groups like Armenians. ... answer to these dilemmas is that first, the very question of compulsion in scattering is difficult to ascertain, particularly as many migrants have seen few economic possibilities-possibilities that would constitute a form of survival-in underdeveloped economies like that of India, or those in Latin America or Africa. Second, diaspora like any other generalised theoretical category, only gives meaning from its cultural and historical specificity, that specify which necessarily produces contras among, say, Jewish, Chinese, or Indian cases. And third, diaspora should be seen not as reflecting a singular state of being or as having a reference to one nation or historical experience, but instead as constructing a space to negotiate many identification. We would use the term Diaspora in the above light.

Migration and Formation of Indian Diaspora

There has been a myth that Indians have rarely migrated. This myth has been substantiated by another myth that Indian villages were self-sufficient and self-contained. However, the practice of village exogamy, the limited number of artisan castes in one village, the pilgrimage centers etc, prove the point that migration of people from one place to another has been part and parcel of Indian society. Secondly, this migration did not begin during the colonial period. Rather it stretches in the ancient times. According to Tinker (1977: 1-2), "yet none of these contacts led to a distinctive Indian population overseas. Indians... married local women, and within a few generations were indistinguishable".

Therefore one can safely argue that Indian diaspora emerged specifically because of large-scale migration of Indians facilitated by European colonial policies during the first quarter of 19th century (Jain 1993, Jayram (ed. 2004). Jayram (ed. 2004: 20) argues that, by the first quarter of the 19th century, the demand for labour was accelerated by the ever expanding colonial economy and because of abolition of slavery by England in 1833, by France in 1848 and by Holland in 1863. Tinker (1974) provides three broad and distinct patterns of Indian emigration in this period: (a) 'indentured' labour emigration (b) '*kangani*' and '*maistry*' labour emigration and (c) 'passage' or free emigration. The indentured labour emigration began in 1834 and ended in 1920. During this period 5 million Indians traveled to different parts of the world. Similarly, the *kangani* system began in the first and third quarter of the 19th century and was abolished in 1838 and restricted to Ceylon, Malaya and Burma.

Further, three patterns can be identified in the post-independence emigration: (a) the emigration of Anglo-Indians to Australia and England, (b) the emigration of professionals and semi-professionals to the industrially advanced countries like the United States of America, England and Canada and (c) the emigration of skilled and unskilled labourers of West Asia (Jayram ed. 2004). In this manner we can observe that the Indian emigrants have settled down as a distinct socio-cultural group keeping their separate identity giving birth to Indian Diaspora. It is estimated that beside 6 million Indian citizens, there are over 20 million people of Indian origin all over the world (Government of India, 2001: 680). Taking 5000 as the minimum figure, overseas Indians are found in as many as 53 countries (Jain 1993: 2-3). However, in 1980 according to '*The Statesman*' news paper there were only five countries in the world where Indians have not yet chosen to stay (*The Statesman*, 5th August, 1980).

Having defined diaspora and process of formation of Indian diaspora let us define the term 'Dalit' which will be used here chapter in defining Dalit Diaspora.

Defining the term Dalit

The Dalits are addressed with different nomenclatures like-*Chandalas, Avarnas, Achhuts, Namashudra, Parihas, Adi-Dravida, Ad-Dharmis*, Depressed Classes, Oppressed Hindus, Harijans etc. But especially after the emergence of Dalit Panther's movement in 1970s in Maharashtra they preferred to be called as Dalits. The definition of Dalits as propounded by Dalit Panthers was a class definition and included members of Scheduled Castes (SCs), Scheduled Tribes (STs), the land-less and poor peasants, Women and all those who were exploited politically, economically and in the name of religion (Murugkar 1991: 237). However for this chapter the Dalit has been strictly used for ex-untouchables of Indian society who have occupied a unique structural location and faced social exclusion in it (Kumar: 2005, Kumar: 2007). The term structure has been used in terms of pattern of inter-related roles and statuses, which the actors of a specific society occupy in the spheres of rights and obligations Nadel (1969:5). Further the term 'social exclusion' has been defined as, "a multi-dimensional process, in which various forms of exclusion are combined: participation in decision making and political processes, access to employment and material resources, and integration into common cultural process. When combined, they create acute form of exclusion that find a spatial manifestation in particular neighbourhoods" (Madanipour et al. 1998: 22). However, in the Indian context as far as social exclusion of Dalits is concerned we have to add to the elements of religious justification of such exclusion based on *Dharma* (follow certain ritual life style) and *Karma* (perform certain duties).

Therefore sociologically, the Dalits can be defined on the basis of three social characteristics:

1. Their Structural location in the Indian Society
2. Social exclusion they suffer in the society
3. And because of structural location and social exclusion the construction of consciousness.

Based on the above elements of structural location, social exclusion and construction of consciousness we can argue that the Dalits are different from poor person, Scheduled Tribes (STs) and Women belonging to caste Hindus that were included in the definition of the Dalits given by the Dalit Panthers. It is so because if the poor person is deprived in economic and political spheres of life, the ex-untouchable is deprived in all the three -social, economic and political realms. And therefore Oommen has rightly pointed out, "If proletarian consciousness is essentially rooted in material deprivations... Dalit consciousness is a complex and compound consciousness which encapsulates deprivations stemming from inhuman conditions of material existence, powerlessness and ideological hegemony" (Oommen 1990: 256).

The social exclusion of an ex-untouchable is so overpowering that even though he attains economic and political mobility or even goes beyond the national boundaries through his hard labour, he is not accepted by the castes located higher up in the caste hierarchy as an equal. His social identity remains stigmatised and his achievements are basically associated with that social identity. Few examples in this regard can make the fact clearer. One, it is a fact that as soon as K.R. Narayanan became the President of India in spite of his high educational achievements and political experience, every one tried to evaluate his ascendance to presidential post only on the basis of his caste identity. Most of them argued the Narayanan was elevated to the post of president because he belonged to Dalit community (Kumar 2007).

Secondly, if we take the Dalit Diaspora as another example, the issue of social exclusion of Dalits becomes further clear. It is true that amongst Indian Diaspora, "that caste was increasingly an aspect of culture rather than social stratification per se...[however] the stigma of caste did not die out completely" (Jain 2003, Kumar: 2004). Jain (2003:74) makes it amply clear how the caste stigma exists with the Dalits even though they have transcended the national boundaries. In his own words, "Women of high caste married to low caste men...looked down upon their husbands ...and even told their children how their fathers were of a lower caste than them" (ibid). The caste stigma and consciousness haunts the Dalits in Diaspora in spite of their economic mobility, whenever they visit their ancestral village. The villagers still looked down upon them.

Therefore we see that the deprivation in the social realm suffered by the Dalits assumes more importance in the construction of their consciousness. And it assumes all the more importance in the construction of consciousness of Dalits living abroad as Non Resident Indian (NRI) or as People of Indian Origin (PIOs). It is so because even though they have achieved socio-economic mobility and have transcended the national boundaries, yet they are not accepted as equals in the Hindu social order by non-Dalits in India and abroad as well. The non-resident Indian Dalits face the same type of humiliation and contempt, as their brothers' face in Indian society, whenever they come back to India. Moreover, their roots in the Indian society remind them of their humiliated, stigmatized, and excluded past when ever they return to India to visit their ancestral place. In this era of information revolution their past becomes alive again and again whenever they read or watch news about the atrocities on Dalits in the print media, on the Inter- net, web site or on the television. Further the NRI or PIO Dalits also face caste discrimination even in countries where they are living with non-Dalits although caste exists neither as a system of social stratification nor as a rigid system of exclusion in the social order of the host country. Therefore one should not be astonished when we use the term Dalits in Diaspora.

Caste in Indian Diaspora

The moot question is how has caste traveled in Indian Diaspora? The answer is not far to seek. Diffusion of Caste as an institution among the Indian Diaspora crystallised because of migration of Indian population. It is a sociological fact that when people migrate they do not migrate only as biological souls. Rather they migrate with their socio-cultural baggage as well. People take along with them their family and caste values as well as their social structures. Caste being the core of Indian's identity and interactional blueprint provides Indians a cushion in times of frustration and alienation which each migrant group suffers in an alien culture.

Migration and Formation of Dalit Diaspora

It is true that Indian Diaspora crystallised because of migration of Indians during colonial period when the Indians migrated as indentured labourers or under the Kangani system to different parts of the world. Same is true for the Dalit Diaspora as well. Migration of Indian Dalits as indentured labourers to different countries is also a fact. The Table 1 below depicts the migration of the Dalit castes as indentured labourers to Mauritius. Migration for Mauritius had started in 1834. These figures are for the period between 1843-73.

Table 1: Dalit Castes Migrants to Mauritius

S. No.	*Name of the Cates*	*Men*	*Women*	
1	Chamars	338	96	
2	Doshad	186	46	
3	Dhangar	68	19	
4	Bhuiya	40	21	
5	Pasi	26	6	
6	Dhobi	25	—	
7	Moochi	23	—	
	Total	706	188	894

Source: Carter Marina, 1995, *Servants, Sirdars, and Settlers: Indians in Mauritius* 1834-1874, Oxford University Press, Delhi, pp. 202-203.

Further, Carter (1995:98) also suggests that, "...out of 1659 individuals traveling from Calcutta to Mauritius between April-July 1872, 38 per cent were respectable agriculture castes, 27 per cent low castes and artisan castes 13 per cent." In the same vein, according to an estimate of 60,965 Indian Indentured labours who migrated to Fiji between 1879, when the migration began until 1916 when it finally ceased, about 11,907 or 26.2 per cent belonged to low menial castes like Chamars, Koris, Pasis etc. (Lal 1984: 126-130). Similarly, Brereton (1974: 26) writes, "To give some figures, between 1876 and 1885 the caste derivation of Hindu arrivals in Trinidad was: Brahman and other high castes 18 per cent; artisan castes 8.5 per cent; agricultural castes 32 per cent; low castes 41.5 per cent". The members of Dalit International Organisation (DIO) Malaysia revealed that the Dalits especially from the then Madras presidency were brought here as indentured labourers some hundred years back by the colonial rulers. They further opined that Dalits here constitute sixty five percent of the ten percent of the total Indian population settled in Malaysia. In this context (Jain 1984: 175) makes an interesting point. Though he accepts that many untouchable castes (Adi-Dravidas) migrated to Malay (as Malaysia was known at that point in time) but he argues that it is difficult to substantiate it statistically.

Apart from migration of Dalits as indentured labourers, the Dalits have also migrated as free labourers to Middle East, European Countries, US and Canada. For instance, the president of the Indian chapter of Apravasi *Dhobi Mahasangh* (Confederation of Non resident Indian *Dhobi* [washerman]) narrated that the *Dhobi* community has been living in Middle-East countries since Second World War when the British forces brought them here as manual labours and some of them as soldiers. Since then they are maintaining a regular flow of the community members in the four countries namely- Iraq, Iran, Bahrain, and Kuwait. In these countries they are concentrated in number of cities like-Baghdad, Albasra, Abudhabi, Dohaquatar, Dubai, Muscat, Sarjaha, Salal, etc. Dalit activists from Punjab narrated that their migration to United Kingdome dates back to before Independence but they could present authentic accounts regarding it since 1960s onwards. This fact is authenticated by Mumman a Dalit from Punjab who in one of his Articles wrote, "I came to Britain in the late 1960s from remote village in India" (Muman, 2000: 71). During this epoch mostly illiterate Dalits migrated as industrial and domestic labourers and got settled there. But today they have gained substantial economic and political mobility. They are in various professions like doctors and engineers and have established their own business.

Today the website www.ambedkar.org estimates about one lakh fifty thousand Dalits living in UK. This Dalit population in UK is quite near to the Dalit population estimates given by Harpal and Tatla (2008: 59-60). They argue that although according to 2001 census Sikhs were 336,179, which for few community leaders are substantial under representation of the Sikhs in Britain, and exact figure is around 5, 00,000. Out of which one-third of Sikhs belonged to the Dalit category (Harpal and Tatla, 2008: 60). Apart from these countries author's own field work in Canada proves the presence of Dalits there. Dalits in Canada celebrated centennial ceremony of their arrival in Canada in August 2006. The souvenir published by Shri Guru Ravidas Sabha (Vancouver) acknowledges that the first group of Dalits came to Canada in the year 1906 and settled on the west coast of Canada. A group of four persons namely Shei Mahia Ram (of Matida), Shri Essar (of Lagiri), Shri Basanta Ram (of Mahilpur), and Shri Gurditta Ram Dhanda (of village Uppalan) hailing form different parts of Punjab are considered to be the 'Dalit Pioneers'. The first group of Dalits did travel via ship as the other Indians traveled with harrowing experiences. The Dalits share experiences of their grand parents with anguish. For instance Darshan Singh Khera, the third generation Dalit from Punjab in Canada argues, "My grandfather would tell us about many hardships he faced. I recall that my grandfather would tell us how they spent the first night in Canada in a horse barn and how difficult was their fist day at the potato farm". Bill Basra the president of the Guru Ravidas Sabha, Vancouver writes, "Many of the pioneers worked tirelessly and they lived in isolation from their families and loved ones for many years. Some of them even faced discrimination because of their race as well as of their caste". The respondents from USA argued that during 1970s the Indian Dalits started migrating to United States of America. Basically they were first generation literate and professional Dalits. We have come across data that proves their presence in countries like-Fiji, Malaysia, South Africa, Surinam, etc. However, because of lack of research we have not been able to elaborate on it. Hence it is pertinent that more research should be taken through this perspective so that new vistas of research can be opened.

Causes of migration of Dalits

The causes of their migration to these countries need a deep research. However few Dalit Non Resident Indians respondents put their migration in a proper perspective, which looks convincing as well. They argued that "we (Dalits) were first to migrate to different parts of the world as we were taken as indentured labourers by the colonial rulers. It happened so that our economic exploitation and social seclusion were enough to force us to leave our place". It is a fact that Dalits were migrating to different parts of the country in search of labourbecause of their abject poverty and sometime because of atrocities and social boycott. They had no property to cling on and hence it was also easy for them to migrate. Contrary to that the Brahmins and other twice born castes were deeply entrenched in their ritual perception that if they crossed the ocean they would loose their castes. And even if they migrated they migrated in small numbers making them insignificant. Moreover, they had economic and social security at home which stopped them to leave their roots easily. It was very late after the advent of Western education that they started going abroad in search of lucrative jobs.

Apart form economic and social reasons the preference of type and nature of labourers also facilitated the migration of Indians as indentured labourers. In this regard, Sandhu (1969:56) has highlighted that, "Of the people of the Subcontinent the South Indian peasant, particularly the untouchables or low caste *Madrasi*, was considered the most satisfactory type of labour...He had fewer qualms or religious susceptibility, such as aversion to crossing the dreaded Kala Pani and food taboos". These castes according to him included Cherumans, Pariyans, Pallars etc. However, Carter (1995:100) argues that high caste status was believed to inhibit migration and to effect Indians in number of ways. It was considered to be a factor in high mortality rates on the emigrant ships. This was revealed by a doctor who had made two trips with indentured labourers. He explained it happened so because the high castes had violated percepts of their religion and defied the anger of their Gods. The passengers told the doctor that they have broken their caste; they have lowered themselves below the level of the lowest Paria. Later she explained that agricultural and artisan castes were considered most suitable for indentured migration.

For Dalits who migrated to Great Britain between 1950 and 1968 when Indians automatically received Commonwealth status and were allowed into the country benefited form the appointment of a Dalit passport officer. Juergensmeyer, describes that, "One would not ordinarily expect the Chamars (Dalit Caste) to have access to international travel in such large numbers...however, the first Scheduled Caste gazetted officer in the Punjab, Ishwar Das Pawar, became the undersecretary for passports...and began handing out passport to Scheduled Caste applicants to emigrate each year (Juergensmeyer, 1982:246)."

Two Types of Dalit Diaspora

From the above based on the nature of emigration of Dalits we can locate two strands of Dalit Diaspora-the 'Old' and the 'New' (Kumar, 2004:114). The 'Old' comprises indentured labourers and assisted labourers who were taken to different parts of Africa like-Mauritius, South Africa, to parts of Asia like-Malaysia, Burma, to parts of Caribbean Latin America like-Trinidad, Guyana, Surinam and to Pacific like Fiji. The contractors and British government facilitated the emigration of Dalits along with other Indians, when the slavery was abolished in 1834. This type of Dalit Diaspora had lost touch with their country of origin and remained aloof till recently when the 'New' Diaspora renewed their links after the globalisation.

The other stream of 'New' Dalit Diaspora includes semi-literate, literate and professionally trained Dalits who have immigrated especially to Europe, United States of America, Canada and Australia. These people went their as industrial labourers, technicians, mechanics, students and professionals like- engineers, doctors, and management experts etc. The 'New' Dalit Diaspora practically the professionals and students have used the modern technology of internet to unite and make the 'Old' and 'New' Diasporas aware of each other. Further, they have helped each other to assert the separate Dalit identity in Diaspora with their own icons, religious and secular symbols. This Diaspora remains in constant touch with the home land running its link with the home land.

Caste Discrimination in Indian Diaspora

If caste exists in Indian Diaspora and Dalits also exist in Diaspora then it is natural that caste based discrimination would also exist within Indian Diaspora. To begin with "There is evidence that some of the traditional methods of showing differences between status still exists. Thus, in Trinidad the residence of lower castes is restricted. In South Africa there is some idea about unclean occupations. There is also some restricted commensality, for example that of the Trinidadian Brahmin priests as rituals, or the Guyanese who told Singer that he would not eat in the home of a low-caste, and restricted feeding of Valmikis in East Africa" (Jain, 1993:15-16). Similarly, "...in Wolverhampton the customer refused to take the change from the vendor lest he found their touch polluting and instead that the change be placed on the counter to avoid contact. On the factory floor, again in Wolverhampton, we know of women of so called upper castes Jats not taking water from the same tap from where the so called lower caste person drink... (in another incident of practice of untouchability) the Sikh temples hold annual inter-temple sports tournaments. One such tournament was held in Birmingham where the *Langar* (sanctified food) will be served by one of the participating temples who happened to be belonging to the Ravidasia community. Whilst their teams participated in the tournament but the Langar did not get eaten by the Jats because it came from the Chamars" (VODI Report, 2000: 73).

Caste Discrimination in British Indian Diaspora

Taking a specific case of UK we can very easily argue that caste discrimination exists in Britain? Caste Watch UK an organisation highlights the existence and spread of 'Caste based discrimination–especially among the Asian Communities'.

Besides it provides a platform to the sufferers of the aforesaid menace to come forward and share their painful experiences to sensitize the larger UK society about the issue.

In an interview with the author in London, the Organisation's head argues that, 'In Britain, caste operates at a much more subtle and sophisticated level. This is the reason why caste discrimination has escaped the attention of the authorities in Britain so far', who are obsessed with countering racial discrimination. Other organisations working for the same issue like-Voice of Dalit International (VODI), International Dalit Solidarity Network (IDSN) etc., endorse the view. They all emphasize the prevalence of multiple forms of caste based discrimination. One of most common form is prevalence of ridiculing Dalits by their caste names from schools to factory. Secondly, restriction on inter-caste marriages between Dalits and castes located higher up in so-called caste hierarchy by the parents of the latter. Caste Watch UK has number of testimonies to prove the caste based discrimination in Britain. In one such testimony, an African from Jamaica argued that his co-brother in law has not been accepted in the family because he is a Dalit while as black I have been accepted. This is so even after he is financially much more mobile than him.

Mark Juergensmeyer in his book '*Religion as Social Vision*' published from University of California reported caste based discrimination against Ravidasis of Wolverhampton way back in 1970s. He wrote, 'on the whole, life is better for the Scheduled Castes in England, but in some ways it is disturbingly the same...the Jat Sikhs do not hesitate to remind the Chamars, even as a personal address. A pub on west End Road, South hall, in the suburb of London has come to be known pejoratively as the Chamar-wali pub because of its clientele'. He had also reported that fights between Sikhs and Chamars have broken all over the industrial England and there have been killings as well. Further, Jat Sikhs have protested against the factory management and refused to work under the Chamar supervisor. But it all went unnoticed. However, the menace is on the rise with number of cases of caste based discrimination increasing in contemporary Britain. That is why the organisations like Caste Watch have also sprung up. In fact, since 2004 this organisation has been organising annual conferences to bring to the people from different walks of life to take active part in the prevention of the growing menace of caste.

Its latest conference was in Aston University, Birmingham on 30th August, 2008 on the topic, 'Caste and Cohesion: Engaging with communities' in which the author also participated with delegates, belonging to academics, NGO, Human Right Organisations, Religious Organisation, etc. The conference accepted the presence of caste based discrimination in different spheres of life. Five categories of caste based discriminations, which exist in Britain, were identified by the participants. One, caste discrimination has crept in schools where Dalit children are bullied by their caste names by their teachers and classmates. Two, when Dalit enters in inter-caste marriage with a girl of a so-called higher caste, he or the couple face isolation, ostracisation, violence and threats by bride's family. In number of inter caste marriage cases the Dalit boys were beaten. Today the young Dalits feel that caste has curtailed their choice of spouse in an otherwise egalitarian society like UK. Three, factories and pubs have seen ugly violence against Dalits and ridiculing of Dalits by their caste names. Fourth, Dalits have been denied equal opportunity and equal status and respect by the so-called upper castes in different organisations based on Indian religions in UK. That has forced Dalits to establish their own organisations and worship places all over Britain. Last but not the least there are songs asserting one's caste identity and pride by the so-called upper castes while being insensitive to the hidden stigmatisation and insult of Dalits in the same songs.

The caste has got new lease of life in the Diaspora because 'New Indian Diaspora' remains in constant touch with mother country unlike the 'Old Indian Diaspora' who lives in the frozen cultural memories because they lost touch with the mother country. The *girmitiyas* of Fiji and Trinidad and Tobago remind us of 'Old Indian Diaspora'. The interaction of 'New Indian Diaspora' with mother country has increased in this era of globalisation because of the information revolution and reduction of time and space with increased transportation. This has further helped the Indian Diaspora to marry their wards in India within their caste and sub castes by flying back to India or having a match with the help of www.shadi.com and other internet sites. This Diaspora calls their relatives in Britain, because of cheap air fairs, which further revitalises caste aspects in Diaspora.

Dalit Diaspora and their organisations

Dalits settled abroad did not remain aloof from each other though they migrated from different parts of India and belonged to different sub-castes. They created their own organisations to develop social solidarity across the different Dalit communities. For instance, the Dalits in UK established *Buddha Vihars* (Buddhist praying center) *Gurudwaras* (Sikh praying place) in late 1960s. While Dalits started migrating to Canada in 1906, the first organisation Dr. Ambedkar Memorial Association was established in 1979 in Vancouver. Later on in 1981 Guru Ravidass Sabha Vancouver came into exixitence. A Buddhist Council was established in the year 1985 here. This council is federation of seven Ambedkarite Organisations working in Britain among the Dalit Indians. Federation of Ambedkarite and Buddhist Organisation (FABO) and Voice of Dalit International (VODI) are also working in UK and are trying to create awareness among the migrant Dalit there, to take action to uplift their brothers back in India.

A more organised effort came in United States of America (USA) from literate NRI Dalits when they formed "Volunteers in service to India's Oppressed and Neglected" (VISION) in 1975. In fact, they aligned with the Black Panther's movement in USA and highlighted their plight, which became the symbol of Dalit and Black unity in USA. It is difficult to delineate the exact date when the Ambedkar Center for Justice and Peace was established in Canada at this point in time. But it is certain that it has been functioning for more than a decade. There are documentary proves that the center has participated in number of conferences organised by United Nation's Human Right Commission. Among them World Summit on Social Development, Copenhagen 1995, World Conference on Human Rights, Vienna 1993, Commission on Social Development at New York, and Sub-Commission at Geneva in 1991 are other significant conferences. The center also helped to produce a documentary titled "The Untouchables", which was released globally with the help of CNN-CBS (VODI Report, 2000: 55).

The establishment of different organisations has not been an easy task and smooth process. People had to sacrifice a lot. Some people had to mortgage their property and some had to leave their job to raise the required funds for buying the land and other material for running the organisation.

Globalisation and its impact on Dalit Diaspora

Dalit Diaspora has become more visible at the international level after 1990s with the onset of process of globalisation, Three important factors have contributed in their visibility:

1. The increased communication facility with information revolution, as an integral part of the process of globalisation, through computers and internet services.
2. The strengthening of civil society with the NGOs, both at the international and national level and their keenness to take interest in the issues related to Dalits and other marginalised sections.
3. Intervention of United Nation Human Right Commission, World Bank, and other international and national institutions for maintenance of human rights of Dalit and other deprived sections of the society.

With regard to the first factor it can be argued that in this era of globalisation, Dalits have snatched an opportunity to unite themselves through Internet service on computer and other International Institutions. At the out set E-mail has given them the much-needed opportunity. Dalits have created their own sites where one can find detail material about Dalits living in India and in different countries world over. In fact, because of E-mail we could establish their presence in different parts of the world. Generally, it was thought that Dalits have not immigrated. If at all they have migrated they are only in United Kingdom and United States of America. But now, thanks to Internet we have come to know that they are present in big numbers in Canada, Malaysia, Middle- East, South Africa, West Indies etc. along with UK and USA. It is because of this media revolution we have also come to know about the Dalit struggles in various countries and at different international forums as well.

Dalit Internet Sites

The few important Internet sites, which help us in locating the Dalits and information about them, are www.ambedkar.org, www.usadalit.org, www.dalitistan.org, ambedkartimes.com etc. The Dalits run these sites on their own. Similarly Dalits also run their E-magazines. Their numbers are increasing day by day. Through these magazines Dalit fraternity the world over keeps itself updated about the latest happenings within the Dalit Diaspora and with the Dalit community in India, which helps them to take prompt action based on these information. It was not possible earlier because they had no link with each other. Another feature of these magazines is that the Dalits from different parts of the countries and the world share there views and air their grievances and achievements. Not only that they are also sharing information about the available job opportunities in different parts of the world. The whole process of sharing of information about themselves which was not there due to want of communication facilities has sensitised themselves and made them conscious that those who are at large distance can easily come together and raise their voice unitedly. And today their efforts are bearing fruits. This can be said on the bases that now they have approached the United Nation's Human Right Commission, which has started taking interest in the welfare of the Dalits.

Dalit Diaspora and Dalit International Conferences

The cognisance of Dalit exploitation in India taken by the Commission in World Conference against Racism, Racial discrimination, Xenophobia and Related Intolerance (August 28th-7th September 2001, in Durban), hereafter WCAR, is testimony to the fact that Dalit organising in this era has reached different levels. In this conference Dalits represented by National Campaign for Dalit Human Rights (NCDHR), which comprised of Dalit Intellectuals, Historians, Artists, Media persons, and Activists, not only from India but also from different parts of the world, participated in big numbers. It is true that never before in the history of Dalit mobilisation Dalit issue has got so much exposure outside the nation (Kumar 2001). Dalits have shown that how international institutions can be used for readdressal of grievances if a national government is not taking care of a group of people. Declaring caste based discrimination and practice of untouchability as crimes against humanity Dalits brought out a programme of action demanding, "measures of reparation for the centuries-old wrong doings committed against these communities" (Declaration of program of Action: 2002). Apart form these the Program of Action went on to demand the redistribution of land, adequate funds for the education, housing, portable water, sanitation and above all appointment of Special UN Rapporteur for examining the complaints and various forms of discriminations against the Dalits.

A unique event of the conference for Dalits was that Dalit women led by National Federation of Dalit Women raised their voice separately, which was later on included in the NGO Declaration on Gender and Racism. They opined, "We declare the Dalit women are victims of caste and gender violence, used by landlords and contractors on construction sites and policemen to 'inflict political lesson' and crush protests, struggle and dissent against centuries old discrimination being inflicted on their whole community. Dalit women are raped and mutilated before being massacred and used as hostages to 'punish absconding relatives'. At a very young age they are forced into prostitution under *devadasi* (maidservant of god) system" (NGO declaration on Gender and Racism). Today NCDHR has a networking of twenty-six international organisations starting from Amnesty International to Human Right Watch along with Heads of many states in European and Latin American countries. The same organisation has raised the issue at the Asia Social Forum meet in India held in January 2003.

However, before Dalits went to Durban, Dalits in United Kingdome had already organised a two-day International conference on Dalit Human Right in London during 16-17 September 2000. The conference was unique in the sense that representatives from all Dalit communities of UK belonging to Shri Guru Ravidassia, Bhagwan Valmiki, Amedkarite and Buddhists and Christian organisations not only attended and participated in the conference but also generously donated money and other resources for the conference. The conference was well attended by the Indian Dalits living in India and abroad. Highlighting the issues concerning the Dalit uplift the conference chalked two pronged approach attacking the problems of the Dalits at the national and international level. The problems to be tackled at the national level included the problem of practice of untouchability, lack of educational, health, food, and other domestic facilities.

Further, concerns were expressed at the fragile Law and Order and Justice Machinery wherein Dalit Human Rights are violated. The conference decided that there should be strong International Campaign in favour of Dalit Human Rights in India. It was also decided that the issues of casteism and discrimination, harassment and atrocities against Dalits are made much more visible, especially in the media and in international forums. Further, it was suggested in the conference that an in-depth "Dalit Research / Information Center" be established in the North to communicate and feed regular information to Governments, Civil Society organisations and other advocacy groups in the north. Similarly, the conference decided that all the Northern Governments, non-governmental aid agencies, Multi and Bi-lateral agencies World Bank, UNICEF, UNDP, and other groups that give aid to India's poverty alleviation program should review their policies and they must see that at least 50% of aid to poverty alleviation programs should be allocated to programs that focus on Dalits (VODI Report 2000).

It is interesting to note that in the follow up of the above conference VODI organised another International Dalit conference in India during 19-20th Feburary 2003. The conference was specially organised on the issue of "Dalit and International Developmental Aid". In this context the conference discussed the role of 'Non Governmental Aid Agencies' (NGAA) in granting aid to Indian NGOs and its use in the Uplift of Dalits in India and other countries where untouchability is practiced. It was deliberated in the conference that the researches of Charity Aid Foundation (CAF) and Voluntary Action Network India (VANI) showed that there were 18000 NGO's in India registered under the 1976 Foreign Contribution (Regulation) Act to receive foreign money without prior permission of Indian government. Further, it was also revealed that these NGOs receive a sum of Rs. 26000 million as foreign contribution but the money is not reaching the Dalits who constitute 90 per cent of poor in India. This money is cornered by the NGOs run by Castes located higher in the Caste hierarchy. Hence the conference decided to launch a campaign to sensitize the NGAAs to ask the NGOs to take special care the Dalits. Moreover, the conference advocated that the relevant organisation and agencies should ensure adequate representation of Dalits in the decision making level and groom the leadership among the young Dalits. The conference pleaded that the Aid programmes should dismantle the service-oriented approach by the NGO like–education, health, income generation, housing, food for work etc., which neglects cultural and identity issues of the Dalits. Instead an integrated right based and service-oriented approach should be practiced so that pace of Dalit empowerment can be much faster.

It is, in this context of establishment of organisations by Dalits abroad Backward and Minorities Employees' Federation (BAMCEF) has also launched its international networking since 1999 and it already has ten branches in different countries of the world. The organisation has already organised conferences in UK, USA, Malaysia, Canada etc. to sensitize their brethren about the wretched conditions of the Dalits back home. They have also sensitised them about the clever manipulations of Vishva Hindu Parishad (VHP) and hence got the grants to VHP stopped and now no more Dalits pay them. This has adversely affected the income of VHP. Moreover, the cadre camps of BAMCEF have further sensitised Dalits abroad about the Ambedkarite movement in India and its benefit to Dalits.

Further Dalit International Organisation had organised first Dalit World Conference in Malaysia on "A Vision towards a Caste-less Society" during October 10th - 11th 1998. The conference was well attended by Dalit leaders and Dalits from India and from different parts of world participated in big numbers. The unique feature of this conference was that the immigrant Dalits contributed their mind, money and man-power for this organisation. It was revealed in the pamphlet that till 1997 the Dalits in Malaysia who are mostly form Tamil Nadu organised Tamil Conferences in league with their non-Dalit Tamil brethren showing their Tamil solidarity and identity. But when they realised the non-Dalit Tamilians are using them for their own gains and political mileage, the Dalit left them and have organised themselves independently. They formed independent Dalit party with the name 'Indian Progressive Front' and organised many rallies under the slogan '*Nidhiketu Nedudhurum Payanam*' (Long March to Demand Justice). Today they revere and highlight Babasaheb Dr. B.R. Ambedkar and have developed a separate political and social identity, which has enhanced their political clout and some Dalits have been nominated to Malaysian Parliament.

The Indian chapter of Apravasi Dhobi Mahasangh (Confederation of Non resident Indian *Dhobi* [washerman]) was another organisation floated in September 2001 to take care of about twenty thousand washermen in the different part of Middle-East. The president of the confederation narrated that the *Dhobi* community lives in perpetual uncertainty in this part of the world as they are not allowed to own any property and therefore they are forced to run their own business in rented shops. The whole arrangement is temporary and depends on the mercy of their foreign owners. In the absence of any government support the confederation is trying to give material and moral support in the hour of crises to the members of their community. They help the individuals and families in case of accidental deaths and injuries suffered by the migrant labourers. In the alien land where Arabic and Persian is the common parlance these illiterate or semi-literate *Dhobis* have tremendous coping capacity with their broken English and are surviving for generations. Today in this era these Dalits are facing competition from the migrant labourers from other third world countries, especially from the Sri Lankan, Bangladeshi and Pakistani migrant labourers. It is because of this reason the Dalit migrants want a helping hand from the Indian government not at the state level but also at the bilateral level between the governments of different countries.

Further, the non-resident Indian Dalits in Vancouver, Canada under the banner of Association for International Dalit Conference Inc. have just organised another World Conference during May 16th – 18th 2003. The Conference was well attended by Dalits from India, U.K., USA, and Canada. Dalit academicians, activists, media persons, politicians, bureaucrats, businessmen, professionals' etc., participated in the conference in good numbers. The theme of the conference was Charting Dalit agenda for 21st Century. The Conference in the end adopted an 11-point declaration with the affirmation that they have been inspired by the great thinker and philosopher of the oppressed, Babasaheb Dr. B. R. Ambedkar. Giving a call to the Dalits world over the Vancouver declaration demands, "The rightful and proportionate share of Dalits and Tribals in India's national institutions, wealth and capital must be recognized. Economic exclusion hitherto practiced in the name of caste must be done away with. The community should have equitable access to means of production and economic empowerment." The conference has taken an important decision that is significant because we are in an era of globalisation where international institutions are becoming important. It demands, "The United Nations and its affiliates, and non-governmental agencies concerned with human rights, social and economic development, must recognize that the Dalits are a special group and create separate Dalit divisions managed by the Dalits themselves. A sustained effort be made at the UN to expedite the process of formally equating caste- based discrimination with racial discrimination. The World Bank and other Financial Institutions should attach conditional special component clause and must ensure the rightful share of the Dalits in the funds they lend to India for socio-economic and sustainable development" (Vancouver Declaration, 2003). It is interesting to note that in a follow up meeting of the conference in India the Dalits from Canada explained their eagerness to help the Dalits in India. In a meeting they told, "we are so far we can help you through our means but cannot come here on regular basis. So you can ask us any help from our side and we will comply". After that the Dalit Diaspora has sent financial help to the Dalits in India and has been maintaining a regular relationship.

Dalit Diaspora and Self-esteem

UK and Canada are becoming the hub of activities of the Dalit Diaspora. As discussed earlier that the Dalits here celebrate Ambedkar's, Buddha's, and Ravidas's birth anniversaries with lots of fun and fare. In every meeting, conference or Seminar they share their struggle and the status they have achieved now. They narrate the miseries and pain their parents and family members have suffered. But feel satisfied with their present achievements. For last three years Dalits have taken an initiative to organize Ambedkar Memorial lecture in Manchester Metropolitan University with a vision of spreading Ambedkar's thought throughout the world. Another unique effort of the Dalit Diaspora in UK in the cultural realm is that on 23rd April 2003, they have established a Ambedkar Museum at Wolverhampton. This museum now houses over 40 items of Babasaheb Ambedkar. The main items include Babasaheb's grey suite, Barrister's gown, umbrella, specks, tie and shirt. Other things include table lamp, clock, cufflinks, paper pins, and puncher besides other things. The most precious of them all, according to Dalits, include Babasaheb's pen, Table Lamp and Parliamentary Pass combined with the personal letters and the Reports he wrote which determined the future of India's Depressed and Oppressed Communities. This Ambedkar Memorial Museum is now the place of Pilgrimage. Dalits visiting UK from different parts of the world visit this museum as the place of pilgrimage. The museum has really become a new cultural symbol for the Dalit Diaspora.

To enhance their self-esteem Dalits in UK and Canada have dissociated themselves from the Sikh *Gurudwaras* as they felt discrimination and realised exclusion from different bodies of the Gurudwara Prabhandhak Committees (Gurudwara Organizing Committees). The reason for separation of Dalits from Sikhs is not ill-treatment meted to them individually rather it has also a religious cause. The Dalits in UK and Canada condemn in strongest possible terms the disrespect shown by the Sikhs to their Guru Ravidas and Guru Valmiki. The Dalits argue that the Sikhs have accorded a lower status to our Gurus by calling them as *Bhakts*. They emphasize that the Holy *Gurugranth Sahib* has versus from Guru Ravidas then how can he be a disciple. Dalits on their part are not ready to accept a subordinated position of their Gurus and hence have opened separate Guru Ravidas Temples and Valmiki Temples. Now they proudly share that in these temples they are the custodians themselves and are free to act independently. By establishing separate Guru Ravidas Temples and Valmiki Temples the Dalits have not only established their independent identity but they have also liberated themselves from caste subordination in foreign land.

The mobility and development which Dalits have attained in the different countries has motivated them to assert that they are not inferior to any one as has been propagated by caste Hindus back home. They have argued when asked, "look we have demystified the ideal type image of Dalits as dirty, drunkard, devoid of any merit, beast of burden etc., accorded to us by others because today Dalits of Indian Diaspora have proved their worth at the international forums by developing themselves without the crutches of the policy of protective discrimination". In the same vein they also narrated that, "by attaining the mobility in different realms of foreign society without the help of the protective discrimination policies Dalits have made a point that nothing is inherently wrong with them. Therefore, it is wrong to say that they are devoid of any merit. Instead it is because of lack of democratic social conditions of the Indian society that they lagged behind. If they are provided a democratic social order they can also perform like any other person and will not need any type of reservations". In their effort to demystify their ideal type image and enhance their self esteem the Dalit boast their contributions to the country by narrating that they also send the foreign remittances like any other group of Indian Diaspora. They argue, "observe the fact that foreign remittances sent to Indian exchequer by general Indian Diaspora and Dalit Diaspora is similar if not equal in quantity".

Conclusions

To conclude at the outset it can be easily argued that the presence of the Dalit Diaspora and their patterns of mobilisation proves the fact that Indian Diaspora is not a monolithic whole as propounded by the Indian academia and Indian government. Hence, the study emphasizes the urgent need to develop a new paradigm and perspective to study and analyze Indian Diaspora. Secondly, the study has revealed the presence of caste based discrimination wherever Indian Diaspora is present. Moreover, Dalits have got a refuge abroad and their exploitation and exclusion is not the same as it used be in the parent country.

Furthermore, the study reveals that Dalit Diaspora has helped the Dalit community to use the most advanced technology-computers, Internet, web-sites etc., for the development of their community in this era of globalisation otherwise there has been nothing to cheer for them in this era. It has helped the Dalits living in Diaspora nearer to their counterparts living in India. It has helped in establishing a new image of the Dalits as Dalit Diaspora has performed without the crutches of reservation in the host country.

Similarly, the analysis in the study brings out a point that the Dalit Diaspora has been performing many important functions. Firstly, the whole process of their organizing at the international level has helped Dalit movement to break the national boundaries and take the Dalit struggle and assertion at the international level. In turn it has made Dalit Diaspora more visible. It is in this context one should realise that as in this era of globalisation the economic exchange takes place through global parameters. Dalit Diaspora with the help of Dalits in India can successfully pressurise the international funding and law making agencies like IMF, World Bank, United Nations etc., to ask Indian government to take up the Dalit issues in right earnest otherwise face sanctions.

On the whole, we can argue that the Dalit organizations at the International level because of presence of Dalit- Diaspora have really questioned the professional credentials of academia, intelligentsia, and media, back home, for keeping the world ignorant about problems of exclusion, untouchability etc., prevailing in Indian society, which have proved detrimental for two hundred million people. Last but not the least, Dalit Diaspora has given the problems of Dalits more visibility at the national and international level.

References

Brereton, Bridget, 1974, The Experience of Indentureship 1845-1917, in John La Guerre (ed.), *Calcutta to Caroni*, Longman Caribbean Limited, Trinidad and Jamaica.

Carter Marina, 1995, *Servants, Sirdars, and Settlers: Indians in Mauritius* 1834-1874, Oxford University Press, Delhi.

Government of India, 2001, *India 2001: A Reference Annual*, New Delhi, Publication Division, Ministry of Information and Broadcasting, New Delhi.

Jain, Ravindra K., (a) 1993. *Indian Communities Abroad: Themes and Literature*, Manohar, New Delhi.

————,(b) 1984, South Indian Labour In Malaya,1840-1920 : Asylum Stability And Involution in Saunders, Kay, (ed.), *Indentured Labour in British Empire* 1834-1920, Croom Helm, London and Canberra.

————, 2003, Culture and economy: Tamils on the Plantation Frontier in Malaysia Revisited 1998-1999 in Bhiku Parekh (eds.), *Culture and Economy in Indian Diaspora*, Routledge, New Delhi.

Jayram, N (ed.), 2004, *The Indian Diaspora: Dynamics of Migration*, Sage Publications, New Delhi.

Juergensmeyer, Mark, 1982, *Religion as Social Vision: The Movement against Untouchability in 20th Century Punjab*, University of California Press, USA.

Kumar, Vivek, 2000, Relating to the Global World, *The Pioneer*, 15th April, New Delhi.

————2001, A blow for Dalit dignity and pride, *The Pioneer*, 25th September, New Delhi.

————2003, Dalit Movement and Dalit International Conferences, *Economic and Political Weekly*, XXXVIII, no. 27, Mumbai.

————2004, Understanding Dalit Diaspora, *Economic and Political Weekly*, No.1, January 3, Mumbai.

———— 2005, Situating Dalits in Indian Sociology, *Sociological Bulletin* (special issue of South Asia: The State of Sociology, Issues of Relevance and Rigor), Volume 54, Number 3, September-December, New Delhi.

————. 2007, Governance and Development in the Era of Globalisation: Understanding exclusion and assertion of Dalits in India, in Kameshwar Choudhary (ed.) *Globalisation Governance Reforms and Development in India*, Sage Publications, New Delhi.

Lal, V. Brij, 1984, Labouring Men and Nothing More: Some Problems of Indian Indenture In Fiji, in Saunders, Kay, (ed.), *Indentured Labour in British Empire* 1834-1920, Croom Helm, London and Canberra.

Madanipour, A, 1998, 'Social Exclusion and Space' in A. Madanipour, G. Cars, and J. Allens (eds.) *Social Exclusion in European Cities*, London, Jessica Kingsley.

Muman, Sat Pal, 2000, Caste in Britain, in Report of the proceedings of International Conference on Dalits Human Rights, Voice of Dalit International, London, UK.

Murugkar, Lata, 1991, *Dalit Panther Movement in Maharashtra: A Sociological Appraisal*, Popular Prakashan, Bombay.

Nadel, S.F., 1969, *The Theory of Social Structure*, Cohen and West, London.

Oommen, T.K., 1990, *Protest and Change: Studies in Social Movements*, Sage Publications, New Delhi.

Saunders, Kay (ed.), 1984, *Indentured Labour in British Empire 1834-1920*, Croom Helm, London and Canberra.

VODI Report, 2000, Report of the proceedings of International Conference on Dalits Human Rights, Voice of Dalit International, London, UK.

National Federation of Dalit Women NGO Declaration on Gender and Racism, Racial, Racial Discrimination, Xenophobia and Related Intolerance, WACR, 28 August –7 September 2001, Durban, South Africa.

Declaration and Program of Action, 2002, World conference Against Racism, Racial Discrimination, Xenophobia and Related Intolerance, United Nations, New York.

Schwartz, Barton Morley (ed.) 1967, *Caste in Overseas Indian Communities*, Chandler Publishing Co., San Francisco, California.

Shukla, Sandhya, 2003, *India Abroad: Diasporic Cultures of Postwar America and England*, Princeton University Press, Princeton, New Jersey.

Shri Guru Ravidass Sabha Community Directory 2007, Vancouver, Canada.

Tinker, Hugh, 1974, *A New System of Slavery: The Export of Indian Labour Overseas* 1830-1920, Oxford University Press, London.

————, 1977, *The Banyan Tree: Overseas Emigrants from India and Bangladesh*, Oxford University Press, London.

9

British Malay: The Untold Saga of Untouchable Plantation Coolies

Tenepalli Hari

The colonial forces from Europe and North America in various periods reached the Asia and Pacific region in order to secure better trade relations. The British defeat of the French and Dutch forces in the Napoleonic Wars permitted Britain to swell its control in South Africa, Southeast Asia, and the southern Caribbean. These colonies soon were turned into centers of the British economic expansion and industrialisation, by exporting raw materials and agricultural goods and importing manufactured and finished products.

They not only emerged as monopoly traders of highly sought spices but they also laid claim to power within a short period. Two main factors had played a significant role for these traders in ultimately turning into rulers. They had enjoyed overwhelming domestic support and justification for colonising, and the prevailing conditions in these colonies provided space for them to emerge as rulers. In the case of India, the existing social system laid a strong foundation for social divisions and turned the vast majority of people into slaves. The exploitation of people had been justified and institutionalised through the caste system. The caste system had historically proved to be a spoiler of the spirit of unity, common brotherhood and enemies among the Indians and ultimately paved the way for the colonial forces to climb to power without any notable resistance from the people. This study tries to explore the British colonial forces' economic policies towards India; starting from its rule and its general impact on the overall conditions in India, and its ultimate impact on Dalits, who were living like slaves to upper castes who now became the slaves of the white men. The white men on the one hand banned black men's slavery, but on the other hand, soon replaced the blacks with untouchable slaves in their place.

The horrible saga of untouchable slaves of the British colonial forces in British Malaya has not been adequately studied yet. It was during the period that for the first time untouchable people were forced to migrate from their native land to foreign territory just for survival. The living conditions on the plantations proved to be worse than the Indian villages social isolation. Upper caste men continued to be their immediate heads, who not only represented colonial interests but also carried caste ideology to subjugate these marginalised people. The British colonial forces and their Indian collaborators through the casteist managerial staff kept the plantation labours in perpetual inhuman conditions by denying them the basic social amenities.

Women and children in the plantation estates worked fulltime to just eke out a small living. The colonial forces also transported innocent women to be introduced into prostitution. Sex slaves of Brahmin temples 'devadasis' who belonged to the untouchable community were also imported to serve the sexual needs of the plantation labourers. The kind of life that these women led and the pathetic and miserable conditions in which they lived had no parallel and they also found no way out from the brutal exploitation. The colonial masters and their collaborators were insensitive to the pain of these people and agony they always looked forward for maximizing profits.

On the eve of the British Invasion

The British defeat of the French and Dutch forces in the Napoleonic Wars boosted Britain's power to expand its rule across South Africa, Southeast Asia, and the southern Caribbean. Before the British colonial forces advance into the Malaya peninsula, the Portuguese in 1511-1641 and later the

Dutch (1641-1824) occupied and ruled the territory by overcoming the local ruling class resistance. The British expansion in Peninsular Malaysia started with the acquisition of three territories; Penang, Melaka and Singapore, in the Straits of Melaka between 1786 and 1824. These territories were, grouped together as the Straits Settlements (SS).

On the eve of the British occupation, Malaysia was like any other Asian country; its economy was completely based on agriculture and there was very little development of other sectors. It was completely a rural based society, self-sufficient village community growing rice and depending upon geographical location, fishing, holding land in common, and to a large extent self-governing. The society was headed by Sultans and he had the sole rights to conduct international trade.

The colonial forces like in other places did not intervene in the social sphere and had allowed the social elites to continue their domination. The collaboration of the traditional elites and new elites tuned the society to the benefit of these few elites. The colonial forces who occupied Malaya gradually turned it into one of their trading centers by developing trading ports, which had emerged as the economic hubs of the colonial economy. Since there was little else in Malaysia which they could immediately convert into cash or export to the international market. First, they had paid attention to tapping the natural wealth by developing the commercial plantations and mining for the rare metals. By the 1910s, rubber had replaced coffee and sugar.[1]

British Colonial Economic Policies towards India before the British occupied India, it was basically a major manufacturing centre for many goods, which had the major share in the export basket. This capability was systematically destroyed by the British conquerors. The British economic policies towards India since the day of their rule were mainly targeted to destroy its well built economic system. As a result of its economic policies all the sections of people were badly affected. The Indian–built ships were prohibited in the Indo-British trade from 1814 onwards. Indians thus ceased to play any major role in the external sea-borne trade of India. These two measures had destabilised the well established Indian industrial establishment and resulted in the decline of many of the industrialists but also more significantly resulted in the loss of customary means of a livelihood for large number of spinners, potters, millers, shoemakers, and such like.[2] The influx of artisans leaving moribund handicraft industries, and the flow of such other elements as the dispossessed or displaced ryots; numbers were also constantly replenished by a large natural increase of pressure on agriculture. In 1891, there were 17,000,000 agricultural labourers in India, in 1901, 35,000,000 and a decade later it had increased to 41,000,000. The pressure on agriculture increased in the face of favourable agricultural conditions which were by no means assured, dependent as they were on the vagaries of the monsoon rains. "Consequently, famines, usually followed by epidemics, were always round the corner, bringing death and desolation in their wake." [3] In addition to the general economic wreckage, the caste structure had also played a tarnishing role by preventing the occupational mobility of a large number of artisan's. The victims of caste system, the landless labourers belonged mostly to the untouchable castes and were pushed into near starvation conditions; historically they owned nothing and the vast majority of them were unskilled labourers. These social communities did not receive any kind of social support from the upper castes whom they had served from generation to generation. Life for them was not so much a question of degree of discomfiture but more a ceaseless struggle just to hang on to the very breath of life. They were left with no other option other than migration to any place just for survival.[4]

The Mode of Labour Contract

The British colonial governments on both the sides first designed policy framework under which the coolies were to be exported from one part to another part. The British India became the second hub for exporting manpower after Africa. The European and North American colonial masters traditionally pursued two policies to fulfill their labour demands. On one side they imported black slaves, whom they had purchased in the international slave market. The other policy was to create a new labour class through various methods within the colony, in the entire Asia and Pacific region.

Except India, there was no wage labour as such; in the entire continent people had land for agriculture or other traditional professions to sustain their lives. To create wage labour class, the colonial powers forcibly confiscated their lands and destroyed their traditional economic structure to throw large number of people into helpless conditions, and later they became coolies in white men's plantations. The saga of Vietnamese under the eighty years of French rule was a perfect example for these kind of historical processes. The French plantations in Vietnam turned to be hell on earth to a large number of people.

The Brahmanical social order had created perfect ground for the colonial forces in many ways. The victims of Brahmanical order were denied education and were not allowed to own property. They lived like slaves to the upper castes. The invasion of the British indirectly led to the ruining of their lives. The general conditions pushed them to starvation. Under these conditions, the untouchable coolies of the upper castes showed interest to migrating to work in white men's profit ventures.

The European investors in Malaya pursued mainly two modes of recruitment to importing coolies from India. In the first period they followed the indentured labour system. Labourers who reached Malaya under this contract were bound by a contract under all conditions and it was almost impossible for them to withdraw from it. The same pattern was followed in recruiting coolies to Ceylone.[5] Under the 'indentured labour' system Coolies mainly migrated to work in sugar production activities in Malaya. This mode of recruitment ultimately landed Indian coolies in horrible conditions. They were paid low wages in comparison to the Chinese workers for the same work. In addition to that, bad and insufficient food, and poor accommodation resulted in horrible living conditions and made their very survival difficult. "The indenture system was "riddled with abuses" as a result of poor living conditions, the questionable means of recruitment and the arduous ship journey, which caused high mortality and ill-health among the surviving passengers. The system was been condemned as "near slavery".[6] The system was disbanded after mounting criticism of its brutality. The indenture system was finally abolished in 1910. An alternative mode of recruiting was developed which was known as the *kangany* system. Kangany is a Tamil word for "overseer" or "superior". Under this new system, coolies were imported up to 1938 and this mode paid way for coolie's entire family moving along with him into Malaya. The Malaya's received large number of coolies under the Kangany mode than the indenture mode. During the period between 1898 and 1938 around 1,153,717 coolies had been recruited under the Kangani system which accounts for an average of more than 28,000 per annum. Even under this new system, the coolies overall position did not improve in any way. The Indian government appointed an inquiry commission headed by Srinavasa Sastri. In his report, he had advised the government stating that the Kangani system was most undesirable and should be ended. A brief-renewal of migration was recorded after 1934. In 1938, the Indian government prohibited the departure of unskilled coolies.[7] Later after the Japanese invasion of Malaya in December 1941 the Japanese forced the Indian government to impose a complete ban on all migration from India for the duration of the war. The British Malaya had passed two Acts in 1953. These Acts on the one side prevented unskilled coolie's migration, while it paved the way for highly qualified professionals and technical personnel to enter the country. Unlike the labour migrants who were mainly the Tamils, the present wave of migrants was more heterogeneous and they hailed from different parts of India.[8]

British India's First Export: Dalits and Backward Caste Coolies

The social divisions in Hindu society not only helped the British colonial forces to gain power but also helped to gain more strength to rule the country for a long period without any major resistance. The Brahmins through their cunning acts prevented other social groups from learning and imposed various fines and forms of prohibition. As a result Brahmin's monopoly on knowledge continued. The Brahmin's knowledge power turned the non-brahmin social communities, mainly the Shudras and untouchable castes as slaves to the social elites; the Brahmin, Kshatriyas, and Vaishyas. This well-established social structure maximised power and privileges of small sections of social elites.

The colonial masters who had conquered the country made no sincere efforts to liberate the victims of Brahmanism. Instead they tried to enhance their hold on the society through help of brahmins knowledge power and the existing social structure. Brahmins not only produced enormous amount of literature in support of slavery of socially downtrodden people to social elites but also extended their support to British administration to keep these people as slaves to old masters and new rulers.

The tropical plantations of sugar, coffee, tobacco, bananas, and tea were the first profit making ventures which the British had pursued in the Asia and Pacific region. The white colonial master's first turned black people in Africa as their slaves. The black people's innocence and their physical strength made them a strong work force for the colonial masters. The black slaves were exported from their native land to all across the world to be employer in white men's ventures.

The British colonial forces on the one side declared the abolition of slavery in its territories in 1833 and at the same time it had replaced Indian coolies whose position was no more better than black slaves. India replaced Africa as major exporter of people for white man's profit making.

Indian convicts from different parts of the country were used as labour in white men's agriculture and construction works in Southeast Asia in the late eighteenth and the early nineteenth centuries. In 1788, British Governor-General of India Cornwallis who had floated the idea of transferring Indian convicts to Southeast Asia. Under his direction the first Indian convicts were transported Malay in1790.[9] As result of this policy, the British colonial masters eliminated the political dissidents in India and fulfilled the labour demands in other colonies of the British empire.

The British colonial rulers in Malaya were not only rulers but they also became the major owners of large tracts of virgin land within a short period. To exploit the nature for their profit they needed the manpower that could fulfill the white man's lust for profit. After assuming formal occupation of Penang in 1786 on behalf of the Crown, the "country trader" Francis Light requested the governor-general India to "supply

. . . one hundred coolies, as the price of labour in Penang was enormous."[10] The European investor's bad experience with Chinese workers made them to turn to India. They had considered India as destination for man power and they also felt that Indians made up cheap and docile labour especially in comparison with the Chinese who were thought to be too independent. South India, because of its favourable geographical position and due to the importance of its colonial ports, had emerged as the major export base for Indian coolies. Sri Lanka, was considered to be the first country where the south Indian coolies were first employed around 1820s. Indian coolie's recruitment for Malaya began around the 1830s.

The planters introduced rubber in 1897 and the demand for rubber in Britain and America prompted the European investors to massively invest in rubber plantations. In Malaya within a short period rubber replaced coffee. The rubber plantation generally required more labour compared to other tropical plantations. Migration of Indian coolies received its greatest thrust with the development of plantation economy and the boom in rubber prices in the international market in the late 1910s and early 1920s. Between the 1840s and 1930s, over 1.9 million Indians entered Malaya. With an estimated 60 percent return migration rate, this produced a net migration gain of about 1.2 million Indians in Malaysia between 1790 and 1957.[11] The inflow of coolies from India was mainly linked to the international market trends. When the price for rubber was booming the plantation owners placed demand for more coolies from India, when market plunged to low, the coolies were pushed back to their native lands.

After the end of the First World War, the Malaya economy registered boom in every sector in line with the more favourable international trends. The world's great depression in the 1930's resulted in the entire world economy being plunged into crisis period. Since the Malaya economy was mainly an export-led economy it was severely affected. In 1930, The planters undertook various measures to save their profits in the wake of world economic slowdown. They immediately reduced production, cut wages, and the coolies from their estates were forced to repatriate to their native lands. In the period between 1930 and 1932 more than 1,50,000 Indian coolies were repatriated, and assisted migrations (Kangani recruitments) were totally stopped.[12] A brief-renewal of migration was recorded after 1934. However, when the price of rubber started falling in 1938, the Indian government prohibited the departure of unskilled labourers. In December 1941, the Japanese invasion had led to an end to all forms of migration from India for the entire duration period of the war. The Japanese invasion of Malaysia had greatly effected Indian coolies in Malaysia more than any other social community. The Japanese invaders forcibly conscripted tens of millions of plantation workers for the construction of the 'death railway' linking Thailand and Burma.**13** As per the rough estimates based on the Labour Records Department in Malaya, about 75,000 Indian estate coolies were taken away. Of them, 45,000 were reported to have been killed; while most of the remaining 30,000 came back to Malaya with virulent diseases such as ulcers, beri-beri, and so on.[14] In Burma, thousands of Indian immigrants died on a forced march, fleeing towards India via Assam to avoid the Japanese brutality. The total number of Indian coolies who had lost their lives due to Japanese aggression is unavailable. The families did not receive any assistance from the British Malaya and Indian government to locate large number of missing men.

The Regional Background of the Coolies

The research work of Adapa Satyanarayana reveals various facts about the south Indian coolies. The coolie's mainly belonged to the three states; Tamil Nadu, Andhra Pradesh, and Kerala. The Tamil speaking coolies were larger in number than any other group. The Tamil coolies were mainly drawn from southern districts of Madras; Trichinopoly, Tanjore, Salem, South and North Arcot districts. Whereas the next dominant group, the Telugu speaking coolies, were mainly migrated from the Ganjam, Vizagapatnam, Godavari and Chittoor districts.

The majority of Indian coolies in Malaysian rubber plantations were mainly drawn from the untouchable castes; the Adi-Andhra and Adi-Dravida untouchable groups of the Mala, Madiga, Pallan, and Parayan and Chakkiliyan castes from coastal districts and Chittoor district of Andhra Pradesh and various adjoining areas of Madras and other port cities.[15] The untouchable castes coolies were historically denied education and learning any profession other than their traditional unclean jobs.

The brutal nature of Brahmanism injected hatred and domination in the minds and body of upper castes, and to maintain that social order it urges the upper caste people to deprive minimum basic conditions to the untouchable castes and not to allow them to have independent livelihoods. The same conditions prevailed in Tamil Nadu on the eve of Tamil coolie's migration to Malaysia. "Here a few high-caste landlords, called Janmis and Mirasdars, respectively, frequently claimed to have a prior right over all land in the village, including the villager's home sites and unoccupied land too. The outcaste or low-caste labourer here had little or no chance of ever acquiring any land and was invariably at the complete mercy of his lord and master, being liable to be expelled from the only land available for the hut sites if he should offend the Mirasdar or Janmi, as the case may be. With increasing monetisation the demands of the landlord on his pannaiyals became even more oppressive. In some of the Mirasi domains, for example, the Pannaiyal was forced to work from sunrise to sunset, and if he was ever dilatory in the discharge of his bond he was confined without victuals and beaten with rods. The vast majority of them led a hand-to–mouth existence in a chronic state of semi-starvation, in perpetual fast. Life for them was not so much a question of degree of discomfiture but more a ceaseless struggle just to hang on to the very breath of life."[16]

They continued to remain left out as unskilled manual coolies in Indian agricultural land and were transported to rubber plantation in foreign lands and in both places untouchable coolies' lived as slaves. Among the untouchable population, occupational mobility was very low. The future generations of this group would largely end their life within the plantation compound.

The backward castes people who had migrated and settled in Malaysia continued their traditional occupations in foreign land without any intervention. Malaysia becomes the only country in Southeast Asia where the caste-based occupations largely spread among the Indian.

Denial of Social Amenities Implies Denial of Future

The untouchable castes in the Indian subcontinent were denied minimum basic human rights. The Brahmanical social order always tried to keep the untouchable castes merely as servants by prohibiting education and promoting social alienation. For centuries, the social elites historically ruled in their narrow self interest. The pain and suffering of untouchable castes was never addressed by these privileged castes. The exploitation of untouchable castes is justified by the vast literature that they produced and through traditions. Brahmins were writers and creators of a dominant culture for their interest to protect their privileges and dominant position in society. The non-Brahmin social communities by accepting the Brahmin's role and by respecting his social norms they become the protectors of Brahmanism. The Brahminised individual and social communities in any religion in the Indian subcontinent turned to be more dedicated than Brahmins in maintaining and promoting the traditional order which subjugates humanity in the name of caste and gender.

The untouchable coolies in Malaysia had never seen Brahmins advocating and enforcing Hindu social order. It was the Brahminised non-brahmins who became dual agents, one side they acted as faithful servants to European plantation owner, and on other side turned into very strong upholders of Brahmanical social order. South Indians from Ceylon had occupied almost all subordinate managerial clerical and technical posts on estates of the European plantation enterprise in Malaysia. Among the various social groups, the Ceylon Tamils once again the dominant group in the field subordinate posts.[17] The social background of all the subordinate managerial clerical and technical staff shows that they mainly come from the backward castes of Hindu social order.

The social and economic setup on plantations completely resembles south Indian village setup. "The social set-up in the plantations was rigidly hierarchical. The status quo of Indian villages be here, viz., the non-Brahmin and Adi-Dravida division was firmly entrenched and it helped the management to run the estate, the Vanniar as "dominant caste" and Adi-Dravidas as the "subordinate castes".[18] "The workers at the bottom of this set-up were treated with scant respect. A labourer must get down from his bicycle when passing a staff bungalow or that a Tamil coolie must not put on shoes, or must groom his hair only in the traditional style. Harsh and inhuman conditions, especially before the Second World War, two generations of workers grew up and lived in an environment that discouraged initiative, independence of thought, or a sense of self-worth. The slightest expressions of dissent to the oppressive set-up were isolated and punished."[19]

The European plantation owners always looked forward to exploit their labour for profit and the Brahminised subordinate staff always sought respect for his dominant status and both the social groups jointly collaborated in exploiting and brutalising the untouchable coolies. The situation in British Malaya resembles the Indian conditions. The social elites comprised upper castes and Brahmins who turned out to be strong loyal workforce of British colonial administration. The vast majority of Indians were forced to serve the two masters; the old social elites who now turned to gloves to the new foreign colonial masters. The Brahmin constructed social structure, not only benefited the traditional social elites who become the major beneficiaries and acted as a strong wall to protect the British empire. The Brahmins and brahminised individuals were their immediate authorities in both places (India and Malaya). They had never shared their brotherhood with fellow Indians but they always acted as mere servants of Brahmanism and the colonial masters. The untouchables in India and in Malaya remained victims of Brahmanism and the brutal British exploitation. These two forces with their joint effort continuously denied basic human rights and humane treatment to untouchables, and they never gave a chance for these groups to escape from their clutches. To protect their hold on power and they denied the basic social amenities to untouchable coolies, to make sure the next generations also remained as captive slaves to them. The coolies were forced to live in cramped and filthy labour lines. Amenities such as clean water and proper facilities for bathing and cooking were unheard of.[20]

Health Facilities

The untouchable coolies mainly lived in owner-provided accommodation within the plantation estate. The plantation estates remained totally isolated from society. Health care facility was not developed for a long period. In addition to that the coolies also lacked natural immune systems, were often poorly nourished, were sometimes diseased on arrival, and were usually placed in working and living situations in which multiple infections were virtually certain.[21] In addition to these conditions, the prevailing conditions further weakened the strength of coolies and most of coolies become victims of various diseases at some point or the other.

"British Malaya was a very unhealthy place in the early years of this century. Malaria, ankylostomiasis or hookworm, venereal disease, tuberculosis, dysentery, pneumonia, beri-beri, cholera and still other diseases accounted for thousands of deaths annually in the I920s. Typically, persons suffered from two or more maladies at the same time. In the Federated Malay States (F. M. S.) "probably more than half of those listed as dying from malaria also suffered from hookworm. Many pneumonia deaths were due to tuberculosis. Chronic malnutrition combined with malaria, hookworm and diarrhoea in many resulted most pregnant women to produce high infant and maternal mortality. The majority of the living were more or less continuously afflicted with disease. Most of the diseases were debilitating and slow to kill. Most were preventable although that was imperfectly understood." (J. Norman Parmer). The coolies faced numerous health problems while clearing virgin lands for establishing new plantations and in maintaining the rubber plantations in a healthy state. The untouchable coolies continually paid high price in maintaining their life in the estate. As result of negligence on part of the management and lack of accessibility to health care in a time had resulted in numerous deaths. By the end of 1918, there were only 8 doctors in the 1006 plantations in the entire Federated Malay States. The Malayan labour code directs that all plantations shall provide medical attendance and a hospital. The plantation managements however never enforced it, and as a result until 1937 only 149 large estates had established dispensaries and hospitals.

The estate managers instead of providing needful health care to its long serving workforce simple opted to dumping dying workers on the roadside, and escaped from their minimum basic responsibility. This inhuman treatment resulted in large number of untouchable coolie's death in the Federated Malay States. As late as 1911, death rates of estate coolies were reported to be around 62.9 per thousand. Where as in the less-developed states of Negri Sembilan, and Pahang the death rates were reportedly very high, 195.6 and 109.5 per thousand, respectively. By 1921, this had been reduced to 18.2 per thousand for the entire country as a whole, these figures however applied mainly to males of working age. It was not until 1929 that births exceeded deaths amongst Indian estate coolies. And it was only in the 1930's that locally settled Indian begans to play a major role in reproducing the labour force. Sandhu had estimated the total death of coolies over a period of ten years to be around 7,50,000.[22]

On the demand of the Indian nationalist movement, the Indian government in 1946 deputed Pandit H.N. Kunzru and P. Kodanda Rao to visit Malaya and Burma and study the conditions of Indian coolies. On their return, they had reported that the economic situation in Malaya was bad, rice rations were quite inadequate, and there was acute scarcity of all consumer goods. Medical relief was the most urgent requirement. Pandit Nehru also visited Malaya in March, 1946, and he had also suggested to the government on the immediate need for the formation of Indian Relief Committee, (George Netto).

The government of India dispatched a Medical Mission consisting of 9 doctors headed by T.S. Sastri, in addition to this, the Congress Party had also dispatched a Medical Mission that consisted of 9 doctors and medical assistants headed by Dr. M. R. Cholkar. Nehru was forced to announce in the Central Indian Legislative Assembly on 29th October, 1946. "It is not intended to lift or relax the ban on emigration unless satisfactory conditions in respect of work, wages, and status of the Indian labourer are assured by the countries needing Indian labour."

As part of saving the interests of plantation owners, the British colonial forces had started initiating various measures specially focusing on the plantation coolies. In·addition to the government intervention, the foreign missionaries also entered the field to provide health care to most of the underprivileged coolies. The government had started opening the Health Branches in 1911, in the rural areas. The British colonial forces like any other colony had laid much stress on promoting western medicines rather than strengthening the indigenous health care system. Indian coolies instead of taking the western medicines had turned to Indian medicines.

Education

The European investors who had imported the untouchable coolies did not pay any attention to providing education to coolies children. The colonial government and its Christian missionaries opened educational institutions mainly in the urban centers, as they had failed to extend that facility in the rural areas where the majority of the people are residing. Only a small section of the feudal classes of the Malays and the middle-class Indians, Chinese, and Eurasians who lived in the urban, had them avail the British English education. The education policy through out the entire period was mainly meant to produce cultural carbon copies and keeping ethnic division intact.[23]

From 1870 onwards, small Tamil schools were started in the estates in province Wellesley Malacca, North Johore, and they eventually spread to other parts of Malaya where the Indian population created a need. The schools, however, were far from satisfactory; mainly because of inefficient, poorly-paid teachers.[24] The government had started opening crèches in 1921 on plantations.

This government's effort had also failed due to non-cooperation of the estate owners. As result of lack of educational facilities on plantations and around, the coolie's children instead of pursuing education turned into child coolies. Child labour had spread all across Malaya plantations. A study on four rubber and two oil palm estates revealed widespread prevalence of child labour. The study found out that over half children working in rubber plantations found their main task in collecting latex and cleaning the cups. Whereas on oil palm estate over half were collecting, loading, and carrying fruit bunches. The government did not make any efforts for eliminating widespread child labour and the investors were mainly worried about their profit margins, and welfare of its workers and their families suffered.

Importing Prostitutes to Gaining Social Stability and Economic Prosperity

The colonial and imperialist forces from Europe, America, and Japan during their process of colonizing the new territories built a huge contingent of army from the native lands they held under their control. To serve their army's sexual needs, they created a large number of comfort zones with a large number of young modest girls. Japanese forces turned large number of Korean young girls into these comfort zones. America had created large number of such zones inside South Vietnam for its allied forces for a long period. The young girls were forcibly dragged into the inhuman practice of prostitution, to serve their narrow interest. In the same way, the British colonial forces instead of turning native girls into such a profession in Malaysia, they imported women from outside for the purpose of prostitution. The brothel houses had spread like wildfire in Malaya to serve the coolie's sexual needs. The Brahmin created devadasis who had been serving Brahmins and other social elites sexual lust, turned into be export items and they soon became the readily available women for brothel houses in the British Malaya.

The colonial Malaya had a much skewed sex ratio. In the Straits Settlements (Penang, Malacca, and Singapore) in 1871, approximately two-thirds of the population was male, with far greater disparity was reported in certain ethnic groups: for example, 83 per cent of the Chinese population, 75 per cent of the Indian, and 98 per cent of the "transmarine" population were male.

The labour forces stability was linked to access to women, there were too few women to become wives despite the work of the government's the Po Leung Kuk Committee on "rescue" work and marriage arrangements. Ultimately Commercial sex was considered as a palliative in the absence of alternative sport and recreation facilities.[25] The Malayan and Indian governments decided to address the disproportionate rate among the sexes. As part of that exercise, the Malayan government reduced the assessment paid on female workers in connection with the Indian Immigration Fund. It also increased the commissions paid to Kanganis for female recruits, and also for married men accompanied by their families. On its part, the Indian government passed the Indian Emigration Act, 1922 and the Indian Emigration Rules, 1923, which were motivated to encourage women's migration compulsory . There should be at least one female emigrant for every 1.5 males selected to emigrate as labourers.[26]

The research work of academicians reveals various facts about the flesh trade in the colonial Malaysia. According to Sandhu: "Indian women had always comprised 25 to 45 percent of the total Indian labour force in Malaysia from the late nineteenth century up to the 1940's, and more than 80 per cent of the women were agricultural laborers. After 1925 Indian female coolies' and child coolies on estates equaled Indian male coolies".[27] Indian female coolies emerged as the largest group of the paid female workers in Malaya before the Second World War.[28] Adpa Satanarayana's research work reveals various facts about the prostitution that spread in the colonial Malaya, which, regularly received prostitutes from India to the new labour settlements". This fact was testified by the colonial authorities; "No Tamil women can go to the Federated Malay States and return with a rag of reputation left". The devadasis or 'temple prostitutes' from Tamil Nadu and coastal Andhra Pradesh also migrated in large numbers to Malaya under British governments encouragement. "A temple was recently built at Coringa in the Godavary district at a cost of 10,000 by a woman of this class who had saved money and returned".[29] The large number of these imported prostitutes ultimately landed on the coffee and rubber estates which employed over 80 per cent migrant of coolie's.

Conclusion

The saga of untouchable coolies of Malaysia highlights some interesting facts.

To escape and save their lives from the centuries-old social oppression and economic exploitation, the untouchable coolies, migrated for the first time in such large numbers to a foreign

PART C : REGIONAL DYNAMICS

10

Beyond the 'Imagined Community': A Study of the Indian Diaspora in the United States

Mohammed Badrul Alam

"The banyan tree has thrust down roots in soil, which is stony, sandy, marshy and has somehow drawn sustenance from diverse unpromising conditions. Yet the banyan tree itself has changed, its similarity to the original growth is still there. But it has changed in response to its different environment."[1]

The Indian community in the United States is one among many ethnic communities, which have been increasingly visible in the last four decades. Although the flow of Indians as new ethnics started first as a trickle in 1895, their impact was really felt in the aftermath of the landmark 1965 immigration legislation. This "new immigration" group has begun to attract academic attention and has also been the focus of research by a number of scholars.

The Asian Indians are an interesting group among the cluster of newly formed immigrant communities; their level of educational standard is particularly impressive; the rapidity of consolidation of economic indicator is remarkable; and the internal mobility of the Asian Indian community is very much viable.

To put it within a larger context, one of the most striking features which have caught the attention of most of the scholars today in this age of globalisation, is the "transnational movement of people" and the "intensification in the creation of diverse diaspora populations in many locations, who are engaged in complex and intercultural relationships with both their host societies and their societies of origin".[2]

It may be useful to clarify the term 'Asian Indian'. The term 'Indian' has both an ethnic and a political connotation. Ethnically, Asian Indians are people who migrated from the Indian sub-continent (from India, Pakistan, Bangladesh, Sri Lanka) and their progeny- are called Indians irrespective of the country of their domicile.[3] Politically, the citizens of the Republic of India holding Indian national's passport could be regarded as Indians. Thus, the term 'Asian Indians' is referred to as the ethnic group and 'Indian' as signifying a specific political status. Asian Indian communities in different parts of the world are more akin to one another than to other communities in their respective countries. A typical Asian Indian community member has generally retained his/her traditional customs, religion, language, forms of worship, food habits, social habits, marriage rites and values. He/she acknowledges his relatives living in India, visits them as often as possible, and returns to them when he/she thinks it is desirable to do so. In terms of blood, emotional attachment and the social value system, he/she is no different from other Indians. It is a rational consideration that differentiates an Asian Indian from the Indian national. The Asian Indian, by conscious and deliberate choice, has opted out of the geographical boundary of India and has transformed his paramount loyalty from the country of origin to the country of domicile.

This chapter analyses and examines the case of Asian Indians living in the United States, in the context of 'cultural pluralism' model. This chapter also addresses and evaluates the Asian Indians' attitudes toward family, education, religion, political participation, ethnic association, media and communication.

To begin with, it is important to understand what an ethnic group is in order to evaluate the position of Indians in the United States. In the *International Encyclopedia of the Social Sciences*, an ethnic group is defined as a "distinct category of the population in a larger society whose culture is usually different from is own."[4] In this sense, the Asian Indian population in the United States does qualify as an ethnic group because its cultural traditions are unique and distinctly different from that of the mainstream United States. However, it should be noted that sub-communities of Indians, for example, Bengalis, Punjabis, Telugus, Oriyas, Tamils, Gujratis, do not form ethnic groups either in India or in the United States. In India, they do not have a distinct culture contrasted from the Indian culture, and in the United States the sub-cultural group or the sub-communities are neither perceived nor recognised for purposes of categorisation or interaction. In fact, this line of reasoning is supported by the fact that there is no equivalent word for ethnic group in Hindi or in any of the major languages of India. The regional or linguistic groups of India are called ethnic groups. It is because the term ethnic group, minority group, and sub-culture are often used inter-changeably. Social scientists in general and sociologists in particular have different perspectives on the same phenomenon depending on the issues that interest them.[5]

In the United States, the term ethnic group refers to a number of characteristics, such as differentiation by race, religion, or national origin. In this context, a succinct definition has been put forward by Milton J. Esman.[6] Ethnic groups have both objective and subjective attributes: objective cultural traits within primordial modes expressed in language, religion, historical experiences, and common institutions and the subjective awareness of identity, belongingness, solidarity, and common interests. Thus, ethnic groups maintain sentimental and material links with the land of its origin. Though it has an objective, ethnicity is contextual in its manifestations, boundaries, intensities, and issues for any group may shift over time in response to changing experiences and problems.

Thus, an ethnic group can be defined as collectivity of people who share some common patterns of normative behaviour. They form a part of a larger population, interacting with people from other collectivities within the framework of a social network system. It refers to the degree of conformity by members of the collectivity to these shared norms and practices in the course of social interaction. By normative behaviour, one can refer to the symbolic formations and activities found in such contexts as kinship and marriage, friendship, ritual and other types of ceremonies of social and religious nature. For example, the differences between the Indians and the Vietnamese are national, not ethnic differences. But when members of these two groups interact in a foreign land these can be referred to as ethnic groups. Ethnicity is thus essentially a form of interaction between culture groups operating within social contexts. Thus, ethnicity is a complex social phenomenon that is inter-locking and involved in cultural, psychological, historical, economic and political realities.

The notion of diaspora is also premised along the above lines. As Cohen points out, "All diasporic communities settled outside their homeland, accept that - the old country- an idea often found in language, religion, custom or folklore- always has some claim on their loyalty and emotions. That claim may differ according to circumstances and history, but the member's adherence to a diasporic community is demonstrated by acceptance of an inescapable link with their past migration history and sense of co-ethnicity with others of similar background. In addition to these traits, there are possibilities which are distinctive and creative thus enriching life in tolerant host countries."[7]

Emphasizing on socio-economic, political, and cultural networks to understand transmigration, diaspora, and its role in the globalisation of production and the increasing spatial mobility of modern times, Sheffer has given a comprehensive definition of diaspora:

"An ethno-national diaspora is a social-political formation, created as a result of either voluntary or forced migration, whose members regard themselves as of the same ethno-national origin and who permanently reside as minorities in one or several host countries. Members of such entities maintain regular or occasional contacts with what they regard as their homelands and with individuals and groups of the same background residing in other host countries. Based on aggregate decisions to settle permanently in host countries, but to maintain a common identity, diasporians identify as such, showing solidarity with their group and their entire nation, and they organize and are active in cultural, social, economic, political spheres. Among their various activities members of such diasporas establish trans-state networks that reflect complex relationships among the diasporas, their host countries, their homelands and international actors."[8]

To place ethnic discourse in the American context, one will notice that American history is the history of ethnic groups. This is increasingly expressed in recent times with regard to the nature and scale of integration of American society. For a long time, observers assumed that immigrants came to America simply to find safe haven from the persecution in home states of Europe. Catholics, Jews, and some Protestants migrated, for example, to avoid religious wars in their respective countries. Others migrated to escape civil and inter-state war, political repression, genocide, ethnic-cleansing, cultural assimilation, and instability, and the abject poverty of their homeland. Many other immigrants chose to migrate to the United States as much because it was considered by many as a land of opportunity and abundance. Whatever their reasons for coming to America, right from the beginning there has been pressure exerted on immigrants to embrace Anglo-American institutions (Anglo Conformity). Despite these pressures, in the case of many groups the "melting pot" syndrome, one of complete assimilation and acculturation has never materialized. Some scholars have subscribed to the idea of "Cultural Pluralism" or "Salad Bowl" suggesting that the United States is not only a nation of immigrants, but it is a nation of immigrant groups of varied cultures and sub-cultures. The notion of cultural pluralism implies that the immigrants in time would become Americanized, but at the same time that they could also retain much that was distinctive and primordial in their own cultural heritage. The "cultural pluralism" model appears to be the more relevant in the context of Asian Indians in the United States. There is a lack of sufficient empirical data to fully support this "cultural pluralism" model. However, there seems to be good social, historical and psychological evidence to argue that the "cultural pluralism" model has greater validity. Gordon's view that assimilation in the sphere of culture has been successful whereas it has lagged behind in the structural sphere is of particular interest to Asian Indian community living in the United States. Moynihan's and Glazer's view that political and socio-economic power keeps ethnic groups together has greater relevance in contemporary American society. But their suggestion that cultural differences are rapidly declining among ethnic groups is not quite true, certainly not for the Asian Indian group.

As indicated earlier, since about 1965 the phenomena of ethnicity has re-emerged in American life and has permeated its social structure. Often this is referred to as the "new ethnicity". The White European ethnics as well as the Puerto-ricans, Filipino Americans, Chinese Americans, American Indians, Mexican-Americans, Asian Indians, etc., have come to share the option that their distinctiveness is no longer a social stigma but a matter of ethnic pride. Not all ethnic groups have experienced this change, however. For example, increased pride in ethnic heritage has led to movements toward separatism among some black Americans. For many American blacks, a situation of cultural pluralism in which they are accorded social recognition, equal access to job, equitable income base, and decent housing, remains the desired goal.

Most ethnic minorities pursue cultural pluralism model including a moderate degree of assimilation as the preferred path. But there is still a visible discrepancy between what they would prefer and what options are available to them as ground realities. The critical question is whether strengthening the ethnic minorities will further divide the nation, or if the greater strengths of the disparate parts of the American society can bridge the social divide. The outcome depends on the manner in which the ideology of pluralism is applied. The theories of the "melting pot" and the "multiple melting pot" and the rest of it have simply not worked. Glazer[9] has rightly observed that cultural pluralism seems to have won out, at least temporarily. He further makes the distinction between "weak cultural pluralism" and "strong cultural pluralism". The former represents an attitude which is basically a form of tolerance or the way to an expected acculturation and assimilation, whereas the latter is primarily based on an ideological view of the position of racial and ethnic groups in American life, a view that emphasises the colonial status and the repression of their cultures by Anglo-Americans. These may be seen as two polar extremes of cultural pluralism. Glazer suggests that there may be a middle grand between the two, which he calls "integration", which he explains by writing, "... integration implies on the one hand, an organic relationship. Just as personality may be integrated, so may a society. On the other hand, it (integration) implies that there is still a clear articulation of the parts that is, some degree of identifiability of each part."[10] He further argues that this form of cultural pluralism would be in the interest of both individual groups and of the entire nation. Here the emphasis would be on distinctive nature of various ethnic cultures, which would be integrated in larger sense with the American experience.

The critics of cultural pluralism have opposed the 'integration' model because it can be divisive and has the potential for disintegration and separatism. This is evident in the black power and the emergent black pride movement of the mid-1960s. Earlier challenges to cultural pluralism came from those who were proponents of assimilation and Americanisation as the most desirable outcome for multi-ethnic American society.

There is another school called 'pluralists' who argue that a multi-cultural society will of necessity contain conflicts and tensions. Thus, managing these tensions, rather than seeking to avoid them, is in the larger interest of the viability and cohesiveness of any society in the long run.

The United States now seems to be moving toward a pluralistic society. However, for pluralism to work, there must be an open society (in the general sense of the term), one in which people with a diversity of backgrounds and characteristics can compete on an equal basis for societal resources. Also, if pluralism is to become the mode of dealing with ethnic diversity, it must be adopted in the America's schools. Under pluralist notion, ethnicity is considered ultimately to be a psychological phenomenon that can be expressed in any identical display. The implication is that ethnicity is a general state of consciousness and identity that is not necessarily obvious, but which can be voluntarily displayed in overt behaviour in a variety of settings.

Varma[11] in his essay on Asian Indians, refers to an "ethnic renaissance" in the United States, and suggests that because of advanced industrialisation, there is a tendency among people to seek escape from machines, tools, and technology. The "new ethnicity" emerges both as result of the standardisation of values in America society, as well as of the opening up of the American mainstream which is becoming more receptive as well as sensitive, to the needs and aspirations of minorities and sub-cultural groups.

The Asian Indians in America not only show a clear preference for the cultural pluralism model, but also see it as the most desirable and acceptable from their point of view, as well as its being in the longer interests of American society. A study of the behaviour patterns of the Indian immigrants does suggest their groups' strong inclination to maintain and enrich ethnic Indian culture and traditions.

Asian Indians in United States can be categorised under three headings: Old Indian Diaspora (constitutes those migrants migrated between 19th century to early part of the 20th century), New Indian Diaspora (constitutes those migrants who migrated after 1965 especially the urban and middle class professionals) and Second Generation Indians (constitutes those Indians born and brought up in the United States).[12] Between these three groups, the latter two - the New Indian Diaspora and Second Generation Indians – continue to have close contact with the families and relatives back home while few of the older generations have lost their contacts with the motherland. Indians have been successful in forming their local, international, formal and informal networks by contacting with their kith and kin around the globe. Their networks are maintained through various mechanisms such as regular communications over telephone, visits and correspondence, remittances, the Internet chat and e-mails, sending and receiving videos on important family events and other celebrations. Although these networks sustain themselves through the proximity of density and distance - which are central to the individual and group interaction - the major stakes by which the transnational networks expand and are established, are through the social, cultural, economic, political and religious spheres.

Attitudes Toward India and the United States

Indian immigrants generally maintain their respect for and faith in the Indian value system and institutions, even though they are critical of India in many ways.[13] For example, they talk about poverty, the population explosion, nepotism, casteism and lack of opportunity for professional advancement in India. However, there seldom is criticism of the basic Indian value system which evolves around major social institutions such as marriage, the family, religion, etc. Their attitude toward India is generally considered more favourable and they try to organise activities to reinforce their Indianness both within the family and outside of it through ethnic Indian organisation. The overwhelming majority of Indians indicate that eventually they wish to return to India born out of nostalgia and '*Phir Bhi Dil Hai Hindustani*' syndrome.

The attitude of the Indian immigrants toward American society is more favourable in the early stages of their residence than later. Initially, they are impressed by American informality, generosity, openness, flexibility and sense of hospitality. The physical environment and the scientific technological advancement of the United States make a profound impact in a positive way. However, as they start moving into the American mainstream and compete for jobs, professional recognition, and social acceptance, the Asian Indians at times experience some prejudice and discrimination. In the post-9/11 environment, some Muslim and Sikh persons of Indian origin have faced harassment as the 'dotbusters' in the early 1980s in New Jersey region of the United States.

The apparent permissiveness of American society and the lack of respect for the elderly (as exemplified by the huge popularity of Bollywood movie, *Baghban*, portraying the same issue) are the most frequently voiced observations made by these immigrants. Interestingly enough, their criticism is not confined to the opportunity structure but is often aimed at basic social institutions such as the family and religion. Many

American values, such as the American attitude towards sex and the elderly, are observed as immoral. On the whole, the values of the Indian immigrants are more favourable toward India and Indian institutional arrangements than they are toward American society and its social parameters.

Attitudes Toward Family

Among the 1965 wave, most of the Indian immigrants were already married when they immigrated. A good number returned to India for arranged marriages (the bride/groom being selected by the parents).[14] In most cases, the wives have taken up outside employment and the husbands share and assist in the household work. Nevertheless, this has not led to change in their attitudes toward each other in any significant way. The husband generally remains at the apex of the decision-making in the family. The immigrants' commitment to the institution of marriage remains strong and they look at marriage as one of life long commitment. Since most of the couples came to the United States as adults, there did not seem to be significant change in their attitudes after migration. Their attitudes toward their children also remain traditional. Most of the children of the immigrants either came to the United States at a very young age or were born in USA.

The lack of change in the attitude of Indian parents and their expectations based on the traditional Indian value system is one of the major sources of discord among the Indian families residing in the United States. Parent-child relationship is one of the most pressing issues confronting the Indian community. As the children are into adulthood, the community has started experiencing the negative consequences of these conflicts. Alternative lifestyles including issues related to Gays and Lesbians have created a new set of challenges for Indian diaspora. Similarly, rising incidents of domestic violence and divorce are matters of concern for the Indian Americans.

Attitudes Toward Religion

In general, it has been seen that the attitude of Indian immigrants toward their religion is favourable since immigration. One of the possible explanations may be that religion also serves social and cultural functions in an alien society. Another change that one can observe is that the Indian immigrants tend to look at religion more as an ideology than as a set of strict dogmas and prescriptions. Nevertheless, it does not necessary result in a decrease in religious observation and practice. Most Indian families have a place of worship in their homes. They also visit temples, churches, mosques and gurudwaras and participate in all forms of religious activity. There are probably as many number of Hindu temples and mosques in the United States as there are super markets such as *K' Mart* or *Walmart*. One can support the hypothesis that religious activity among Indian immigrants has not declined as a result of immigration. On the contrary, there is a greater religious consciousness and a need to practice religious rituals individually as well as communally. The popularity of *Vishwa Hindu Parishad* in the United States is a testimony to it.

The social life of Hindus in the United States revolves largely around temples, and therefore, construction of temples is called the part and parcel of Hinduism in America.[15] The first Hindu temple in United States goes to the credit of the Vedanta Society that was established in San Francisco in 1906. The Sikh Temple at Stockton in the state of California was built in 1915 followed by the Hollywood Temple in 1938, and the Santa Barbara Temple in 1956 (see www.vedanta.org). Two important temples in the United States today are 'Maha Vallabha Ganapati Devasthanam' in Flushing, New York and the Sri Venkateswara Temple in Pittsburgh, Pennsylvania. Besides these, there are hundreds of Hindu temples that are found in and around the United States and these construction activities by Indian immigrants are on the increase. Presently, there are over 450 Hindu temples in the United States. Hinduism in the United States shows every sign of being a flourishing religion. These temples do make honest efforts in fostering a sense of community among Hindus in the United States.

Attitudes Toward Economics

Most of the Indian immigrants have more than average education and professional backgrounds.[16] Because of high educational standards, it has become relatively easier for the Asian Indians to find employment and improve their economic profile in the United States. While the per capita income of Indian immigrants is much higher than that of the average American, their consumption pattern is lower than that of Americans on the comparable income level. This is due to their conservative attitude toward spending. Their savings level is almost two to three times higher than the national average. They put a great premium on savings as well as on investment. Most of the Indians in U.S. are highly qualified persons having 43.6% in professional and managerial positions, 33.2% in the technical, sales and service sectors and the remaining 23.3% are skilled labourers. The total per capita income of Indians in U.S. as per 2000 census is estimated at US $ 17,777 compared to the average per capita income of US $ 14,143. While poverty rate in the United States is 13%, for the Asian Indians, the average is 9.7%. More than half of the Indian immigrant community own houses. This may be considered as an indication of this ethnic group's intention to settle permanently in the United States. The practice of remitting money to India for parents and other family members is quite evident. This also supports the assumption that the close link and bonding with family members in India is maintained despite migration to the United States. It would be fair to suggest that in the sphere of economics as well as in other areas, one finds the continuation of traditional values and attitudes on the part of Indian immigrants, particularly for those who have migrated in the post-1965 phase.

Attitudes Toward Education

Most of the Indian immigrants put heavy premium on academic excellence. Since American society also emphasizes on the importance of education, there is no conflict there with prevailing American norms. But there is a perceptible difference in the attitudes between the Indians and the Americans. The Indians' attitude to higher education is closely tied to a family's prestige and status and strong desire for upward social mobility accrued from it. Moreover, instead of being a 'brain drain', Indian Americans are being considered as 'brain banks' who are assets to the country of their origin (India). Children of the Indian immigrants (especially of the first generation) are doing exceedingly well in all aspects of academia. In all major US universities, the number of Indian students and faculty members are quite substantial. Among foreign students entering the United States, India currently ranks as number one. However, in certain quarters, there is some doubt about the children's continued success because of the influence of external factors. It is argued that as the children assimilate in the new society, they become more independent and act more in terms of their own values rather than those of the family-based values which are very strong in India. This provides some basis for suggesting that education is not considered as free an enterprise and as individualistic in nature by the Indian immigrants as it is perceived and practised by the larger segment of the host (American) society.

Attitude Toward Political Participation

The Asian Indian group in recent years has taken proactive interest in the political process of the country. During Kennedy's Administration, Dilip Singh Saund, a member of the Indian ethnic community, was successfully elected to the House of Representatives of the U.S. Congress. Since then, a number of persons of Indian origin have contested for various political offices under both party tickets (Democrats and Republicans). This political participation by Asian Indians and their affiliated groups, is also being reflected in the 2008 Presidential races of Republican John McCain and Democratic contenders in the primaries namely Barack Obama and Hillary Clinton. In a way, it shows the maturity of the Indian ethnic community in the United States and their willingness and determination to participate in the politics of America. A number of organisations, such as India League of America and the Association of Asian Indians in North America have taken leading steps in this direction. In 1994, Kumar Brave and Upendra Chivukula - the first Indian Americans - from Maryland and New Jersey respectively were elected to their respective state legislatures. In the year 2000, Satveer Choudhary became the first state senator to be elected in Minnesota. He was re-elected in 2006 as well. Iowa State Representative Swati Dandekar, Democrat, also won for the third time. Several Indian-Americans have held the position of mayor as well. They include: Bala K. Srinivas in Hollywood Park, Texas, John Abraham in Teaneck,

New Jersey, and Arun Jhaveri in Burien, Washington. Number of Indians has also become prominent at the national level. For instance, during Clinton administration, Dr. Arati Prabhakar was appointed as the Director of National Institute of Standards and Technology, Neil Dhillon as the Deputy Assistant Secretary of Transportation and Dr. Rajen Anand as Executive Director of Centre for Nutrition Policy under USDA. Similarly, Bobby Jindal was appointed as the Assistant Secretary of Health, Gopal Khanna, Chief Technology Officer of Peace Corps while Karan Bhatia was appointed as the Deputy Under Secretary in the Department of Commerce in the George Bush, Jr. administration. In the election held for the U.S. Congress on 6 November 2006, bucking the anti-Republican trend, incumbent Bobby Jindal won a thumping victory and got re-elected to the House of Representatives from Louisiana's 1st District, securing 88 per cent of the vote. Subsequently, Bobby Jindal was also elected as the Governor of Louisiana, thus becoming the first ever person of Asian Indian origin to hold such an august office. Jindal's name was also short listed for the position of Vice Presidential running mate for Sen. John McCain of the Republican party in the 2008 US presidential contest. All of these Asian Indian candidates for various electoral races were actively supported by the Asian Indian diaspora residing in the United States. In the past few elections, Asian Indian donors have financed and campaigned for members of both political parties. In some cases, Asian Indian donors are supporting candidates from both the Democratic party and the Republican party in a single Congressional district. In the Barack Obama presidential team, the following persons of Asian Indian origin have occupied prominent positions: Nick Rathod, Arati Rai, Anjan Mukherjee, Parag Mehta, Rachana Bhowmik, Subasri Ramanathan, Natasha Bilimoria, Puneet Talwar, etc. President Obama has also appointed Dr. Sanjay Gupta in the high profile position of US Surgeon General and Preeta Bansal as Senior Policy Advisor in the Office of Management and Budget. It will still take some time before Indians make their presence felt more visible on the political landscape.

A coalition pattern, in conjunction with other ethnic groups, such as Italian Americans, Greek Americans, Japanese Americans, Mexican Americans, etc., along with proactive courting of India Caucus members who number more than 100 in US Congress may be an ideal type for the Asian Indians to pursue. At the formative stages of building up a political front, these steps leading towards ethnic solidarity are net plus and an interesting proposition.

Attitude Toward Media and Communication

While Asian Indians have ventured into almost every field of profession in the United States, one such successful foray by Indians, is in the field of media and communication. Eminent writers, journalists, musicians and filmmakers have made noteworthy contribution in their respective fields. Writers of English with international repute includes Jhumpa Lahiri, whose work *Interpreter of Maladies* won the Pulitzer Prize in 2000. Besides Lahiri, Salman Rushdie, Vikram Seth, Gita Mehta, Bharati Mukherji and Anita Desai are included in the list of celebrated international writers of Indian origin. Similarly, Fareed Zakaria who earlier became the Editor of the prestigious *Foreign Affairs* is now in charge of the Editorial board of *Newsweek*. The names of Pankaj Mishra and Shashi Tharoor are also widely acclaimed in this field. In music, the credit goes to Pandit Ravi Shankar, Ali Akbar Khan and Zakir Hussein who have settled in US and yet have brought Indian music into American mainstream by winning critical public acclaim and in creating fusion music between Bollywood and Hollywood. Zubin Mehta's success in New York Philharmonic Orchestra is also a tribute to the talent of Indian communities in the United States.

In filmmaking, Indian Americans also have great names. Important in the list are: Pratik Basu's *Welcome To The Family*, Punam Sawhney's *The Goddess Method*, Mehreen Jabbar's *Beauty Parlor*, David Dasharath Kalal's *Five Minutes To Cloud Boundary*, Anmol Chaddha and Sonya Mehta's *Yellow Apparel: When The Coolie Becomes Cool*, besides Mira Nair's *Mississippi Masala*, *Salaam Bombay* which has been appreciated all over the world. Mira Nair's movie *Monsoon Wedding* has won the Venice Film Festival *Golden Lion Award*. Like icing on the cake, *Slumdog Millionaire,* the movie with Indian cast members, lyricist and music composer won eight Oscar awards in 2009. Prominent Hollywood production houses such as

Warren Brothers, Columbia Pictures, Walt Disney, etc., have entered in a big way into collaborating in the Indian film making enterprise.

Asian Indian ethnic media plays an important role by keeping in touch with fellow ethnic members in the diaspora. The Indian ethnic media in the United States has evolved gradually from radio, to print and then to ethnically owned radio and TV channels. Some of the important Indian ethnic media that have flourished in the United States today are recorded during the annual Pravasi Bharatiya Divas that meet at various Indian cities each January.

The important media outlets are as follows:

Newspapers, Journals and Magazines: *India Abroad, News-India Times, Globe, Awaz, Biz India, Desi Talk, Express India, Greet Gujrati, Gujarat Mitra, Gujarat Samachar, Gujarat Times, Himalayan News, The Hindi Times, Hindi Jagat, Hindu Vishwa, Indo-US Business Journal, India Currents, The Indian Express (North American Edition), India Focus, India Journal, Indian Life and Style Magazine, India light, India Living Magazine, India Monitor, India Positive, India Post, India Reporter and World News, India Today, India Tribune, India Weekly, India-West, Jhankar, Khabar Magazine, Lokmat, Lokvani, Malayalampathram, Malayalee Sabdam, Mantram, Marathi Vishwa, NRI Times, NRI Today, The Pittsburgh Patrika, Prasaar Bharati, Punjab Times, Rajani, Ranauk Mela, Rang Taranga, Sandesh International, Sher-e-Punjab, Silicon India, Spirit of India*, etc.

Radio: Bharat Vani, Jhankar (Hindi), RBC Radio, Vividh Bharati Radio Programme. **Television:** Channel-80 Aap Aur Tum, Chitrahar Broadcasting, Darshan TV, Ektara Television, Kerala Television, Manoranjan Channel 30, Namaste America, News India TV, Sanjha Punjab TV Network, Sikh TV/Sohna Punjab, Sony TV (EABC), S.R. Video and so on. The High Level Committee on the Indian Diaspora chaired by Dr. L.M. Singhvi has made some recommendations to strengthen links between Indian organisations and ethnic media as well as prominent Indians in the foreign media. The important recommendations include creating a data bank on the ethnic media and a facilitation mechanism for interaction with the Indian ethnic media, and so on.

Ethnic Associations

The steady growth of Indian population in the United States including the heavily populated ethnic enclaves of 'Little India' in mega metropolitan cities such as New York City and Chicago over the years have contributed to the emergence of various cultural, religious and regional associations. The first major community based group was initiated in New York with the formation of Association of Indians in America (AIA) in 1968.[17] After ten years, in 1978, the Federation of Indian Associations (FIA) was formed as an umbrella organisation in New York. In 1980, the Association of Indians in North America (AIINA) was formed in New York. Besides this, the National Federation of Indian-American Associations (NFIA), the American Indian Associations (AIA), and the Indian American Forum for Political Education (IAFPE) was established to pursue and promote Indian interests in a more organised and sustained manner. Other important organisations, which have emerged to enhance and safeguard the Indian interests, are: Global Organisation of People of Indian Origin (GOPIO) and the National Association of Americans of Asian Indian Descent (NAAAID). There are larger political organisations like American Indian Foundation and various professional organisations like The Indo-US Entrepreneurs, Indo-American Chamber of Commerce, Network of Indian Professionals etc., which function as umbrella organisations.

The ethnic, linguistic, and cultural diversities among the Indians in the United States have manifested in the formation of separate associations over a period of time. Among these are: the Bengali Association, the Bihar Cultural Association, the Tamil Nadu Foundation, the Telugu Association, the Punjabi Cultural Society, the Maharashtra Mandal, the Kerala Associations, Gujarati Association, Kannada Koota, Oriya Society of America, Rajasthani Association, etc. There are organisations which have striven very hard in evoking a more comprehensive notion of 'Indianness' among Indians in the United States such as Indian Classical Music Circle, which sponsors recitals by major Indian musicians, and the Chicago chapters of various professional organisations of Americans of Indian origin.

The religious, regional, linguistic and caste factors plays an important role in the everyday lives of the Indians in the United States. For example, besides the language and religion, the caste and sub-caste identity of Telugus provides them an additional forum for closer interaction among themselves and among other ethnic Indians hailing from other regions of India. Telugus are generally classified into several caste groups, the important among them being the Brahmin, Reddy, Kamma, Kapu, Naidu, Mala, Madiga, Yeraka and Yanadi. These caste differences are manifested in the socio-economic and political interactions among the Telugus in the U.S. For example, the members of Kamma caste dominate the Telugu Association of North America (TANA) while the Reddy caste on the other hand promote the American Telugu Association (ATA).

Conclusion

This study aims in establishing a baseline for observation of the sociological parameters of the Asian Indian community. Proponents of assimilations have always taken the stand that rapid Americanisation is the most desirable goal. Even if one accepts its viability, one is never sure what it means or connotes. If it means a monoculture, then obviously the assimilationists have reason to be utterly disappointed. Even in the days when the assimilationists' view was dominant, diversity in American society was very much in existence. In the final analysis, it is safe to conclude that there is room for flexibility, tolerance, freedom, openness and opportunities in American society. From Asian Indian perspective, one can argue that the American society may not be fully ideal, but it is fair to suggest that it has been considered better than many other societies of the world. This is validated by the continuing flow of legal immigrants (including those who come under family unification and skilled persons category of H-1B) to the United States from various parts of the world, representing diverse languages, religions, regions and cultures.

The major flow of Asian Indian immigrants started in 1965 in the aftermath of change in the immigration laws that removed the quota system. The Indian population is marked by its high educational credentials, concentration in professions, known history, strong family ties, and at the same time represents splendid diversity in terms of language, religion, custom and religion. They represent a rich history which strongly recognizes the Indian motto of 'unity in diversity'. In spite of the existence of internal diversity, there is still that sense of Indianness that has solidified this diasporic community. This aspect is also clearly noticeable to outside observers.

The Indian population recognizes a pluralistic society as a desirable goal, and wishes to flourish as a 'strategic asset' without the pressure for Americanisation. Government policy in the United States today is maintaining foreign languages and cultures through various bilingual and multicultural programmes. Despite its diversity and preference for pluralism, the Indian population shows its clear commitment to participate actively in the structural side of it, that is in the spheres of education, economics, mass media, and slowly but surely, in political arena as well.

Asian Indian community which is more than 2 million strong wants to become part of the mainstream of American society by exhibiting itself as a 'model minority'. The Indian experience has also shown that neither complete assimilation or acculturation, nor separatism or alienation, have any place in the context of American society. On balance, the cultural pluralism model certainly has the potential to bridge the societal and cultural divide and in helping Americans of all backgrounds to take pride in maintaining and enriching their identities. As agents of 'cultural pluralism' model, the Asian Indians want to become full, proactive participants in the American society. There is near unanimity on the 'salad bowl' or cultural pluralism model, at least in the context of the Asian Indian population. The real challenge is to work out a suitable middle ground which can provide for support to the basic institutional arrangements of American society and at the same time fulfill the wishes and aspirations of those who are Americans, yet Asian Indians.

Annex:

The Government of India had set up a High Level

3. For details, see K.N.Vaid, *The Overseas Indian Community in Hong Kong*, Center for Asian Studies, University of Hong Kong, 1972, pp. 5-6.
4. H.S.Morris, "Ethnic Groups," in *International Encyclopedia of the Social Sciences*, ed. David L. Sills (New York: Macmillan and Free Press, 1968), p. 167.
5. For a theoretical analysis of the Caste systems, see Baidya Nath Varma, 'The Caste System of India," in *Contemporary India*, Asia Publishing House, New York, 1964, pp. 59-81.
6. Milton J. Esman, *Ethnic Conflict in the Western World*, Cornell University Press, Ithaca, New York, 1977.
7. Safran, W. "Diasporas in Modern Societies: Myths of Homeland and Return" *Diaspora*, Vol. 1, 1991; also, see, Harpreet Kaur, "Diaspora: Some General Expositions", *Punjab Journal of Politics*, Vol. XXX, No. 1, 2006, pp. 109-120.
8. Sheffer, G, *Diasporas Politics: At Home Abroad*, Cambridge University Press, London, 2003; also see, Ma, J.C and Cartier, C, *The Chinese Diaspora: Space, Place, Mobility and Identity*, Rowan and Littlefield Publishers, Lanham, 2002.
9. Nathan Glazer's article, "Cultural Pluralism: The Social Aspect," in *Pluralism in a Democratic Society*, Melvin . Tumin and Walter Plotch, eds; Praeger, New York, 1977, p. 248.
10. *Ibid.*
11. B.N. Varma, *The Sociology and Politics of Development: Theoretical Study*, Routledge and Kegan Paul, London, 1988.
12. See, Ajaya K.Sahoo, "Contemporary Appraisal of Indian Diaspora in the United States", *Man and Life*, Vol. 30: Nos. (3 and 4), July-December 2004, pp. 81-92, ISRAA, Kolkata.
13. M.K. Mohapatra, "Overseas Indians in Urban America: A Study of their Attitudes and Experiences involving Discrimination in American Society," *Nagarlok*, Vol. 11, No. 1, 1979, pp. 120-41.
14. Parmatma Saran, "New Ethnics: The Case of East Indians in New York City" in *Sourcebook on the New Immigration: Implications for the United States and the International Community*, Roy Simoh, Bryce Laporte, ed. (New Brunswick, N.J.) Transaction Books, 1980.
15. Lal, Vinay, 1997, 'Ambiences of Hinduism in the Wild West of America: Perspectives from Two Citadels, The Grand Canyon and Las Vegas', *Suitcase,* Vol. 1, No. 1-2, pp. 84-97; also, see, Prentiss, Karen Pechilis, 2004, 'The Pattern of Hinduism and Hindu Temple Building in the U.S.'. Committee on the Study of

Religion, Harvard University, www.pluralism.org., see, *Ibid*, Ajaya K. Sahoo, No. 9.

16. Mohapatra, *Ibid*, also, see, Ministry of External Affairs, 2001, *Report of the High Level Committee on Indian Diaspora,* New Delhi: Indian Council of World Affairs.
17. Abraham, Thomas, 2003, *The Power of Community Involvement: Successes in Indian Communities Across America*. Keynote address at the 40th Anniversary of India Association of Nashville, March 8, 2003., see, Ajaya K. Sahoo, *Ibid*, No. 9.

11

Diaspora and Motherland: Explorations into the Role of Indo-Canadians in India's Welfare Programmes

Prakash C. Jain

This article seeks to sociologically study the role of the Indo-Canadian individuals/ NGOs which are active in the welfare activities in India in such areas as education, environment, health care and aging, community and infrastructural development. The following are the objectives of this study: (i) To study the nature of involvement of the Indo-Canadians in India's welfare programmes. (ii) To analyse the structure and functioning of the concerned NGOs/ agencies. (iii) To highlight the difficulties such agencies face in their operations in Canada as well as India. The field work was conducted in the Vancouver city. The article is put within the wider conceptual framework of diaspora-homeland relationship as briefly detailed in a subsequent section.

Indians in Canada

Currently there are about 1.3 million people of Indian origin in Canada which constitute about 3.7 percent of the total population of Canada (estimated at about 35 million in July 2010). The available data suggests that about one-third of them returned Punjabi as their mother tongue in the 1996 Canadian census (statistics Canada 2001: 2). Originating in

North India, particularly Punjab, most Indians are settled in Ontario (51.2%) and British Columbia (32.5%). According to the Census of Canada 1996, of the total foreign-born population of Canada 4.7 per cent were born in India. The overwhelming majority of them (94.3%) preferred to settle in the English-speaking provinces of Canada. About 90 per cent of Indian immigrants migrated to Canada in the 1970s, 1980s and 1990s – almost in about equal proportion in each decade.

About two-thirds of Indian immigrants in Canada had 12 years or more schooling. A small section of Indian immigrants (15.6%) were educationally better qualified (that is, those with 18 years or more schooling) than any other group of immigrants or Canadian-born. Occupational distribution of Indians suggests that about 20 per cent of them are professionals and senior and middle level managers; 37 per cent comprised middle level occupations and 43 per cent in lower level jobs such as semi-skilled manual workers and sales and service workers. The presence of Indians in the Canadian agriculture sector is also noteworthy, particularly in British Columbia. Not surprisingly, mean or median income of male Indian immigrants is comfortably higher than that of their counterparts from other parts of Asia, Africa, Latin America etc., but far lower than those from the U.S. and Europe and the Canadian-born population. On the contrary, the income level of the Indian females was comparatively the lowest of all the immigrant groups in Canada. Still, only 23.8 per cent Indian immigrants lived below the poverty line in 1996 compared to 36.6 per cent of immigrants from other parts of the Third World (see Grenier 2001).

What role these Indians play in Indo-Canadian relations in general and India's socio-economic development in particular? Do they represent only a 'brain' depriving India of its vital human resources, or provide an outlet and opportunity for India's educated underemployed and unemployed? How significant are their remittances and investments to the Indian economy? Is Indian community a "bridge" between Canada and India? What hurdles Indian activities pose in improving Indo-Canadian relations? These are some of the questions which have been raised and speculated about but never empirically researched. This article partly attempts to rectify this situation.

Indians in Vancouver

Vancouver, as already pointed out, hosts the oldest Indo-Canadian community in Canada. A commemorative postal stamp was released on 21st April 1999 by Canadian Prime Minister Jean Christian on the occasion of the completion of 100 years of the arrival of Sikhs in Canada. Beginning with only a few unknown pioneers the South Asian Community in British Columbia (BC) rose to 2,623 in 1907-08. Most of these early immigrants were from the district of Jallandhar, Hoshiarpur and Ferozepur in Punjab. Most were Sikh. Rural indebtedness in Punjab as well as job opportunities in BC both factors were responsible for immigration into the area.

North America's first Sikh religious organisation Vancouver Khalsa Diwan Society was formed in 1907 that built a year later North America's first Gurudwara. Racial discrimination, anti-Oriental Riots, disenfranchisement, the Continuous Journey legal provision and finally the infamous Komagata Maru incident — all had their due share in rendering the South Asian population decline in British Columbia. As late as in 1951 there were only 2,148, South Asians in Canada overwhelming majority of them, that is 1,937 (90%) settled in British Columbia alone.

The quota and the point systems led to fundamental change in South Asian immigration. The Indian communities in Canada since 1960s have been extremely diversified in every respect of the term. There is predominance of Punjabis in British Columbia, (nearly 80 percent). Other noticeable groups include Tamilians, Bengalis, Goans, Keralites and immigrants from the Hindi heartland in idea. Others who are originally Indian include 50,000 strong Indo-Fijian community and the sizeable number of Indians from Uganda, Ghana and Mauritius.

The Survey of Literature

There exists a voluminous literature on overseas Indians in Canada covering such themes as immigration and settlement, socio-economic and political status, ethnic/ race relations situations, social organisational aspects such as transformation or disintegration of the caste system and joint family (see Buchignani 1977, 1989; Jain, 1983, 1999). Various aspects of religion among overseas Indians have also been studied.

A brief review of literature on the subject suggests that although there is enough concern shown by scholars about 'brain drain' from India to the U.S., Canada, the UK and elsewhere, its positive aspects have not been fully appreciated (see Jain 1989, Oommen 1989; Sukhatme and Mahadevan 1988). Helweg (1986) and Weiner (1990) are some of the exceptions who have speculated about the beneficial role of the overseas Indians to India. These writers have approached the problem from the perspective of modern diaspora formations and their role in international relations (see also Sheffer, 1986). They argue that ethnic diasporas play an important role in international trade and commerce, economic investment and remittances and political interests.

Seen in this perspective, the role of Canada-based Indians is illuminating and instructive (Jain, 1999). India can look towards these emigrants not only for their remittances and investment but also for their skills. Their participation in voluntary developmental projects is also important. So also their role as lobbyists in India's favour.

Conceptual Framework

"Diaspora" means dipersal and until recently the term referred to the Jews living in different parts of the world outside Israel—their ancestral "homeland". Of late, however, the purview of the term diaspora has been broadened to refer to any population group settled abroad but maintaining close links with its homeland. Following Gabriel Sheffer (1986: 3), diasporas can be defined as "ethnic minority groups of migrant origins residing and acting in host countries but maintaining strong sentimental and materials links with countries of origin-homelands".

Modern organised diasporas constitute trans-state triadic networks involving ethnic diasporas, their host countries and homelands and as such they have significant ramifications for international relations and international politics, and other activities. As Gabriel Sheffer (1986:6) put it :

> Ethnic diasporas are involved not only in national and trans-state politics, but also in cultural educational and religious affairs and consequently they establish specialised organisations to promote and defend their linguistic, cultural, religious and economic interests in both their host countries and homelands.

These triadic relations, however, are not always smooth, consistent or uniformly strong. Besides socio-political and economic conditions in the host countries as well as homelands, such factors as capabilities of the diaspora, the objectives of the diasporas activities, and sources of mobilisation and activation of diasporas may affect the triadic relationships and the behaviour of a diaspora. Thus, whereas the study of the degree of economic, social and political "integration" of a particular diaspora into its host society can give us the idea of the state of relationship between the diaspora and the host country, diaspora-homeland relationship can fruitfully be investigated in terms of contact the diasporic communities maintain through visits, remittances, trade and transfer of skills and technology and political lobbying for the homeland.

Methodology

In pursuit of realizing my research objectives I planned to collect primary as well as secondary data in the greater Vancouver area, which hosts the oldest and the second largest Indo-Canadian community in Canada. As already expected there was hardly any secondary data (library material) on the subject as the research proposal was placed in an area which still remains virtually unexplored. In other words there was a real 'knowledge gap'.

My main focus of research therefore was meeting and systematically interviewing the concerned Indo-Canadians who have been involved in welfare programmes in India. In the absence of any directory on the subject initially it was difficult to identify the respondents. However, slowly with the help of the office bearers, the Indian associations in Vancouver area a number of such respondents were identified and interviewed.

The whole process was not very smooth and in the beginning it was full of frustration on the part of the researcher, specially given the time constraint and the city bus strike during the same time.

An ongoing bus strike in the Vancouver city hampered systematic and comprehensive fieldwork among the Indo-Canadians who are largely concentrated in Surrey, Richmond and other areas – far away from the UBC campus where I was located. Commuting to these areas was the major problem. Taking lift a couple of times turned out to be extremely inconvenient, having a taxi quite expensive and relying on some of the willing respondents to pick me up from the campus to their offices/ homes and back was a daunting and impractical task. A couple of respondents were kind enough to come to see me on the campus. A few others sent me relevant literature by fax or by post. In most cases therefore I had to rely on telephonic interviews which were short and for want of time and other eventualities. Thus, I was able to collect some data which are not as extensive, uniform and consistent as desired.

CASE STUDIES

1. Budh Singh Dhahan

Mr. Budh Singh Dhahan and his son Mr. Bajr Singh Dhahan are actively involved in health and educational projects in rural Punjab. The senior Dhahan had migrated to Canada via California in 1959. The family has been into construction real estate, oil and other businesses. Ever since his arrival in Canada Mr. Budh Singh Dhahan has been greatly inspired by the work of Canadian Charities and volunteers. He set himself a goal of uplifting the poor and less educated, especially young girls and women in rural Punjab. With his social work experience in British Columbia in the 1960s and '70s, in 1984 Mr. Dhahan along with local support in Punjab operated a 40-bed hospital in Dhaham –Kaleram villages in Nawashahar district. The hospital called "Guru Nanak Mission Hospital" today has 150 beds. In 1987 an elementary and secondary school was started. Subsequently the Guru Nanak College of Nursing was started in 1993 which has been upgraded to a baccalaureate degree and training college for 50 students since 1998. The college has entered into partnership with the Guru Nanak Dev University, Amritsar and the University of British Columbia.

These projects were executed through two charitable societies, one each India and Canada: The Guru Nanak Mission Medical and Educational Trust, Dhahan-Kaleran (India Trust") and the Canada-India Education Society ("the Society"). Needless to say, there has been a committed group of volunteers in Canada and India behind these projects. In India, local villagers along with professionals in health care and education have contributed a vast amount of time and labour and money since 1982 in construction of the infrastructure and development of programmes. The village councils of Dhahan and Kaleran had donated 30 acres of land to the India Trust. The market value of the land is estimated at over two million dollars. An additional 22 acres are also available for future expansion of facilities. Among a number of land donations to the India Trust the largest – a strip-male market in Banga (about 5 km from Dhahan-Kale ran) - was made by an Indian family from Fiji. The market value of this property is about 2 million dollars. In Vancouver, the society is made up of volunteers who raise all the funds and seek out other Canadian volunteers for assignment in Punjab. To date, about three million dollars have been contributed by Canadian donors. Donations have also come from the Punjabi/Sikh donors in Norway, Fiji and the U.K.

In April 2001, Mr. Barj Dhahan was pleased to announce the launch of a one-year project to develop a primary health care plan in Nawanshahar and Jullandhar districts. The project is undertaken with the financial support of the Government of Canada provided through the Canadian International Development Agency (CIDA). The project will be carried out by the Society and the India trust. The overall goal of this new project is to contribute to improving health in rural Punjab through strengthening primary health care. The first step will be to conduct a community survey to assess existing health services in 70 villages and to determine priority health concerns. When the survey is completed, the findings will be used to create a long- term plan for primary health care. The Trust has set up a Primary Health Care Project Committee to coordinate the project. Throughout the year, committee members and staff will have opportunities to gain experience in project planning, monitoring and evaluation.

2. Chinmaya Mission, Vancouver

A worldwide mission founded in 1951 by Swami Chinmayanand, follower of Advait Vaidant, the Chinmaya Mission is active in Canada since 1975. The Halton Region chapter Ontario came into existence in 1981. The Mission is recognised by the Canadian Government as registered charity since 1990 and the Canadian International Development Agency (CIDA) has been giving grants to it since 1994. The Mission is involved in a variety of welfare activities in India — two medical centers, an orphanage, and projects on child adoption, immunisation, family planning, clean water, education and training, tree planting and environmental awareness.

Of the several projects in India run by the Chinmaya Mission two are noteworthy one each in north and South India: Chinmaya Rural Primary Health Care and Training Centre, Sidhabari, Himachal Pradesh and Chinmayaranyam, District Cuddapah, Andhra Pradesh.

Chinmaya Rural Primary Health Care and Training Centre. The Centre was launched under the aegis of the "Chinmaya Tapovan Trust". It is primarily aimed at empowering women at various levels. At its inception, it was recognised that the poor state of women's health in the country is linked to a host of problems such as poor nutrition, lack of education, absence of women in the economic and political decision making processes and low self esteem etc., which affect their lives on day today basis. To address these issues the development programmes at the Centre attempted to combine training with motivation and follow up, to bring about a change in the health and socio-economic conditions of the women in the Kangra district of Himachal Pradesh. With these objectives in mind the following specific programmes have been launched by the the Centre:

1. Clinics for Health Care. At the Trust's Central Dispensary services are provided at a nominal cost. These involve training rural midwives in aseptic birthing practices, oral dehydration, child care and general hygiene. Such simple steps have resulted in drastic reduction in the infant mortality rate in the area.
2. Self Help Groups. The Centre helps poor rural women to form groups and mobilise savings. Each women gives a small amount (less than a dollar per month) and becomes eligible for a bigger loan from a pool fund – a source from which they can borrow. The Centre helps them link with local banks to increase the credit available to them. This not just links women with each other but also links them with formal systems which otherwise ignore their needs. There are 140 women's micro-banks mobilising savings and credit.
3. Income Generation, Training and Motivation. The trust trains women in conducting small businesses at home which they themselves manage, earn and control. This training motivates women to become entrepreneurs and use the Self Help Group Credit for economic activity.
4. Play Schools. These schools act like crèches while women attend group meetings.
5. Political Awareness. Local self government training enables women to get elected to village councils and acquire leadership role. More than 60 women trained by the trust have won local elections. The biggest challenge before these women is to deal with the problem of alcoholism and family violence. To combat alcoholism there are training programmes based on Alcoholics Anonymous and Al – Anon to provide support to the dependents of alcoholics.
6. Adolescents Girls Groups. Teenage girls learn to deal with issues such as dowry, caste system etc., in addition to the training they receive in health, hygiene and leadership.
7. Other Activities. The Trust is also involved in programmes for environmental awareness, adult literacy,

family planning education and motivation. The future plans include the starting of a community-based Rehabilitation Programme for the disabled.

According to Raj Kapahi, president Chinmaya Mission, Vancouver the target was to raise Canadian $50,000 in 2001 in Vancouver for this project. A similar amount of money was raised in the year 2000 also. For every dollar received from donors, an additional two dollars come from the CIDA.

Chinmayaranyam. The project which aims at land reclamation is located in Andhra Pradesh and was started in 1985. Chinmayaranyam, which means Chinmaya forests, is a hamlet of villages sheltered over 24 acres which was declared a "disaster zone" in 1975. Land declared useless after years of draught was irrigated with digging tube wells. Today the land has been converted into a lush orchid of bananas, oranges, lemon, mangoes, rice paddy fields and flower gardens. Besides tree planting, the objectives include promoting environmental awareness children and adults and imparting training in forestry education the goals are (i) to sponsor tree planting in the new 86 acres donated to Chinmayaranyam, (ii) to nurture tree growth for fruit crops, (iii) to sink three more bore-wells, (iv) to create a sub-soil irrigation network in the complying, and (vi) to build security fencing around the land.

Chinmayaranayam also supports an orphanage for about 60 boys and girls and provides them education to Grade 8 followed by vocational training in brick making, land reclamation, etc. There is also a "hospital" run by a physician and two nurses, which requires further expansion and equipment's for the benefit of the Chinmayaramyam residents and neighbouring villages. The expansion goals have been set at providing health care in villages (immunisation, birth control, eradication of child marriages, primary health care etc., and promoting "third world technologies" to the village clusters of Chinmayaranyam (bio-gas plants, reforestation).

3. Operation Eyesight Universal

Operation Eyesight Universal is a Canadian organisation that works to restore sight and to prevent blindness in countries of greatest need. Since 1963 their Gift of Sight programmes have helped 25 million people all over the world. In the 1930's, Dr. Ben and Evlyn Gullison left Canada for Sompeta, a village in southern India, known for its high rate of disease- leprosy in particular. While conducting a medical survey of the area, they were surprised to discover a large number of people who were blind. In this small area consisting of only 200 small villages, there were about 200,000 people blind with cataracts. These people could be cured with a simple operation, but unfortunately they did not have access to medical care. Dr. Gullison and a local eye-doctor opened an eye clinic and people in need strained in-but the two doctors could not meet the need. In 1963 Dr. Gullison returned to Canada and made an appeal for help to a group of business people in Calgary and Operation Eyesight Universal was born. From humble beginning in Sompeta, OEU now finance projects in 43 programs in South Asia, Africa and South America OEU's work is concentrated in two main areas — sight restoration and blindness prevention.

For a $35 gift, OEU is able to restore sight to one blind person in the developing world through cataract surgery. A cataract occurs when the ordinarily clear lens of the eye becomes cloudy-resulting in a lack of light entering the eye eventually leading to blindness. In some cases cataract surgery is performed at hospitals affiliated with OEU. Sometimes our partners "take the hospital to the Patients" by packing equipment and supplies into vans called mobile eye units and setting up free eye camps in remote villages. The second main thrust of OEU's work is blindness prevention among children. In the developing world children are in great danger of losing eyesight due to malnutrition and disease. Operation Eyesight not only helps by providing vitamin A but in many cases provides a comprehensive eye care programme including medicine, vaccinations, training, equipment and nutrition counseling. This work can either be done at a base hospital or in a rural area through an eye screening camp. Similar to surgical eye camps, these are free clinic at which hundreds of people can have their eye sight examined. Simple problems are treated on the spot. Patients with more serious conditions are taken back to the base hospital for treatment. Operation Eyesight has recently joined forces with other eye care organisations to form Vision 2020. This joint effort, started by the World Health Organisation and the International Agency for the Prevention of Blindness, aims to eliminate avoidable blindness by the year 2020.

4. Gill Brothers

Surjit and Gurdip Singh Gill are into lumber industry, farming, transport and other businesses in British Columbia / Vancouver. They have been in Canada since the early 1960s. Their major contribution lies in raising funds to the tune of about Rs. 4 crore for a Women's College named "Guru Harrai Sahib College for Women". Located at Chabbevaal a small town in Hoshiarpur district on the main road between Chandigarh and Hoshiarpur, the college is a literal arts degree college for women which was started in March 2000. The classes started in July 2001. It is built on the Panchayat land, with 2500 sq ft. built in area. The college is managed by a local trust registered in the town. Rs. two crore has already been spent on the college and there are plans for its expension. The College is likely to be affiliated with the Punjab University, Chandigarh. There were no major problems in the execution of the project. With an annual contribution of about Rs. 50,000, the Gill brothers also organise annual soccer tournaments at Mahalpur in Hoshiarpur district.

5. Tara Singh Bains

Seventy eight year old Tara Singh Bains is a prominent Indo-Canadian in Vancouver. An Indian army Veteran, he migrated to Canada in 1953 and subsequently worked in lumber factory and as a farmer. Tara Singh Bains is a co-author of a book with Hugh Johnston, a professor of history at Simon Frazer University. Entitled "The four Quarters of the Night: The Life-Journey of an Emigrant Sikh" (McGill-Queen's University Press, 1995), the book is more than one man's life story", . . . a compelling narrative presenting "an evocative picture of a newcomer's experiences in a land of foreign customs, culture and religious beliefs". Mr. Bains has been active in fighting against racism, and for immigrant rights and speaking out for the Sikh faith in Canada.

Tara Singh Bain's major contribution to Indian welfare programmes is a school at village Kultham in Nava Sahar district of Punjab. The school named "Guru Nanak Adarsh Model School", is built on half-an-acre of land and has been in operation since 1992 (The Grade started in April 2001). The building so far has 14 classrooms, well-equipped office and a library, a computer room. It employs 14 teachers and has about 250 students on its rolls who commute from the neighbouring villages. According to Bains, admission and tuition fees are very moderate compared to a private commercial school which initially tried to create obstacles but eventually was unsuccessful. The school also imports moral education, but developing secular-orientation among the children is encouraged. The school is financially a viable proposition and is worth Rs. 40 lakhs, excluding land. Mr. Bains had also contributed Rs. 2 lakhs for Mr. Budh Singh Dhahan's Nursing Home in the nearby village.

6. Dr. G.S. Gill

Gurdev Singh Gill is a general physician, a UBC graduate of 1957. Befitting of his vocation, he has completed in 1999-2000 a project called "Village Life Improvement Project" benefiting above 128-130 household in the Kharoudi village in Hoshiarpur district. In project under the auspices of "Indo Canadian Friendship Society, British Columbia" (a charitable, non-profit organisation registered, in 1974) involved in filling up of a big pond constructing Septic tanks with facility for pumping out water and filtering the water for general use) tanks and underground sewerage, laying telephone cables and installing solar panels for street light. Simultaneously, a drinking water project for seven villages was also completed. These projects were completed at a cost of about Rs. 60 lakhs, of which only about Rs. 16 lakhs came from the Punjab government. With great sentimental links with his native village, Dr. Gill himself supervised the projects to completion keeping the local bureaucracy at bay. According to him, this is perhaps the only village in Punjab, which has undertaken a comprehensive sanitation project.

7. Venilal Sisodraker

Just retired from business, Venilal Sisodraker was instrumental in getting completed "Handiya Baba Children Hospital" at Allahabad (U.P.) in 1994 for poor people. Since then he has been busy with 3 orphanage projects at Gandhi Nagar (Gujarat), Hyderabad (A.P.) and Kalyamkundam (Tamil Nadu). About 500 orphans have been benefiting from these projects. With a contribution of U.S. $ 50,000 from the Edmond Hilary Foundation in addition to money raised in Canada, Japan, the UK, etc he has also been helping Tibetan refugees at Dharamshala (Himachal Pradesh). "Child Heaven international", a registered society also runs a *ashram* in Navasari (Gujarat) since 1985 where presently about two dozen adopted children have been living.

8. Drs. Ram and Susila Reddy

This husband-wife team of doctors has been active in supporting a 15 bed general hospital outside the Bangalore city which is visited by about 50 outdoor patients daily. Named as Swarnamukhi Hospital, it has 3 doctors, three nurses, and is well equipped with a pathological laboratory x-ray machine and an operation theatre. A retired government hospital employee in Vancouver, Dr. Ram Reddy is active in philanthropic work through a network of Rotary clubs in Vancouver. He secures a variety of used equipments from hospitals in Canada and sends them to the needy hospitals in India. Dr. Reddy has instituted two scholarships for best students for further studies at Renuka High School, Bangalore, Karnataka. He had also raised $22,000 for AIDS awareness programmes in South India.

9. Dr. Satyen Banerjee

A retired Professor Emeritus from the British Columbia Hospital, Dr. Banerjee has been actively engaged in a number of welfare activities in India through "Aghornath Foundation", which was registered in 1994 and is named after his grandfather. The foundation provides scholarships to high school students at Nalahati in Berbhum district of West Bengal. A few lakhs rupees have been put in bank fixed deposits whose interest money is distributed as scholarship.

At Vishwabharati University, Shantiniketan, West Bengal three inter-related projects are run by "Vidyasagar Janakalyan Samiti" (a registered society): (1) About ten destitute women are given training in sewing, knitting, etc. (2) Mentally challenged children (some of them being wards of faculty and staff of the university) are treated for various ailments, and (3) a fully equipped medical van visits neighbouring Santhal tribal villages. Almost every year Dr. Banerjee visits India and himself sees thing running smoothly. In addition to these activities, Dr. Banerjee has also instituted two scholarships at post-graduate (M.Sc.) level in the Agriculture Faculty of the University of Calcutta in the name of his teacher Prof. P.K. Sen. He also runs a primary school for poor students in Kolkata under the aegis of "Kalyani Samtat Siksha Niketan" which grows every year by one grade. Teachers serve voluntarily and lunch for children in provided free of cost.

10. Dr. Anup Singh Jubbal

A resident in Canada since 1968 Dr. Jubbal's is a well-settled family in Vancouver. Through Rotary Clubs in Canada and India he has been instrumental in carrying out about 40,000 cataract operations in north India. He is a regular donor to an eye hospital at Kabliji, near Gurgaon, Haryana. Presently he is planning two major projects, one each in Amritsar and Lucknow, converting his ancestral houses into charitable eye hospitals. This is being done following his mother's death wish to set up a trust for the purpose in India after her name. He already has Rs. 10 lakh funds with appropriate grant from CIDA and a committee to execute three projects.

11. India Mahila Association

The Association has been active in Vancouver since 1973. In relation to India its major programme has been to raise funds for a nine-bed hospital at Rurka Kalan village in Jalandhar district. The project was started in 1999 and will be completed in a couple of years. So far over $ 50,000 have been raised in Vancouver and efforts are on way to raise more funds in the US. and the U.K. According to Harminder Sangera, president of the Association, her father and her brother Mahinder Singh Sandhu are also involved in the project. It is being executed through "Bhai Sandhu Charitable Trust" in India. The Sandhus are in real estate business.

12. Dr. Vinod J. Mody

Resident in Canada for over 40 years, Dr. Vinod J. Mody is a renowned aeronautical engineer and a Professor Emeritus at the University of British Colombia, Vancouver. He is an internationally recognised authority in the area of spacecraft dynamics and control. Currently his research efforts are aimed at the international space station, a collaborative project involving the USA, Canada, Japan, Russia and the European Space Agency. The space station with six astronauts abroad is scheduled to be operational in year 2002.

Apart from his international reputation as an aerospace engineer, Dr. Modi has gained worldwide recognition as an award winning photographer. In 1957 he received President Eisenhower's prize for use of photography to promote international understanding. His photographs have been exhibited around the world including at the famous Nikon Center, Japan. He was invited to arrange an exhibition of his photographs in honour of Queen Elizabeth's visit to Vancouver, Canada, in 1983. In 1985, Dr. Modi was invited by the Council of Museums and Art Galleries of Los Angeles to make presentation on the Evolution of Buddhist Architecture.

Dr. Vinod J. Mody's vocation and hobby have both been instrumental in serving his motherland. In 1978 he held a photographic exhibition in Bombay called "God's Prayers to Time", which was based on the pictures of monuments. The sale of these photographs earned him $24,000 which he donated to the National Association for the Blind. In the year 2000 he held another exhibition in Mumbai titled "This Moment Has 21 Days". The photographs were based on the life of a small village near Pune where Dr. Mody lived as a "participant observer" for 21 days. This time the exhibition raised $32,000 which he donated to the National Association for the Blind to be used for the purchase of a mobile van library equipped with brail books.

Besides a variety of professional contacts and contributions to India institutions and organisations pertaining to science, engineering and space research, Dr. Mody's recent philanthropic activities include the following: (1) donation of Rs. 8 lakh and a large number of books and periodicals. In 1995 to the library of the Indian Institute of Science, Bangalore; (2) donation of Rs. 12 lakhs for the library of the National Institute of Advanced Study, Bangalore in 2000. Additionally, he also plans to donate about 3,000 books on philosophy, literature, etc.

13. Sudarshan Baxi

Mr. Baxi has been working through an NGO called Janata Sevak Society" in Canada registered in 1988) and "Nishkam Seva Ashram" in Ludhiana, India. The Ashram has been instrumental in organising eye operation camps, dental care and operation camps, knitting and sewing classes for women, besides arranging simple marriage ceremonies for girls who cannot afford spending much money on such ceremonies. Mr. Baxi is a frequent visitor to India. Besides raising funds for various causes in Canada as well as India, Mr. Baxi is presently involved in $ 6 million project for a funeral house in Vancouver. According to him, the hall can accommodate about 1,000 people. In project so being carried out through a registered body called "Five Rivers Community Services Society" of which Mr. Baxi is a senior Vice-President. The House will be ready some-time next year.

14. Dheeru Desai

Such programmes are not without their detractors. Mr. Dheeru Desai, born in India, brought up in South Africa and now a long time resident in Vancouver is a well settled and widely traveled person. He happens to be a disillusioned individual in so far as the impact of such welfare programmes on India is concerned. Now he is extremely critical of the socio-political situation in India-its politicians, bureaucracy and even the people in general. He is almost cynically negative about doing anything for India. This year he was in India for about three months and was shocked to see the tents sent for earthquake victims in Gujarat being "used" by politicians and others. Mr. Desai thinks that he has links with India because he was born and initially brought up there. But according to him, his children and grand children' are not going to have any links with India. Presently he is involved in building a hall in a school in South Africa.

15. Dr. Bakul Dalal

Resident in Canada and presently working at the Department of Pathology of the Vancouver General Hospital since 1979, Dr. Dalal has been active in organising every year international medical conferences in such areas as blood diseases, cancer, etc., at different cities in India. He is also involved in the activities of the Operation Eyesight Universal.

16. Vancouver Kingsway Lions Club

For about a decade now the Club has been organising eye operation camps in India through Operation Eyesight Universal. It also collects used eye glasses for distribution in India. The Club had raised funds for earthquakes victims in Latur and in Gujarat. The Club is planning to build a hospital near Faridabad in Haryana.

17. India Club of Vancouver

The organisation has been involved in organising eye operation camps and dental care camps in India, particularly in Gujarat, Rajasthan and Bihar for the past 16-17 years. The eye camps are organised through Operation Eyesight Universal. Additionally, used medical equipments are collected in Canada and sent to hospitals in India.

18. India Cultural Centre, Canada

The Centre is active since 1984 and has about 90 members. The Centre has been instrumental in sponsoring a mobile medical van/hospital equipped with pathological laboratory in Mumbai. Its cost Can $80,000. Another van is planned for Chandigarh. The Centre is also planning a school in Gujarat but the place is yet to be decided. Earlier its members contributed generously for the Latur and Gujarat earthquakes victims.

Analysis

1. The "Myth of return" on the part of "brain drain" type émigré is being replaced by frequent and extended trips to India. Funding community development projects back home may well be one of the outcomes of such movements. An increasing number of chartered flights from Canada, the U.K. and the U.S.A. to India and private bus/taxi service bye-passing regular bus/train service – all testify to this trend.
2. Almost all the individuals involved in the welfare projects are retired gentlemen – generally in their sixties and seventies. "Most of these men were retired, and at a point in their life where they could afford a significant amount of time to be either in Punjab overseeing developments or travelling to overseas sites of Punjabi settlement in order to raise more funds" (Walton-Roberts 2000: 22). Most of the respondents had the support of their extended family members who appeared to be very well-settled in Canada.
3. It is significant to note that although these projects have been initiated by successful emigrant male members, quite a number of projects are directed towards improving the lot of rural women in Punjab and elsewhere in India. This attempt at gendered social engineering not only underline patriarchal social formation in India but also point out the changed worldview and renewed concern (the desirability of the just and equitable socio-economic development) on the part of the diasporic communities in western societies.
4. In India's context the diasporic linkages are best expressed through regional-linguistic ties such as Punjabi, Gujarati, etc. It should not be surprising therefore that a large majority of respondents have done what they have done for Punjab. With the same logic, Dr. Satyen Banerjee and Dr. Vinod Mody originally coming from Bengal and Maharashtra respectively have chosen to do their bits for their respective provinces. Indeed

regional-linguistic basis has been the preffered mode of socio-cultural organisation among the overseas Indians.

5. The Indo-Canadians do not seem to have any major problem in raising funds, etc., in Canada or elsewhere for doing community development projects in India. On the contrary, many of the respondents did mention a number of problems they faced in India. Most of these were related to usual bureaucratic hurdles in seeking permission to start the project or getting no objection certificates from local, district or state level authorities. In some cases the Punjab government, for example, did not release the matching grant it had initially promised. In others, land transfer proved extremely difficult as the applicants had to go through complicated rules and regulations.

Conclusion

The case studies presented above more than adequately highlight the deep involvement of Indo-Canadians in a variety of welfare activities in India. Besides these a large number of Indo Canadians have also made generous donations perhaps running into several lakhs of dollars to the Latur and Gujarat earthquakes. These activities should be understood in their proper perspective. They are not merely philanthrophic activities or acts of charity but a natural urge on the part of the diasporic communities to do something for their motherland. These findings are a remarkable theoretical feedback in the context of a wider diaspora-homeland relationship. There is need for further research in this area.

Given these motherland-diasporic linkages and recognizing the fact that they are particularly beneficial to India, the least the Government of India or Indian provincial governments can do is to compile a directory of various projects in which diasporic individuals/NGOs are involved. As already pointed out, there was no such directory even in a city like Vancouver where a number of Indo-Canadians have been involved in various welfare and development projects in India and were generally unaware about each other's works.

References

Bains, Tara Singh and Hugh Johnston 1995. *The Four Quarter of the Night : The Life Journey of an Emigrant Sikh*. Montreal: McGill-Queen's University Press.

Buchignani, Norman, 1989. "Contemporary Research on People of Indian Origin in Canada", *Sociological Bulletin*, 38(1), pp. 71-93.

Buchignani, Norman, 1977. "A Review of the Historical and Sociological Literature on East India in Canada" *Canadian Ethnic Studies*, ix (1), pp. 86-108.

Grenier, Gilles 2001. "Indian Immigration in Canada: A Comparative Analysis", paper presented at the Summer Institute of Canadian Studies, University of Ottawa, Ottawa (mimeographed).

Griffin, Kelvin 1993. Vancouver's Many Faces: Passport to the Cultures of a City. Vancouver/Torento: Whitecap Books.

Helweg, Arthur W. 1979. Sikhs in England: The Development of a Migrant Community, Delhi: Oxford University Press.

Helweg, Arthur W. 1983 "Emigrant Remittances: Their Nature and Impact on a Punjabi Village", *New Community* 10: 435-443.

Helweg, Arthur W. 1986. "The Indian Diaspora: Influence on International Relations", in Gabriel Sheffer (ed.), Modern Diasporas in International Politics, London:Croom Helm, pp. 103-29.

Helweg, Arthur W. 1990. "Sikh Politics in India: the Emigrant Factor", in N. Gerald Barrier and V.A. Dusenbery (eds.), *The Sikh Diaspora*, New Delhi, Chankya Publications, pp. 305-36.

Jain, Prakash, C. 1983. "Racism in Canada: Some Recent Surveys", *India Quarterly*, 39 (2), pp. 193-98.

Jain, Prakash C. 1989. "Emigration and Settlement of Indian Abroad", *Sociological Bulletin*, 38(1), pp. 155-68.

Jain, Prakash C. 1999. "Indians in Canada:........and How They Have Influences Indo-Canadian Ties", *Encounter*, 2(2), pp. 99-113.

Judge, Paramjit S. 1994. *Punjabis in Canada: A Study of Formation of an Ethnic Community*, Delhi : Chankya Publications.

Khemani, R.S. *et al.* 1982. A Socio-Economic Profile of the Indo-Canadian Community in the Ottawa-Hull Area, Ottawa: NACOI, Ottawa Chapter (Mimeo).

Oo mmen, T.K. 1989. "Brain Drain or the Migration of Talent : The Indian Case", *International Migration*, 29(3), pp. 411-25.

Sharma, Kavita A. 1997. *The Ongoing Journey: Indian Migration to Canada*. New Delhi: Creative Books.

Sheffer, Gabriel (ed.) 1986. Modern Diaspora in International Politics, London: Croom Helm.

Statistics Canada 2001. *Census at a Glance: 2001*. Ottawa: Statistics Canada.

Sukhatme, S.P. and I. Mahadevan, 1988. "Brain Drain and the I.I.T Graduates", *Economic and Political Weekly*, 23, pp. 1285-93.

Thakkar, R. 1994. "Indo-Canadian", in J.S. Grewal and Hugh Johnston (eds.), *India-Canada Relations*, New Delhi: Sage Publications.

Walton-Roberts, Margaret "Returning, Remitting, Reshaping: Non-Resident Indians and the transformation of Society and Space in Punjab, India", Peter Jackson (ed) *Transnational Spaces*. London: Routledge.

Weiner, Myron 1990. "The Indian Presence in America: What Difference Will it Make? in Sulochana Raghavan Glazer and Nathan Glazer (eds.), *Conflicting Images: India and the United States*, Glenn Dale, Maryland, The Riverside Co., Publishers, pp. 241-56.

12

Gulf NRIs as a Factor in Strengthening Indo-Gulf Relations

Anisur Rahman

Introduction

The significance of the Gulf NRIs is increasing as the role of Indian Diaspora is gaining momentum in the age of globalisation and liberalisation. It is evident that the NRIs in the Gulf are not only working there but also now more actively investing their surplus money for the better return. Not only this, it is also found that India has realised its significance and is now taking steps to facilitate the Diaspora to take part in this new business and investment climate. TheGulf NRIs are found to be the major engine for the economic growth and development in this region. Indian Diaspora in the Gulf countries which consists of Non- resident Indians and Peoples of Indian Origins. But overwhelming majority of them fall in the category of NRIs. There were only 53, 000 PIOs whereas the number of NRIs was more than 3.2 million in 2000(GOI, High level Committee on Indian Diaspora, 2001). At present, over 5 million Indians are engaged in the Gulf countries for different activities such as employment, business and trade.

It is rightly said that the recent economic role and contribution of NRIs in the Gulf is mainly because of the liberalised policies of the respective governments both in India and the Gulf countries. Moreover, this new liberalised business climate has also attracted the Gulf investors towards India. In this respect, the NRls are playing the major roles by showing their hard work and sincerity in enhancing confidence amongst the Arab entrepreneurs. The major aim of this study is to highlight the main contributions of Gulf NRIs in Indian and Gulf economies. How do their contributions would be effective to bring them closer would be examined in this study. It would also be examined as how are the Gulf NRIs playing an important role for building confidence amongst both sides? Finally, it would be analysed, how far they would be instrumental for strengthening relations between India and Gulf countries for their mutual benefit and development.

Some Aspects of Indian Diaspora

Today there are over 25 million Diasporic Indians consisting of People of Indian Origins (PIOs) and Non-Resident Indians (NRIs) settled in about 110 countries (Ministry of External Affairs, 2001-02). Demographically, Indian Diaspora constitutes the third largest group which stands next to the British and the Chinese Diaspora. It is found that people of Indian origin constitute more than 40 per cent of the population in Fiji, Mauritius, Trinidad, Guyana and Surinam. They are also found to be in Malaysia, South Africa, Sri Lanka, Uganda, UK, USA and Canada in minorities (www.uohyd.ernet.in/sss/cinddiaspora/india.html). There are over 5 million NRIs who are presently living in the Gulf countries. They constitute one fifth of the total Diasporic Indians living abroad.

The Gulf NRIs are one of the most important components of Indian Diaspora today. Indian Diaspora is considered to be a unique social force globally which, in fact, came into being mainly due to the subjugation of India by the British and its incorporation into the British Empire. Indians were taken over as indentured labour to many parts of the empire in the nineteenth-century. Since then they have been living over there as culturally distinct communities. They have their deep roots in the ancestral land and still maintain extensive cultural links with India. In a way, it is considered to be a part and parcel of the Indian culture and civilisation. Thus, the Indian way of life and culture is just not confined to its geographical boundaries, but rather it has its presence wherever Indians have emigrated along with their socio-cultural heritage. The dispersal of Indian labour and professionals has been witnessed as a world-wide phenomenon especially after the World War II. South Asians especially Indians provided the labour that helped in the reconstruction of war-torn Europe, particularly the United Kingdom and the Netherlands. Indians have also made their presence visibly felt in the many professions in some industrially advanced countries such as the United States, Canada, and Australia. Since the early 1970s, unskilled and semi- skilled labour primarily from India has been the major force in the transformation of the physical landscape of several countries of West Asia. Myron Weiner rightly described this unskilled and semi-skilled Indians as "incipient Diaspora" which is still continuing to go to the Gulf region.

The presence of Indians has been established in West Asia, especially to the Gulf region since ancient times. Indians are known to have gone to Bahrain in pursuit of trade as early as 3000 B.C. when their ships used to go from Harappan settlements to Oman and Bahrain, on their way to Mesopotamia. Indian settlement in this region has been, however, established only since the sixteenth century. There were few Indian communities relating to trade and business called Baniyas were traced in contemporary Iraq, Iran, Oman, Yemen and Saudi Arabia in the seventeenth and eighteenth centuries. In the nineteenth century, Indian merchant communities prospered in a number of towns in the Gulf countries under the British influence (Jain, 2005:124) . Some Indians were also found to work as bankers, importers and exporters, customs farmers, agents for local merchants, government contractors, financiers, etc. The Indians settled in the Persian Gulf region imported Indian goods and redistributed them throughout the Arabian Peninsula (Weiner, 1982:13). Before 1980, there were 3,000 Indian merchant families in Dubai which was the major trade centre in the region. Bahrain and Oman had some special Indian connections during the British rule in India. They were made British protectorates and were controlled by the Government of India (Nair, 1986:68). During that period Indian merchants were also settled in

Bahrain who imported rice, tea, sugar, etc. Indians also began to migrate to work as clerks, technicians and nurses during the 1930s with the development of the Bahrain Petroleum Company. The Indian merchant community had also dominated the economy of this region even during the nineteenth century.

Table 1. Outflow of Indian Workers Abroad for Employment during 2004-09

Year	*Number of workers (In lakhs)*
2004	4.75
2005	5.49
2006	6.77
2007	8.09
2008	8.49
2009	6.10

Source: Government of India, Ministry of Overseas India Affairs, Annual Report, 2009-10

Following the Second World War and more decisively after the independence of the Gulf countries, it was found that the Gulf countries began to emerge as oil-producing and exporting economies. As a result, there was a huge demand for labour in the Gulf. This demand in fact, changed the size and complexion of the Indians and other expatriate communities in the region. With the increase in oil prices in the mid-seventies, Indians began to migrate in large numbers into the Gulf countries for a variety of jobs. This trend has been continuing since then with some variations till today as shown in Table 1. It is expected that it will continue in future also. It is thus noted that every year a large number of Indian workers migrate to the Gulf countries to earn more money in order to raise their standard of living and make their families happier and prosperous. In a way India is benefited enormously in terms of remittances due to the outflow of Indian labour in the Gulf countries. Today a significant number of Diasporic Indians are living in this region.

Composition of Indian Diaspora

Indian Diaspora in the Gulf countries consists of Non-resident Indians and Peoples of Indian Origins. It is however, found that overwhelming majority of them fall in the category of NRIs as shown in Table 2. There were only 53, 000 PIOs in the entire region whereas the number of NRIs was more than 3.2 million in 2000: NRIs in Saudi Arabia were about a million and half who were the largest Indian passport holding community abroad. The number of PIOs was nil in Saudi Arabia. NRIs constituted 7 percent of the total population of the country in 2000. The Indian communities in Saudi Arabia are well received and accepted at all levels of the Saudi Society as stated by high level committee. The Indian Diaspora in UAE was significant as the number of NRIs was about 1 million and PIOs was about 50,000. The NRIs at that time constituted over 50% of the country's expatriate workforce followed by Pakistan with 22%. The Indian Diaspora in the UAE constituted about one third (32%) of the total population in the country. The UAE had the largest number of Indians in terms of percentage as compared to any other Gulf countries (ICWA, 2001). This trend is still continuing in case of the UAE.

We further observe that out of nearly 2.2 million population of Kuwait, there were about 65% foreign nationals in 2000. The Indian Diaspora constituted the single largest expatriate community in the country. They constituted of almost 13% of the total population. All of them are NRI as foreigners do not normally qualify for local citizenship. They were about 1,000 PIOs in Kuwait. Out of Oman's total population of 2.3 million, the Indian community in this country constituted about 15% of its population. Indians were the single largest expatriate group in Oman. There were about 58 percent foreign population. The Indian Diaspora consists of 25% unskilled, 30 semiskilled and 35 skilled manpower in Oman. The remaining 10% constituted highly skilled professionals such as doctors, engineers, bankers, financial experts and managers.

The size of the Indian community in Qatar was almost one fourth of the total number of residents in the country. A major chunk of the Indian expatriates is engaged in unskilled or semiskilled work. The annual remittances from Qatar to India were estimated to be around Rs. 1,200 crores in 2000. Bahrain is the smallest of GCC countries with a total population of

643,000 persons, Bahrainis number only 391,000. There were nearly 130,000 NRIs in the country and are mostly from Kerala and South Indian states. The NRIs constituted one fifth of the total Bahrainis population.

Table 2. Composition of Indian Diaspora in the Gulf countries, 2000

Country	*Population*	*No. of NRIs*	*PIOs*	*% of Popul-ation*
Saudi Arabia	21,500,000	1,500,00	NIL	7
U.A.E	2,800,000	900,000	50,000	32
Kuwait	2,200,000	287,600	1,000	13
Oman	2,200,000	340,000	1,000	15
Bahrain	643,000	130,000	NIL	20
Qatar	525,000	125,000	1,000	24
GCC	29,868,000	3,282,600	53,000	11

Source: Indian Council World Affairs, *Report of the High Level Committee on Indian Diaspora*, 2001 (Gulf Region) accessed through internet, http://indiandiaspora.nic.in/contents.htm

The Indian migrants are going to different parts of the World from every nook and corner of the country. Gulf NRIs are from almost all Indian states. But there are some states like Kerala, Tamil Nadu, Andhra Pradesh, Maharashtra, Rajasthan, Punjab, Uttar Pradesh and Bihar that dominate in the process of migration. These are the states that send a considerable number of migrants abroad every year. Out of these, Kerala, Tamil Nadu and Andhra Pradesh send more than fifty percent migrants. While, in 1970s and 1980s, migration was dominated by Kerala which alone sent about 50 per cent migrants to the Gulf countries. But now, its share has declined due to the entry of other Indian states in this arena. Despite all, Kerala is still at the top in sending maximum migrants abroad followed by Tamil Nadu. It is observed that south Indian states are still far ahead in terms of sending more migrants outside the country.

The Role of NRIs in Economic Development

It is evident that India has acknowledged the potential of Overseas Indians and has initiated a dialogue with them. In order to use their full potential, the new ministry namely, Ministry of Overseas Indian Affairs (MOIA) came into being in

2004. One of the focus areas of the Ministry over the last few years has been the promotion of investments by Overseas Indians including innovative investment and policy initiative. This Ministry has established a Centre called Overseas Indian Facilitation Centre (OIFC). This centre is working in collaboration with the Confederation of Indian Industry. The main objective of OIFC is to promote Overseas Indian Investment in India and facilitate Business-to Business partnership between Indian Business and Overseas Indians. This centre is also providing a number of advisory services such as consular questions, stay in India, investment and financial issues, etc., to Indian Diaspora.

It is noted that NRIs now have started investing in retail stores, gold and textile trade, hotels and restaurants, IT companies and joint ventures following the diversification of industrial and commercial activities in the Gulf countries. The Free Zones promoted by the Gulf governments have provided an attractive environment for investments with no taxes, no restriction on foreign investment, and top class infrastructure. Gone are the days when the only jobs that Indians took up in the Gulf were of the 'ABC' variety – namely the 'ayah, butler and cook jobs (Pravasitoday.com). Similarly, the trend of top-level Indian executives, professionals and doctors is also going down. The Indian presence in the Gulf is no longer primarily focused on services. They have in fact made significant contributions into big business over the last two decades. Thus, the profile of the Indian immigrant to the Gulf is undergoing a steady transition, with Indians having an increasingly influential economic role in the region.

Now the time has come that the Gulf NRIs must be engaged more and more for investment in Indian economy. For this venture, the Indian government must take care of their welfare? As is rightly highlighted by many NRIs that the Govt. must consider the plight of millions NRIs specially lower income workers for their welfare and pooling their resources for the nation building process. By providing all these incentives, NRIs could be engaged for the development of infrastructure, technological innovation, industrial and economic growth of India. This could be made possible only by evolving specific and purpose-oriented schemes to attract their capital and

Gulf Immigration Policy and Human Rights

The Gulf labour importing countries are completely perplexed about their labour immigration policy. On the one hand, they need these workers for their economies and have become accustomed to the benefits of greater money incomes and wider personal services that such migrants make possible. On the other hand, they fear being overwhelmed by the inflow of migrants from other countries. They worry about losing their cultural values on account of the overwhelming presence of migrants in their countries. They also have the great fear for the possibility of political activism by the migrant workers. We see no indication that this contradiction will be resolved soon. It is likely that the Gulf countries will remain dependent on migrant labour for years to come and they will also continue to dislike their dependence on foreign workers. It was found that migrants form the majority in almost all GCC countries except Oman (Seale, 2005).

In case of Kuwait, the proportion of migrants was set to fall to below 50 percent in every plan. But this has never been achieved except when the second Gulf crisis occurred. As a result of this crisis, it was found that about 1.5 million of non-Gulf Arabs were expelled because they favoured Iraq. But as of today, the proportion of foreign workers in Kuwait is back to earlier proportion. We further see that the proportion of expatriates in Dubai of the UAE is about 95 percent, while the locals are only 5 percent. This city is an outstanding economic success. It has become the pride of the Arab World. This is made all possible due to the contribution made by expatriates. Hence they deserve better treatment at home as well as at host countries.

The migrant workers suffer at both the places. It is reported that unscrupulous recruiting and travel agencies exploit workers in their own countries. In the host country, employees do not execute proper job contracts, nor pay them promised salary. They even fail to provide adequate shelter and food to the workers. They are sometimes treated like slaves and are forced to work 18 hours a day. This is an open violation of the International Convention on the Protection of the Rights of All Migrant Workers and Members of their families. As the Article

24 of the Convention states: "Every migrant worker and every member of his or her family shall have the right to recognition everywhere as a person before the law" (Gilmore, 2003). The migrant workers cannot become citizens of the Gulf states no matter how long they reside in the country. Their children also cannot get citizenship even if they are born there (Kishore and Khan: 87). Citizenship may be rarely given only by the ruling Sheikhs. The policy of not giving this right is uniformly applied to Palestinians and to other Arabs who have spent their entire lives within the Gulf States, as well as to non-Arabs. The foreign workers are not permitted to own property. They cannot own a business, purchase a house, or acquire land. But Oman and now Dubai are only exceptions where non- citizens can own these assets. Now the time has come for the entire Gulf States to liberalize their policies in favour of giving migrants' rights. They must follow international norms and conventions in order to prevent any malpractice against migrants. This is in the interest of both migrants and host countries.

The Gulf countries are however, following the policy which does not allow migrant workers to be integrated into their own societies politically and socially. They rather create a sense of insecurity and impermanence among the migrants even though they treat the migration process as an enduring one. There is no free labour market. Migrant workers receive work permits only after obtaining NOCs from the government. They can not change their jobs without the consent of their employer and the Ministry of Labour and Social Affairs. If they do so without consent, they are liable to deportation.

Social Conditions of the Gulf NRIs

The working and living conditions of Gulf NRIs are not much satisfactory in the Gulf countries. It is also reported that they are discriminated in many ways. As a result, the rules and regulations for the recruitment of workers in the Gulf region were laid down by the Government of India. The policy of the Indian Government regarding the recruitment of highly qualified experts in such recruitment should be on a government-to-government basis. Semi– skilled and unskilled workers were found to be discriminated in terms of wages and salaries, working conditions, work, and security and welfare facilities.

The Indian Government also got information about the miserable working conditions especially from those migrant workers who were recruited by unauthorised agencies that used false passports, visa and work permits. There were also many complaints about high fees charged by these unauthorised agents. In response to these problems, the labour Ministry prepared a draft model agreement for use by migrants and recruiting agents. Foreign employers are required to provide free roundtrip passage, free furnished accommodation commensurate with the category of work, free medical care, free transportation and other benefits. The employment contracts also contain provisions for over time wages, hours of work, terminal benefits, compensation for accidents, etc.

In spite of these requirements and provisions however, malpractices and contract violations are continued. After reaching the Gulf, the migrants find themselves to be discriminated against, despite all these measures taken by the Government of India. It is also reported that a Westerner is paid double the salary of an Asian, even though the Asian is employed in the same capacity. A British reporter employed in the UAE was paid twice the salary of an Indian reporter (Nair, 1983). The work contract between employers and emigrants are often violated by employers. Persons who were promised the job of an electrician were put to the work of an ordinary unskilled labourer (Nair, 1983). According to a report published on 25 May, 1983, the Government of India received 274 complaints pertaining to wide variety of subjects including cheating by recruiting agents, repatriation of contracts and poor working and living conditions (IE, 1983). There was a survey recently conducted by the team from CDS, Trivendrum on the working and living conditions of Indians in the UAE. It was found that the major problems faced by several Kerala emigrants in the UAE were non-payment of salaries, denial of wages and non-wage benefits stipulated in their work contracts, refusal to release passport and nonpayment of air-ticket fare for return to Kerala. Nearly one-third of the Kerala emigrants live in worker camps and in the majority of cases, the number of persons per room range from four to six. The survey found that 36 percent of the emigrants had a monthly saving of less than 500 Dirhams (Rs. 6,000) and another 37 percent a monthly savings of 500 to 1000 Dirhams (Rs. 6000 to Rs. 12000) (Zachariah, Prakash and Rajan, 2002:326).

Although the migrants working in the Gulf region are a part of its economy but do not enjoy rights of political or social participation. They live in their own enclaves and cannot obtain citizenship, even property or join trade unions. They have thus restricted social benefits and excluded from participation in the political system (Weiner, 1982:6). Since labour legislation and social security institutions are not yet fully developed in many countries of the Gulf region, the employment contract, to some extent, depend on honesty and integrity on the part of employers in respect of the terms and conditions of the agreements. Moreover, wage and salary are not determined by the force of demand and supply. The host countries' government can dictate how migrants are to be admitted, what qualifications they must have, how long they can stay, what wage should be paid, what rights and benefits should be provided, and whether they should be exported from Arab countries or not. For all practical purposes, the power to regulate is primarily in the hands of the labour importing countries not of labour exporting countries (Weiner, 1982:8).

Despite all these limitations and restrictions, Indian migrants rush to the Gulf countries for getting lucrative jobs and they receive wages which are several times higher than what they might receive in India for similar work in addition to free housing facilities, food and medical care. Workers are able to save large part of their wages income. Since in Gulf region, opportunities for costly entertainments such as bars and gambling-houses are non-existent. The prices of consumer durables are much lower in the Gulf than in India (Weiner, 1982:8).

Moreover, Indian migrants know that their employment is purely of temporary nature and they are also aware of the constraints of the Indian Government regarding their protection in the host countries. The Government of India is rather more interested to get benefit from the Gulf NRIs in terms of remittances. Gulf NRIs send a great deal of remittances to

India which help to earn foreign exchange and thereby adds to the foreign exchange reserves in India. There has been increase in terms of foreign exchange which led to the increase in the foreign exchange reserves. The amount of remittances increased from 3.6 billion US dollars in 1991-92 to over 12 billion US dollars in 2001-2002. This remittance further increased to 21.7 billion by 2005 (GOI, 2004-05:33). In 2008, it was found that India received 27 billion US dollars in terms of remittances from abroad. India in fact, tops the list of remittance-recipient countries in the World as data provided by the World Bank's Migration and Remittance Fact book, 2008 (HT, 2008).

This increase, has however, resulted mainly because of the remittances from the Gulf countries. Indians living in other parts of the World remit only a tiny proportion of their savings. The Gulf money has also improved the income level of the migrants' households considerably. This rising income level has directly affected the consumption and investment and saving patterns of country due to the inflow of Gulf remittances. The Gulf NRIs are in fact, an asset to India. Eve then, India is doing little to address the grievances of NRIs in the Gulf.

It is reported that India is planning to sign the bilateral agreements with the Gulf countries. The same kind of the pact has already been signed with the UAE which has been successful. These agreements would provide opportunities to protect the interests of Indian workers in the host countries. These agreements would provide the Indian workers security and housing benefits as rightly highlighted by Vayalar Ravi, Minister for Overseas Indian Affairs. He further said, "The main achievement of the UAE agreement is that the workers duration of stay is not connected with the employers' contract. They are free to change jobs and visa would be extended accordingly" (HT, 2008). Thus, many positive provisions are in place which would provide them a legal cover. The pact would also help fight illegal immigration in this region.

Conclusion

We conclude by saying that NRIs' presence in the Gulf Countries is very significant. Currently, the Gulf NRIs are the major source of remittances and foreign exchange to India. They are not only helping to reduce the situation of unemployment but also earning a great amount of foreign exchange. They also play the vital role in their household economy. On the other hand, Gulf countries are benefited by the NRIs' vital contribution in their economies. Thus, the benefit of NRIs' presence in the Gulf is beneficial for India and the Gulf as well. Thus the population mobility has had positive impact on India's employment, balance of payments, commodity export, business profits and government earnings. The inflow of the Gulf remittances is playing a major role in this direction. The Indian business and government have been benefited in many ways. It is thus fully realised that Gulf NRIs are assets to the host and home countries.

References

Al-Tayer, Ahmad Humaid, 8 December 2004, "GCC should talk to US on free trade." *Gulf News*.

Bhuyan, Aroonim, "Foreign Workers should be treated at Par with Locals http://www.indiaenews.com/nri/20070803/63783.htm

Birks, J.S and Sinclair, C.A., 1980, International Migration and Development in the Arab Region (Geneva:ILO) Centre for the Study of Indian Diaspora, Indian Diaspora, University of Hyderabad, Hyderabad, http://www.uohyd.ernet.in/sss/cinddiaspora/Indian.html, p. 1

Ecevit, Zafer and Zackariah, K.C., 1978, "International Labour Migraton", *Finance and Development*, Vol. 15, No. 4

Gilmore, Kristin, 2003, Convention Establishes Rights of All Migrant Workers and Their Families, accessed through internet, http:/www.un.org/ Pubs/chronicle/ 2003/webArticles/070203_migrantworkers.html

Government of India, Ministry of Overseas Indian Affairs, Annual Report 2004-05 and 2008-09.

Gour, Devashu, Economic Role of Indians in the Gulf, http://www.pravasitoday.com/economic-role-of-indians-in-gulf

Gulf NRIs promise to invest$10b in AP, http://www.thehindubusinessline.in/2003/07/29/stories/2003072901391700.htm

Gulati, I. S., and, Mody, Ashok, 1983, Remittances of Indian Migrants to the Middle East: An Assessment with Special References to

Migrants from Kerala State, Working Paper, No. 182, Trivandrum: CDS, p. 12.

Hindustan Times, June 1, 2004, "Indians in the Middle East", New Delhi.

Indian Council of World Affairs, 2001, Report of the High Level Committee on the Indian Diaspora, New Delhi.

Indian Express, 25 May, 1983, "Migrant Workers Complain of Ill-treatment".

Jain, Prakash C, 2007, "An Incipient Diaspora: Indians in the Gulf Region", in Prakash C Jain (ed), Indian Diaspora in West Asia: A Reader,(New Delhi: Manohar), p. 179.

Jain, Prakash C., 2005, "Indian Entrepreneurs in the Gulf Countries: Some Case Studies", *India Quarterly*, New Delhi, p. 124.

Kapiszewski, Andrzej, Arab vs. Asian Migrant Workers in the GCC Countries, accessed through internet, http://www.un.org/esa/population/meetings/EGM_Ittmig_Arab/P02_Kapiszewski.pdfhttp://www.un.org/esa/population/meetings/EGM_Ittmig_Arab/P02_Kapiszewski.pdf.

Kishore, M.A, and Khan, Shandan Zeb, "Human Rights of Migrant Workers in West Asia", *Journal of West Asian Studies*, (Aligarh) p. 87.

Mathew, E.T.., and Nair, P.R.G., 16 July, 1978, "Socio-Economic Characteristics of Emigrants' Households: A Case Study of Two Villages", *Economic and Political Weekly*; Commerce Research Bureau, Emigration, Inward Remittances and Economic Growth of Kerala: Report of a Survey, Bombay, 1978; Prakash, B.A, 8 July, 1978, "Impact of Foreign Remittances: A Case Study of Chavakkad Village in Kerala", Economic and Political Weekly; Radhakrishnan, C. and Ibrahim, P., Jan-March 1981, "Emigration, Inward Remittances and Economic Development", *Manpower Journal* (New Delhi).

Mattar, Khowla, 2006-07, The Rights of Migrant Workers ignored, Gulfnews, accessed through internet http://archive.gulfnews.com/articles/07/06/12/10131775.html.

Ministry of External Affairs, Government of India, Annual Report, 2001-02, New Delhi.

Nair, P.R.G. 1983, Asian Emigration to the Middle East: Emigration from India-Report of the State of the Art, Trivandrum: Centre for Development Studies.

Nair, P.R.G. 1986, "India" in Godfrey Gunatilleke (ed) *Migration of Asian Workers to the Arab World* (Tokyo : The United Nations

University), p. 74

Nair, P.R.G. 1986, "India" in Godfrey Gunatilleke (ed) *Migration of Asian Workers to the Arab World* (Tokyo : The United Nations University), p. 15.

Nair, P.R.G. 1986,"India" in Godfrey Gunatilleke (ed) *Migration of Asian Workers to the Arab World* (Tokyo : The United Nations University) p. 68.

Nayyar, Deepak, 1994, *Migration, Remittances and Capital Flows: The Indian Experience*, (Delhi: Oxford University Press), p. 30.

NRI from Gulf wants justice from Indian government, http:// www.nriinternet.com/ MIDDLE % 20 EAST / Dubai/2006/ 4_06_Do_justice.htm

Prakash, B.A, 8 July, 1978,"Impact of Foreign Remittances: A Case Study of Chavakkad Village in Kerala", *Economic and Political Weekly*, p. 110.

Rahman, Anisur, 2001, *Indian Labour Migration to the Gulf: A Socio-economic Analysis*, Rajat Publications, New Delhi, p. 19.

Rahman, Anisur, 1999, "Migration of Indian Labour to West Asia: Trends and Effects". *Manpower Journal*, Jul- Sep., IAMR, New Delhi, p. 991.

Rahman, Anisur, 2008, " Migrant Workers and Human Rights: Astudy of the Gulf Region", in Vijapur, Abdulrahim P. (ed.), *Implementing Human Rights in the Third World:Essays on Human Rights, Dalits and Minorities*, Manak Publications Pvt Ltd., Delhi, p. 453.

Seale, Patrick, 2005, The Challenges Facing Arab Gulf States, accessed through internet http://www.genceglobal.com

The Hindustan Times, April, 9, 2008.

The Hindustan Times, March, 21, 2008.

Weiner, Myron, March-1982, "International Migration and Development". *Population and Development Review*, Vol. 8, No.1, p. 13

Weiner, Myron, March-1982, "International Migration and Development". *Population and Development Review*, Vol. 8, No. 1, p. 6.

Zachariah, K.C., Prakash, B.A., Rajan, S. Irudaya, 2002, Gulf Migration Study: Employment, Wages and Working Conditions of Kerala Emigrants in the United Arab Emirates, Working Paper No. 326, March, Centre for Development Studies Thiruvananthapuram.

13

Indian Diaspora in East Africa: Entrepreneurships and Philanthropy

Rajneesh Kumar Gupta

Introduction

A fundamental characteristic of people is their movement from one place to another place; anthropology has recorded nomadism as a stage preceding human settlement as communities. Even after their evolution as communities, throughout the civilisation, human beings have been experiencing temporary, seasonal or permanent migration from their original habitat either voluntarily or forced. Migration is closely related to a variety of socio-economic, demographic and political factors. People who migrate also carried their socio-cultural heritage with them and protect their distinguished identities. There is an increasing trend among scholars to study migrant communities having sense of their motherland and a differentiable identity, under the fabric of 'Study of Diaspora' or 'Diasporic Study'. Originally associated with *Jews* migration, term Diaspora has received acceptance to study such kind of migrant communities from any of the political boundary.

In his editorial preface to the first issue of Diaspora, Khachig Tololian writes, "the term (Diaspora) that once described Jewish, Greek, and Armenian dispersion now shares meanings with a larger semantic domain that includes words like immigrant, expatriate, refugee, guest-worker, exile community, overseas community, ethnic community." Encyclopedia of Diasporas gives a very broad and liberal definition of Diaspora, "a people dispersed by whatever cause to more than one location. The people dispersed to different lands may harbour thoughts of return, may not fully assimilate to their host countries, and may maintain relationship with other communities in the Diaspora." This study aims to study Indian Diaspora in East Africa with special focus on their entrepreneurship and philanthropy in their land of destiny.

Migration and Settlement

Traces of Indian migration to East African coast goes back to at least three thousand years. Blanche D'Souza in her book *Harnessing The Trade Winds: The Story of The Centuries-old Indian Trade With East Africa Using The Monsoon Winds* gives a detailed account of trading links existed between India and East Africa before beginning of recorded history through small sailing boats called *dhows* propelled by the *monsoon* winds (referred as trade winds) which continued throughout history. Since, movement of *dhows* were dependent on monsoon winds they had to stay in East African coast for several months. Thus, she argues that there is every reason to believe that migration and settlement of peoples from India to the East African coast is taking place since pre-historic times.

Similarly, Prof. Mangat points out that, in ancient period Indian merchants supplied cloth, beads and simple manufacturers to East Africa, in exchange for ivory, gold, gum copal, incense, and after the fourteenth century, slaves. The writing of the Venetian traveler, Marco Polo also produces proof of the trade relations between the Malabar Coast of West India and Zanzibar in East Africa in the time of his visit. At this point it is noteworthy that presence of Indians was not limited to coastal region, they also ventured inner-land. As Cynthia Salvadori writes –

"When Vasco da Gama sailed into Mombasa in 1498 he noted the presence of 'four vessels belong to Christians from

India', and it was a Badala Muslim pilot from Cutch whom da Gama encountered in Malindi who showed the pioneer Portuguese navigator the way to India. A Dutch traveller noted *'Mesticos'* (i.e. Goans) along with 'Portingales' in Mombasa in the 1580's. A Badala captain is recorded to have settled there in 1705; another Cutchi Muslim pilot was noted as being in the employ of the Sultan of Mombasa in the early 19th century. In the records of the brief Britisn Protectorate that captain Owen declared over Mombasa there are numerous references to the 'sizeable community of Indians (e.g. Muslims and Banyans)' then in the town".

However, migration and settlement of Indians in the region is certainly linked with the expansion of British colonialism in both regions. In 1841, British established consulate in Zanzibar, in 1872. They introduced a regular steamer service between Bombay and Zanzibar and a British Indian Post Office at Zanzibar. In 1873, Bombay High Court acquired appellate jurisdiction over British Indian subjects in Zanzibar. In the same year the control of Political relations with Zanzibar and of Consular appointment it was transferred from the Bombay government to the government of India. All the above development facilitated trade linkages and so free migration and settlement. By the year 1887, population of Indian settlers in East Africa reached 6345 and Business communities of India like Khojas, Bohras, Sindhis, Memans, Parsis etc., emerged richest and the most influential businessmen in the region.

Later, Indians migrated to East Africa as 'indentured labours' for the construction of 'Uganda Railway'. Final report of the Uganda Railway reveals that, although the number of Africans working on the railway never exceeded 2600, the total Indian employees rose from 3948 in 1896 to 6986 in 1897 and to 13003 in 1898, the high point occurred in March 1901 when 19742 Indians and 2506 Africans were employed. By Sep.1903, when the Uganda Railway committee was dissolved, 319883 indentured servants had been imported for work on the railway. Of these 16312 had been repatriated on the expiration of their contracts or through dismissal, 6454 had been invalided to India and 2493 had died (Table 1).

Table 1. Labourers on the Ugandan Railway, 1896-1903

Year ending June	*No. of Lab. Imp-orted to the End of the Year*	*No. of Locally Engaged Lab. At The end of the Year*	*No. reparti-cipated To end Of each Year*	*No. of Invali-ded Men to End of Each Year*	*No. of deaths to End of Each Year*	*Total Casualties To end of each Year*	*Av. No. of lab. through out Year*	*Av. No. of Effective Lab. in Year*
1896-1897	4269	1349	---*	200	121	321	3398	--*
1897-1898	7131	1372	--*	705	340	1045	6377	6085
1898-1899	15593	2509	773	1206	611	2590	11485	10365
1899-1900	23379	2690	2761	3424	1164	7349	17116	15350
1900-1901	31646	2506	4109	5811	1984	11904	20484	18853
1901-1902	31983	2335	9616	6354	2367	18337	19114	18154
1902-1903	31983	1865	16312	6454	2493	25259	12275	11725

* Detailed figures not available *Source:* P.P., Cd. 2164, Final Report of the Uganda Railway.

The importation of indentured Indians did not cease, with the completion of the trunk line from Mombasa to Kisumu in 1901 or the dissolution of the Railway Committee in 1903, Indians continued to be imported under contract until a new Indian emigration bill was enacted in March 1922. The most important factor, for the attraction of Indians in this period, was Indians who returned told stories of their vast opportunities in Africa and a certain number, together with friends and relatives, who could afford it, subsequently migrated at their own expense. The construction of the Uganda railway enhances opportunities, to extend their trade activities in land. Indian commercial men and petty traders of whose ancestors had traded along the coast for generations and financed the caravan trade with the interior followed the railway as it advanced towards the lake.

In 1939, the Asian population in East Africa exceeded 100,000. Their number had increased, both by a free flow of immigrants attracted to East Africa by prospects of economic betterment, and by natural growth estimated at two to three percent per annum. By 1948 Kenya had a population of about 97,000 Indians, Uganda 35,000, and Tanzania 62,000 the greatest proportionate increase since 1921 having occurred in Uganda. This trend was continued till the independence of these countries. Rattansi and Abdulla estimate that by 1963 the Asian population in East Africa was placed at 3,72,000 with the distribution between the three countries as follows: Kenya 1,80,000, Tanzania 1,10,000, and Uganda 82,000 - the rate of increase between 1948 and 1963 was on an average 4.2 per cent per annum.

In post independent period, Indian Diaspora faced tremendous crisis. Uganda's expulsion in the 1970s, Kenya's policy of discrimination and its 1982 riots and Tanzania's economic stagnation under anti capitalist policies have lead to a sharp reduction in the Indian population in East Africa. Indigenous debate in 1990s in the Tanzania has further created fear among Indians settled in that country. Due to unfavourable treatments in East African countries and better prospects available in other countries, especially in developed parts of the world many Indian settlers further migrated from East African countries. Nevertheless, migration from India to East

African countries has been a continuous phenomenon. As, Aparajita Biswas notes,

> "...There were two discernible trends towards the middle of 1970s. One was the expulsion of Asians from Uganda and the exodus from Kenya and Tanzania; the other was a sizeable fresh inflow of Indians into these very countries as well as several other developing countries of Asia and Africa. The new immigration was a result of growing demand for certain categories of middle- and high- level manpower and enterprising skills which were not available locally but could be located in South Asian countries. This demand rose considerably, and was backed by the projected developmental needs identified by Kenya and other neighbouring countries. Even President Idi Amin of Uganda had called back Indians. This migratory process gathered further momentum as the years rolled by as a result of which the Asian population in Kenya started swelling again. These were not businessman but professionals such as doctors, teachers, accountants who took assignments in Africa on contractual basis they were highly educated and hailed from different parts of India."

Some years back *The Analyst* (a Kenyan magazine) reported, "While official figures show that only 1918 (731, 703 and 484, respectively) work permits were issued between 1995 and 1997, unconfirmed reports state that between 30,000 and 40,000 immigrant workers from the Asian sub-continents have entered Kenya in the past four years. Continuation of migration is also evident in the survey conducted by author in various parts of Kenya. Total 99 per cent of the respondents stated about their citizenship. Out of those 99 per cent, 64 per cent of the respondents were Kenyan citizens, 21 per cent, Indian citizens and rest 15 per cent were citizens of other countries. In the citizens of other countries category majority of them were British passport holders but in this category small segment of USA, Australia and Tanzania is also included.

Findings of the survey are further supported by latest available data on Indian overseas communities. If we compare data provided by the High Level Committee on Indian Diaspora

(2001) and data of Ministry of Overseas Indian Affairs (2011) can clearly observe ongoing migration of Indian communities in East Africa. In 2001, total size of Indian Diaspora in the region was placed at about 2,04,500 out of those 1,77,000 were PIO's, 25,000 NRI and 2,500 stateless. According to current estimates total strength of Indian Diaspora in the region is 1,49,700. Though, in absolute term diasporic strength has declined but it is mainly due to further migration of PIOs, as now there are only 91,900 PIOs. Contrary to this number of NRIs has grown to 57,800.

Contributions to the Country of Adoption

Peoples of Indian Origin in East Africa, constitute a tiny minority and their total population do not exceeds even 0.5 per cent of the total population in either of the countries of East Africa. They have migrated in different capacities and in different bursts and do not form a homogenous group. In-spite of this diversity one thing is common among all PIO's and that is their contributions to the land of their new destiny. They have contributed positively to every stratum of East African economy, polity and society. They participated in national movement and made significant contribution in the nation building process. The success stories of entrepreneurs are legendary and they are playing a key role in industrialisation process of these countries. From hi-tech manufacturing industries to traditional restaurants, from renowned hospitals to famous educational institutions, from popular games to leading think-tanks -everywhere contributions of PIO's is visible which, is an obvious result of skill, dedication and hard work. Nevertheless, Indian Diaspora has shared their economic prosperity for the socio-economic welfare of their land of destiny through philanthropic activities. Let us concentrate on their entrepreneurship and philanthropic activities.

Entrepreneurship

There have been divergent views with regards to economic role of Indian Diaspora. While, people like Idi-Amin have bitterly criticised Asians in general and Indian Diaspora in particular on account of its exploitative nature towards local people and economy; on the other hand scholars such as J K

Jhaberi, Nitin Mehta, Prof. Bihari Lal etc., have fairly appreciated the role of Indian Diaspora. There have been number of arguments and counter arguments regarding their economic contributions, but it is un-doubtful that Indians are considered an economically affluent community having entrepreneurship skill and expertise. It would be appropriate to take a look on economic history of Indian Diaspora to analyse their entrepreneurship in East Africa. Broadly speaking, in-spite of the ancient trade links between India and East Africa, Indian settlement increased rapidly only with the beginning of construction of Ugandan railway. Viewing from this perspective any analysis of economic contribution must start with the beginning of construction work of Ugandan railway. In almost two centuries of the Indian settlement, we see five distinct patterns in economic history of Indian Diaspora in the region-indentured labours, *dukwallah* (petty shopkeepers), economic elite, small scale industrialists and in present context their engagement in vivid occupations.

Indentured Labours : In the late nineteenth century as the British assumed the control of the interior parts of East Africa, the Indians were given important part in the development of East Africa. The founders of the British East Africa company-Sir William Mackinnon, Sir Donald Stewart, Sir John Kirk, William Burdctto Coutts, Robert Palmer Harding and George S. Mackenzie- thought that the East Africa would provide an outlet for India's surplus population. Thus, when construction plan of railway line finalized, human resource available in India was an obvious choice of colonial officer to fill up lack of skilled and semi-skilled human resources in East Africa. Even Sir Harry Johnston described East Africa as a possible '*America of the Hindu*', or contemplate the growth of Entebbe as the future Calcutta, a new capital on the Mau plateau as the Simla, Mombasa as the Bombay and Fort Portal as the Darjeeling of the new East African Empire'.

However, construction of the railways was not an easy job; indentured labours faced many hardships and dangers. Soon after the beginning of work in the humid coastal lowlands, they suffered from malaria, jiggers, dysentery, scurvy and various liver complaints. In the early years, fifty percent of the Indians contracted malaria. Often an average of 10 percent of the labour force was on the sick list. Despite of these difficulties Indian indentured labours were able to complete the 572-mile long railway. It will be interesting to quote Sir Charles Eliot who has acknowledged, important role of Indian indentured labours in these words:

> "The railway was built almost entirely by coolies brought over from India; and though the cost of transport and of providing the food to which men were accustomed was considerable, I do not think the necessary labour could have been provided in any other way. After nearly nine years the natives have become so far familiarised with the railway, and the idea of working for Europeans, that they are able to perform the class of work required for maintenance; but it may be doubted even if now they could be used for purpose of construction and it certainly was out for the question when the railway commenced. The jungle which surrounded the first part of the line is particularly uninhabited and to have brought labour down from Uganda would probably have been a more lengthy and difficult task than to bring it from India, to say nothing of difference in efficiency".

Dukawalla : Indians came to East African coast as traders long before the European colonizers. But unlike colonial powers, they were content to barter goods and return to their homeland. The permanent settlement of Indians began with the construction of Ugandan Railway; petty merchants who were spread all along the railway lines or moved to newly established posts. 'These may be called the real founders of the Indian commercial enterprises in the interior of East Africa, who helped to create trade, initially in a small way, and than in a large way; in areas where none had existed before. With considerable fortitude and perseverance against all kinds of odds, they pioneered the establishment of '*dukas*' (derived from the Gujarati word '*Dukan*' means a shop), local trading centers and bazaars in different localities. The introduction of a variety of imported items to the local population and later on the rupee as currency provided incentives for greater production as well as a transition from barter to money based economy.

For several years "*dukawallah*" had to pave his way through very trying and tough conditions indeed. There were no proper transport facilities and only a patchwork of footpaths leading to the interior African habitats. Some of African tribes were still considered to be dangerous by the unfamiliar strangers and above all diseases and death were commonplace. Malaria, Black water fever, Plague, Sleeping sickness were the most dreaded diseases and were widespread. They went to the unknown areas and settled in isolated areas in order to start trade with strange and primitive natives who mostly had no previous knowledge of money and trade. Despite of these circumstances a "*dukawallah*" carried the mechanism of monetary economy in the interior to create new methods in the process; he introduced a set of new values of mark for money, to produce for the market, to cultivate economic crops and to manufacture other goods not merely for exports but also for the expanding domestic market.

Since the Indian '*dukawallah*' or shopkeeper was a characteristics feature of townships and urban centers throughout East Africa for the decades, it is necessary to say something about it. To a typical "*dukawallah*' living in a remote township, life offers few excitements, and hard work pays little compensation. The working day was long, usually starting at 7 a.m. and continued late till the evening. The shopkeeper, who generally used to live in a small brick house adjoining his shop, and will typically be helped in his chores by his relatives; but he may barely manage to save enough for his children's education or for his daughter's dowry. Life in the township offers few amenities; there is very little by way of organised recreation and entertainment. The tedium of enforced leisure may partly and occasionally be relieved by social calls on the few Indian families in the neighborhood. But, in general, there is little colour or variety in his dreary routine.

Economic Elite : From ancient period, Indians links with East Africa were mostly for the purpose of trade. These links acquired new dimensions by the construction of Ugandan Railway and aftermath. Further economic depression after First World War, gave new opportunities to Indian business communities in the region. The first two decades of the twentieth century witnessed a rapid growth of the Indian role in the interior of East Africa based on the twin foundations of the middle level employment and commercial enterprises.

Though, Indians were still characterised as '*dukawallah*' living in remote parts of the country. Today their main economic contribution is the supply of middle level manpower and of capital. This combination of capital and technical know how in one section of the population is a great potential asset to the economy. According to Guy Hunter's estimates, in mid 1961 there were 67,500 skilled persons in East Africa, divided into two categories: the first consisted of just over 18,000 professional men of graduate or equivalent level, senior administrators and senior managers in commerce and industry; and the second category covered about 49,500 in the next layer of skilled manpower, including technicians and sub-professional grades (for example, the second echelon in agricultural extension work), executive grades in the civil service, middle management in industry and commerce and teachers with secondary education but without a University degree. Hunter's estimates shows that Asians provide a little less than forty percent of the population in category I, and about fifty percent of those in category II, in the whole of East Africa. There were small numbers of business families, such as Mehtas, Madvanis, Mainis and Hindochas of Uganda and the Karimjee and Jivanjees of Tanzania who were rich by world standards. There were also some top professionals (specialist, doctors and lawyers) who also belonged to this category.

The booming economy, rising employment opportunities, particularly in the middle-level skilled labour roles, the high saving propensity and consequent reinvestment by Asian business and their expansion led to an expanding demand for goods supplied by such businesses. Expanding income also gave rise to some manufacturing industries and with the increase in middle level labour market needs; the Asians filled these. This created a virtuous circle of expanding industries for Asians. Nevertheless there were some Asians, who were excluded from these improvements. These were members of the large families with low or negative saving propensities, thus the economic picture of the Indians in the early sixties as the East African territories advanced towards independence was a mixed one.

Small Scale industrialist : After independence, measures taken by successive governments in East African countries largely prevented Asian communities to venture in remote areas. They were discouraged to purchase agricultural land or conduct business in the remote areas. As a result the Asian community people migrated to the urban areas in these countries. Further, retail shops of certain commodities were reserved for native people. In these circumstances Indian Diaspora moved towards small scale industries for their livelihood. Because of their predominance in commerce and their knowledge of African market, Indian communities were in a position to explore new opportunities and over come with the Africanisation policy of successive governments.

Indravadan Chandaria's study (1962) of fifty-eight manufacturing enterprises with over fifty employees reveals that 67.2 per cent of these companies were owned by Indians, 24.1 per cent by Europeans, 5.2 per cent by interracial partnership, and 3.4 per cent by international firms. David Himbara conducted a survey of one hundred manufacturing enterprises in Kenya in the year of 1989-90. Findings of his survey demonstrates that almost two-thirds (63 per cent) of the manufacturing firms sampled in 1989-90 had been established since 1970; almost four-fifths had been established since 1960. 71 per cent of manufacturing companies established before independence belonged to PIO's. In 1960s the proportion established by PIO's increased to 79 per cent; in 1970s it fell down to 70 per cent; in 1980s it rose sharply to 85 per cent. For the years 1964-1990 as a whole share of new manufacturing companies owned by PIO's was 78 per cent; while from 1977 (when East African Common Market collapsed) to 1990 the proportion rises to 84 per cent. Figures of the overall result in the various period of growth (since independence to 1990) shows that PIO's owns 75 per cent in all manufacturing companies and 73 per cent of the manufacturing companies with over one hundred workers. They own 86 per cent of manufacturing companies with a capital of over Kenyan Shs 100 million. His survey also studied ownership of the companies in the sample which were in financial or mismanagement difficulties (i.e. under receivership) in 1989 and 1990 and found no PIO's owned companies in this category. Findings of Himbara's survey indicates that while the role of PIO's in commerce and industries has continued to increase, the performance of private Africans and state parastatals has ranged from mediocre to total failure.

Now, Indian Diaspora is a major stakeholder in the small scale industries of East African countries. A survey conducted by Vijaya Ramachandran and Manju Kedia Shah on enterprises ownership in five African countries also reveals the fact that minority communities own more industries then indigenous people (Graph-1).

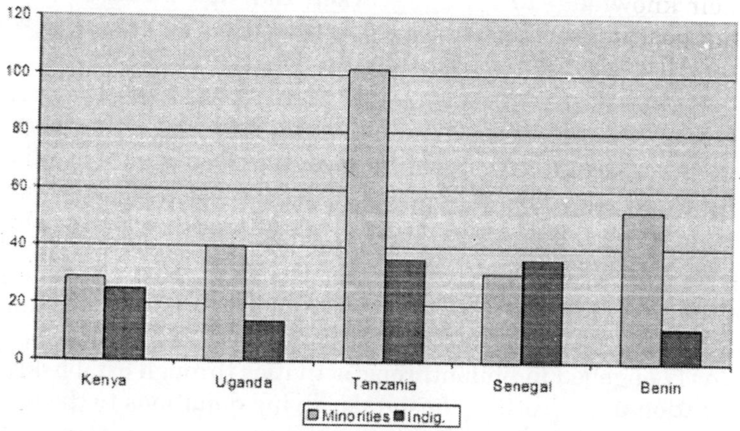

Graph-1. Ownership of Industries- Indigenous vs. Minorities

Source: Ramachandran Vijay and Manju Kedia Shah, *Why Are There So Few Black-Owned Firms in Africa?*

Present Context- It is a common notion that Indian Diaspora in East Africa is an economically affluent community engaged in trade and industries. However, contrary to general belief Indian community in East Africa is not a monolithic homogenous community. It is true that some of the pioneer industrialists of East Africa belongs to ethnic Indian community but since there arrival in the region there has been huge diversity in their occupation. Robert G. Gregory provides detailed analysis of occupation of the economically active Asians in East Africa during the period of 1957-62. He observes that apart from businesses, Indians were also engaged in agriculture, government and private jobs and a large section was getting livelihood by providing services such as plumber, manual worker, electrician, teaching and so on. Findings of my own survey regarding livelihood of Indian communities in East Africa have been indicated in Graph-2.

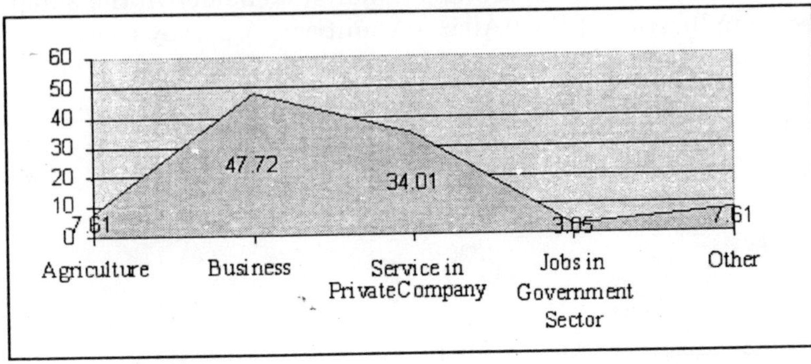

Graph-2. Occupation of Indian Diaspora

Philanthropy

Literally, 'philanthropy' means 'love of mankind', which involves service of humanity as per capacity of individual or group. Philanthropy has been an integral part of the Indian way of life. People of Indian Origin in East Africa have been actively engaged in philanthropic activities through establishing educational institutions, hospitals, giving donations to the poor and needy people and providing relief in natural or manmade calamities. It would be noteworthy to quote Robert G. Gregory's remark on philanthropic activities of Indian Diaspora-

> "Unlike in Western societies, where philanthropy, at least in the industrial age, has been associated with a relatively few, affluent members of society, philanthropy among the Asians tended to be general through the society. It was not confined to any one religious community, nor to people in any distinct level of capital accumulation. On the whole, it was practiced by both rich and poor. It was as though everyone had assumed an obligation to give, and to give according to his means. Thus, Asian philanthropy is explained not so much by factors that determined the unique motivation of individuals, as by those that affected the society as a whole."

Education: The first and foremost among philanthropic

endeavors of the Indian Diaspora, is their contribution to the promotion of education in East Africa. Initially the Indian Diaspora established their own community schools to educate their children in accordance with their own cultural ethos, as colonial educational setup was inadequate and unsuitable for them. Later, they started admitting children of indigenous communities as well. Now, Schools like Arya Boy's School, Arya Girl's school, Shree Sanatan Dharm School, Ismaili School, Goan School, Khalsa school, Allidina Visram High School, Aga Khan Academy etc., are primarily established and funded by Indian Diaspora and they are providing cheap and quality education to the children of Indian Diaspora as well as to children of indigenous people.

During the establishment of University of Nairobi, Indian Diaspora were major contributor in terms of funds as well as intellectual resources. In-fact proposal to establish a university for providing higher education to citizens of East Africa first mooted by Indian Diaspora, leading industrialist Nanji Kalidas Mehta wholeheartedly supported this idea and expressed his view that:

> "We should go in for a scheme of East African University to commemorate the name of Mahatma Gandhi...There could be no discrimination. Indians, Africans, Arabs, Europeans and in fact any person who calls himself or herself an East African citizen should have full freedom to avail of this facility".

Apart from this, Indian Diaspora have established libraries such as Desai Memorial Library, Asian-African Heritage Trust Library, Oshwal Library, East African Ramgarhia Board Library etc., in various parts of East Africa with the substantial collection of books and other resources which are being used by PIO's as well as indigenous people.

Medical facilities: It is a well established fact that healthy citizens lead to prosperous nation. Health is duly regarded as an important criterion of the development. The Human Development Index (HDI), released by United Nations Development Programme on yearly basis considers health in three most important segments of human development. Adequate medical facilities are the foremost necessity to maintain good health of the people. These consist of establishment of well equipped hospitals, availability of skilled doctors and other medical staffs, and costs of medical care in the reach of ordinary citizens. Contribution of Indian Diaspora is noticeable in every aspect of adequate medical facilities.

To provide proper and affordable medical facilities they are running various hospitals, dispensaries and clinics such as M.P. Shah Hospital, Aga Khan Hospital, Parkland Nursing Home, Pandya Memorial clinic, Guru Nanak Hospital, etc. In these hospitals qualified medical staffs take care of health of the people and majority of the beneficiary are indigenous people. Ethnic organisations of Indian Diaspora like Hindu Council of Kenya, Ramgarhia Youth Club, Associations of Ismaili Khojas and believers of Agha Khan also organize Free Health Camps on different occasions.

Relief works and other charity activities : In case of any calamity Indian Diaspora undertake voluntary services and often reach to victims to provide them relief. Here two of such examples can be cited, the first is linked with manmade calamity and second is related to a natural calamity. In August 1998, ethnic Indians organised "All Africa Hindu Conference" in Nairobi, as the opening session was underway on 7th August, news came that there is a major bomb blast in the city centre of Nairobi at American Embassy. Organizers got together and suspended further programmes of All Africa Hindu Conference and diverted all attention to the national tragedy. Immediately all food that was prepared for the participants of the conference were taken to the bombsite to help the rescuers. A 24-hour food centre was set up immediately and people were immediately requested to donate blood as the extent of this blast became apparent. In 2006, when Kenya was facing severe famine situation Hindu Council of Kenya launched "Food for Education Programme" and reached over 2,00,000 children within a period of eight weeks and with the collaboration of Eagle Foundation, Switzerland distributed 400 tones of highly nutritious food. It would be appropriate to quote President of Kenya Mr. Kibaki's appropriation to the charitable work of Dr. Manu Chandaria that is equally important for the philanthropic activities of PIO's in general:

"...I am particularly gratified that Dr. Chandaria continues to, actively support charitable causes, including assisting destitute children, the sick and disabled. I would like to mention, in particular, his support for my Government's efforts at settling street families. As Chairman of the Street Families Rehabilitation Trust Fund, and the Watoto Kwanza Trust, he will no doubt continue to work, with us to solve the eyesore of begging children on our streets. Finally, I must mention that no one can succeed on his own. The support from family members and the community is crucial. Often, however, this may go unnoticed to the casual observer. The Chandaria family started from humble beginnings, but due to strong family discipline and hard work, they have succeeded in business. Their interests have spread out beyond East Africa, to other regions. This clearly shows that hard work and discipline pays."

Conclusion

Indians have enjoyed a long association with East Africa. Despite of age old linkages, modern settlement of Indians in the region is certainly linked with the colonial exploration of the region. In the colonial period migration occurred in both ways- by force as well as by choice. These people went with limited resources and physical and climatic conditions of the region were usually very difficult. However, all those hardships were proven gnome with the courage, hard work and dedication of Indian Diaspora. Entrepreneurship skills made them an economic affluent community from 'indenture labour' or petty shopkeepers as they were labelled during the time of migration. Nevertheless, they have shared their economic prosperity for the well being of their fellows in the land of destiny. Philanthropic work undertaken by Indian Diaspora has not only got due recognition of local people and government but have also prompted the attention of scholars all across the world.

Notes

1. Tololian Khachig, "The Nation State and its Others: In Lieu of a Preface" *Diaspora*, Vol. 1, No. 1, (1991), pp. 4-5.

2. Melvin Ember, Carol R. Ember and Ian Skoggard (eds.), *Encyclopedia of Diasporas*, (Yale: Yale University Press 2005), p. xxvi.

3. Mangat, J.S., *A History of the Asians in East Africa c. 1886 to 1945,* (London: Oxford University Press, 1969), p. 1.

4. The book of Ser Marco Polo tr. Henry Yule (London: 1903), pp.411-12. Cited in, Tirmizi S.A.I., *Indian Sources of African History* (New Delhi: South Asia Books, 1988), p. 9

5. Salvadori Cynthia, *Through Open Doors-A View of Asian Culture in Kenya* (Nairobi: Kenway Publications, 1989), pp. 7-8.

6. Gregory Robert G., *The Rise and Fall of Philanthropy in East Africa* (New Jersey: Transaction Publishers, 1992), p. 18.

7. Morris, H.S., *The Indians in Uganda* (London: Garden City Press 1968), p. 9.

8. Mangat, J.S., No. 3, p. 140.

9. Rattansi P. and M. Abdulla, "An Educational Survey" in Ghai Dharam P. (ed.), *Portrait of a minority Asians in East Africa*, (Nairobi: Oxford University Press, 1965), pp. 127-28.

10. This survey was conducted by author during June-July 2007.

11. *Report of the High Level Committee on the Indian Diaspora* (New Delhi: ICWA, 2001), p. 94.

12. *Estimated Number of Overseas Indians,* Ministry of Overseas Indian Affairs, Government of India (www.moia.gov.in accessed on 24 July 2011).

13. Mangat, J.S., no. 3, p. 63.

14. McDermott P.L., *British East Africa or IBEA* (London: 1893). Cited in Robert G. Gregory, *India and East Africa: A History of Race Relations within the British Empire, 1890-1939*, (London: Oxford University Press, 1971), p. 55.

15. Eliot C., *East Africa Protectorate*, (London: Frank Cass and Co. Ltd, 1966), p. 215.

16. Desai N., 'Asian influence in East Africa', in J.K. Motwani, Mahin Gosine and J.B. Motwani (eds.), *Global Indian Diaspora Yesterday, Today and Tomorrow* (New York: GOPIO, 1993), p. 127.

17. Ramchandani R.R., *Uganda Asians: The End of an Enterprise*, (Bombay: United Asia Publications, 1976), pp. 89-90.

18. Ghai D.P. and Y.P. Ghai, 'Asians in East Africa: Problems and Prospects', in Anirudha Gupta (ed.), *Indians Abroad: Asia and Africa*, (New Delhi: Orient Longman, 1971), p. 194.

19. *Ibid.*, p. 195
20. Gupta D, "South Asians in East Africa: Achievement and Discrimination", *South Asia* Vol. XXI, Special Issue, (1998), p. 128.
21. Indravadan Chndaria, *The Development of Entrepreneurship in Kenya*, B.A. Thesis, Department of Economics, (Harvard: 1963). Cited in David Himbara, *Kenyan Capitalists, the State and Development*, (Nairobi: East African Educational Publishers Limited, 1994), p. 44.
22. David Himbara, Ibid. pp. 45-51.
23. Ramachandran Vijay and Manju Kedia Shah, *Why Are There So Few Black-Owned Firms in Africa?*, (Washington DC: Centre for Global Development, Working Paper Number 104, January 2007), p. 4.
24. Gregory Robert G., No.6, pp. 21-25.
25. *Ibid.*, p. 206.
26. *Ibid.*, p. 127.
27. ________*Virat Hindu Samagam Souvenir*, (Nairobi: HCK, 14 January 2007), pp. 61-64.
28. Kibaki M, President of Kenya, speech July 2003 at Oshwal Centre Nairobi, published in *Awaaz*, Issue II, (2003), p. 7.

14

Indian South Africans: Political Affiliations in the Post Apartheid Era

Ruchita Beri

The people of Indian origin in South Africa or the "Indian South Africans" (ISA) as they would prefer to be called have a long history. There appear to be differing accounts of the arrival on the Indians on the South African shores. Some South African historians like Dr. Cyril Hromnik, claim that Indians had settled in southern Africa more than two thousand years ago. Also in his view the term "Bantu" is derived from the Sanskrit word *Bandhu* (friend) that the Indians used for their African helpers. Studies on slavery in South Africa conducted by scholars from Britain, United States and South Africa have shown that Indians constituted a large proportion of the slave population at the Cape in the 17th century.[1] They were mainly from the coastal region of Bengal, Malabar and the Coromandal in India and were brought to the Cape of Good Hope by the Dutch in the 1650s. These findings challenge the claim that Indians arrived in South Africa only in the 1860s. Though it is true that the maximum number of Indians were brought as indentured labourers in the Natal province of South Africa by the Natal government between 1860 and 1911. Around 105,529 Indians arrived as indentured labourers during this period on a five years contract. It is believed that around fifty percent of these chose to stay after their contracts expired. There was another stream of Indians that migrated to South Africa. These people who paid their fare for the passage to

South Africa and have been often referred as the "passenger Indians". The "passenger Indians" were mainly traders and professionals. Most of the Indians settled in the Natal province and established small businesses and shops. Some of them migrated to Transvaal province after discovery of gold in Witswatersrand.

Today the majority of the Indian South Africans who were born in South Africa regard it as their home. There are around 1.2 million people of Indian origin in South Africa and they form 2.5 percent of the total South African population. Thus, within South Africa they are an ethnic minority. Politically, there is a long history of collaboration and support between the ANC and Natal and Transvaal Indian Congress in the apartheid era.[2] Indians and Africans fought together against the apartheid rule. Over the year's number of prominent Indians like Yusuf Dadoo, Monty Naicker, Yusuf Chachalia, Cassim Anwar Ahmed Kathrada, Ismail Meer, Mac Maharaj, and Fatima Meer were part of the larger alliance with the ANC. However in the post apartheid era apparently there has been a shift in the support of the Indians for the ANC. It has been reported that generally the Indians have voted against the ANC in the 1994 and 1999 elections.[3] It seems in the 1994 elections most of the Indians voted for the National Party while in 1999 elections the Indian votes shifted towards the Democratic Party and the Minority front. This study will explore and analyse the political affiliations of the ISA in the post apartheid era.[4]

Pattern of Political Support

Since the triumph of democracy South Africa has been the focus of much of media and academic attention for the last ten years. There are a number of empirical debates on the nature of voting behaviour in South Africa.[5] They are either based on the reported voting pattern during the national elections or public opinion polls. So what is the pattern of the reported Indian vote during the 1994 and 1999 elections? We can draw a number of conclusions from Table 1. First, that Indians appeared to have split the votes between the White and the black parties in both the elections. Second and more importantly, the ANC does not have overwhelming support of the Indians. In the 1994 elections 24% of the Indians voted for the ANC while in the 1999 elections there was a slight increase to 30%.

Table 1: ISA Reported vote 1994 and 1999 Elections (%)

Party	*1994*	*1999*
"White" Parties	50	34
Democratic Party	0	18
National Party	50	16
Other White	0	0
"African" Parties	42	30
African National Congress	25	30
Inkatha Freedom Party	17	0
Other African	0	0
Other	8	36

Source: Table based on Ferree (2004).

A look at Table 2 makes it abundantly clear that ISA voting intentions depict similar trend overtime.

Table 2: ISA Voting Intentions

	Sep / Oct 1994	*Apr -99*	*Jul / Aug 2000*	*Sep / Oct 2002*
ANC	28	10	14	18
NNP	51	34	30	11
DP/DA		16	21	10
MF		7	11	2
FF		1	4	2
ACDP		0	4	0
AMP		0	4	3
UDM		2	2	0
UCDP		0	1	0
IFP		1	0	0
OTHER	3	2	0	0
UNDECIDED	0	16	0	14
WOULD NOT VOTE	6	1	0	30
REFUSED TO ANSWER	12	10	2	10

Source: *Afrobarometer* Briefing Paper No.6 July 2003.

The ANC appears to have gained some popularity by October 2002 and has emerged as the leading party amongst the ISA voters for the first time. However its support within the ISA has gone down from 28% in Sept/Oct 1994 to 18% in 2002. Further it is important to note that about 54% of the Indian voters are in the "undecided" or "would not vote" category. What is the reason for these changing political affiliations? Why is the ANC not so popular? There are various arguments/ factors to explain this situation.

Racial Credentials of the Party

Race has often been seen as a predictor of elections in South Africa. So much so that the elections are referred as a "racial census." Which suggests voters had in fact affirmed their ethnic identity through voting. If this logic is followed then Africans should vote for the ANC because they see the ANC as an exclusive "African" party and whites should vote for the Democratic Party (DP) / Democratic Alliance (DA) because they see DP/DA as exclusive "white parties". Similarly Indians should vote for Minority Front (MF) because they see it as an exclusive "Indian" party. Is that really the case with the Indians? A close look at both Tables 1 and 2 shows that in the case of the Indians, race does not appear to be predictive of voting behaviour. Generally they have split the votes across parties supported by whites (like the NNP and DP) and the parties supported by the Africans (ANC, IFP). While the Indians do have the option of supporting an exclusively Indian party i.e. the Minority Front, they have not opted to do so in large numbers. Further, surveys done by IDASA in 1994 and 1999 indicate that most Africans perceive that the ANC is an inclusive party representing the interests of all in South Africa. Similarly whites perceive DP and NP/NNP as parties representing all in South Africa. Thus, it appears that most of the South Africans are not overly interested in affirming their racial identities through political parties at election time and that they support the parties that are inclusive.

How do you explain the South African more particularly the ISA voting behaviour? Ferree argues that though race does not play an important role in the sense that while South African do not see the parties they support as their exclusive racial representative but they hold racialised views of other parties.[6] Thus while Africans perceive ANC as an exclusive party- 100 % Indians associate it with Africans and 85 % of whites associate it with Africans.[7] The same holds true for the NP/NNP and DP. While most whites and many Indians view the NP/NNP as inclusive, Africans viewed it as exclusive in racial terms representing interest of the whites.[8] If we follow this argument then the reason why Indians did not vote for ANC was because they perceived it as representing the African interest and supported NNP and DP because they perceived these parties would represent their interest.

Material Issues and Interests

While racial credentials of the party may have influenced the voters, there are other material issues that affected the Indian South Africans voting pattern. Most of the political parties in South Africa and the media have assumed the Indian vote as homogenous. However, an elaborate study on Indian and coloured voting pattern has revealed that this was far from the truth.[9] There appears to be a significant heterogeneity within the Indian community. Further there was a distinct correlation between income categories and voting behaviour of the Indian South Africans.[10] For example, Habib and Naidu argue that in Indian residential areas like Phoenix and Chatsworth in Kwazulu Natal province where the majority of residents had an average household income of less than Rs. 2,500 were decisively won by the DP and the NNP. On the other hand, in areas like Lenesia in Gauteng province where the average household income was more than Rs. 2,500 the ANC did well. Traditionally the blue-collared workers and the poorer support the parties to the left while the middle class and more privileged class support the parties to the right of the political spectrum. This logic when applied to South Africa would imply that the ANC receive the support of the working class and DA and NP receive that of the middle and upper class. However, Habib and Naidu argue that in case of the South African Indian community this logic has been reversed. The more privileged section of the community has voted for the ANC while the under privileged votes have gone to white parties like DA and NP.

This trend has emerged primarily due to two sets of policies followed by the ANC government in the post apartheid era.

Affirmative action

The ANC government has launched the policy of affirmative action, aimed at redressing the apartheid-induced imbalances in South Africa's work places. While it is true that affirmative action is necessary to correct past discriminatory policies unfortunately it is perceived to have a negative impact on lower income Indian communities. These groups were in a weak position because of their lower levels of skill, education and training. As a result they have often been replaced in their place of employment when their companies/ institutions are under pressure to enforce the " black empowerment" policy. By contrast the affirmative action policies have less impact on the upper income persons of Indian origin. The main reason for this is because this group of people are either self- employed or have higher skills that make their replacement impossible. This category of Indians have flourished in the post apartheid era and apparently their annual incomes have risen exponentially after 1994.

Neo liberal Macro Economic policy

The ANC before coming to power in 1994 had espoused the macro economic policy of growth through redistribution. The Reconstruction and Development Programme (RDP) plan launched in 1994 outlined a nation –building strategy driven by the public investment to meet basic human needs. It promised housing, sanitation, health care and education for South Africa's long disenfranchised majority. However, the government discarded these policies in favour of a neo liberal economic policy that has resulted in higher levels of unemployment, restricted economic opportunities to the poor.[11] Critics argue that the Growth Employment and Redistribution (GEAR) policy, which replaced the RDP in 1996, militates against redistribution.[12] It aims to improve economic growth by lowering restrictions on capital movement to and from South Africa and by lifting protection on the local companies so that global corporations can compete with local companies as equals. However this has not led to the improvement of the conditions of the poor even more people live in destitution now compared to 1994. Therefore the working class communities are pitted against each other over the declining economic opportunities. An Afrobarometer survey, "The Public agenda" done by the Institute for Democracy in South Africa (IDASA) done in 2002 indicated that unemployment was the most important challenge facing South Africa, across all races - 78% of the Indians, 86% blacks, 85% coloured and and 75% whites.[13] While the blacks/ Africans are still optimistic about their future and trust the ANC in its promises, the Indians have lost hope and are feeling doubly vulnerable as a result of these policies. The political parties like DA, NNP and MF have in the past capitalised on this state of affairs and promised different ways to protect minority interests.

Crime in South Africa

This fight for economic opportunities has also led to increase in crime in South Africa. Violent crime appears to be one of the most debatable issues in South Africa. This debate is often coloured by race, statistical manipulation, extreme secrecy and political rhetoric. It is an issue that the media has kept alive. The crux of the matter is that the South African crime rates are among the highest in the world. Crime was one of the most contentious issues in the recent elections in South Africa. The present government led by President Mbeki has claimed that the number of homicides has come down since the 1990s. This claim is based on the latest crime statistics churned out by the South African Police Service (SAPS).[14] The statistics show that the rate of murders has gone down from around 52 per 100,000 citizens in 1994 to 47 per 100, 000 citizens in 2002.[15] Nevertheless the situation continues to be grim. While South Africa is no longer the murder capital of the world, it is still comparable to the most dangerous urban are in United States, Washington D.C. However, the police statistics are often considered to be unreliable. Primarily due to the fact that the statistics from the ten worst affected areas still continue to be a secret.[16] A supplement to the police statistics is the National victims survey. The latest National Victims Survey collated by the Institute for Security Studies (ISS), Pretoria, suggests that 53 percent South Africans feel that the crime has increased in the last three years.[17]

More alarming is the statistics related to the people of Indian origin. Around 32% of Indian South Africans felt they were "very unsafe" walking in their neighbourhood in the day time as opposed to 4% Africans.[18] Similarly, another survey done by the Institute for Democracy in South Africa (Idasa) called the Afrobarometer survey reports that 57 % of the Indians feel that crime and security was a challenge to South Africa *vis- a- vis* 25 % of the Africans. Why do the Indian South Africans feel so?

It appears that the Indian community at large feels that they are targets of a hate campaign and that has resulted in the increase in crime against them. This is particularly true in the Kwazulu Natal province. Incidents like the release of an anti Indian song by controversial playwright Mbogeni Ngema in 2002 have fuelled negative feelings against the Indians. In this song called "Amandiya", Ngema calls for "strong brave men to confront Indians" and says that " Indians have conquered Durban- we are poor because they have been taken by Indians" and he also claimed that whites are better than Indians".[19] While Ngema withdrew his song he was defiant saying problems existed between Indians and Africans. Specially focusing on economic success of the Indians he says, " In the major towns of Kwa Zulu Natal shops are owned by Indians". However, he stressed that the song was meant to stimulate discussion around Indian - African relations and to promote reconciliation between the two groups. The song drew extreme reactions from the Indian community. Sociologist and author of President Nelson Mandela's biography, Professor Fatima Meer of the Institute for black research dismissed the song as a " disgusting bit of racist diatribe which has no truth to it"[20]

The South African politicians have tried to water down the controversy. Veteran Indian politician Amichand Rajbhansi leader of the Minority Front in Kwazulu-Natal, conceded that there was widespread suspicion among Indians that the cold blooded killings in Chatsworth was motivated by Ngema's song. "There is widespread anger in the community" he said.[21] However, he was loath to link the killings to the song. "Africans are also being killed by the criminal elements in our society, so we should refrain from attaching a racial tag to these incidents," he said. The then Inkatha freedom party's agriculture minister in Kwazulu Natal, Narend Singh, echoed his views. He did not believe that "the song had anything to do with the attacks on the Indians," and that "people of all races were being attacked and killed."[22] Mitholephi Mthimku provincial spokesperson of the African National Congress in Kwalulu Natal too dismissed the linkage.

However most of the residents of Chatsworth feel otherwise. Ron Reddy, a prominent personality in Chatsworth remains convinced that the upsurge in attacks against Indians is linked to the song. He feels that incidents attacks against Indians have become commonplace following the release of the song.[23] Some Indian South African academicians support this view. They fear that the illiteracy among the Africans, a legacy of the apartheid rule, is responsible for the rise in these attacks.24 Most of the Africans may not understand the intentions that Ngema claims behind writing the song and may interpret it literally as a license to kill Indians.

Another reason for the escalation of crime against Indians has been the influx of Africans from the neighbouring countries. These migrants have entered the borders of South Africa and set up squatter camps in Indian neighbourhoods. The opposition parties particularly the Democratic Party and the National Party have played on the Indian fears. Their campaigns have focused on the rise of crime against the Indians, giving a racist angle to it.[25]

Inkatha Freedom Party (IFP)/ Buthelezi Factor

The ISA anti- ANC stance can also be explained by the fear of reprisal from the IFP. It appears ISA have been caught in the power struggle between the Xhosa dominated ANC and the Zulu led IFP in the Kwazulu natal province. As explained earlier most of the Indians live in the Kwazulu Natal province, the stronghold of IFP. The Indians have resisted voting for ANC for the fear of retribution from the Zulus in the province. Traditionally the Zulus in the province are diehard supporters of the IFP. While the Zulus residing in the urban areas out side the province have supported the ANC. The IFP chief Gatsha Buthelezi is perceived as anti-ISA.[26] Buthelezi has alienated the ISA by his "hostile references to the activities of the Indian politicians and organisations and has warned the Indian community not to forget the events of 1949"; referring to the appalling anti-Indian Durban riots.[27] In 1949, riots broke out between Indians and Africans, almost 142 people (87 African and 50 Indian) were killed and 1087 were injured (about half Indian and half African).[28] There was a tremendous loss of businesses and property. One factory, 58 stores and 247 dwellings were destroyed and two factories, 652 stores were damaged. These riots were the result of the growing misperception among the Africans about the Indian community at that point of time. The Africans perceived the ISA merchants as exploitative. These feelings were stoked by the strong anti-Indian campaign by the National Party that came to power in 1948.[29] Further the growth of an Indian merchant class was a challenge to the economic dominance of the white commercial class and they encouraged such perception to grow.[30]

The Zulu tribe is the largest in South Africa now numbering seven million. And even if not all of them belonged to Inkatha, they were still Zulus and the common Zulu resented the common Indian's relative prosperity. This attitude is the crux of the anxieties of the Indians in Kwazulu Natal region.[31] Despite the ANC ruling the center, IFP will continue to play a dominant role in the Kwazulu province. Therefore there is a natural reluctance on the part of the Indians to openly declare their loyalty to either the ANC or the IFP.

Meanwhile IFP on its part has been trying very hard to dispel this image and acknowledged the role of Indians in the nation building. It has been argued that Buthelezi's comment of "remember 1949 "to a group of Indian students at the University of Durban Westville in late 1970s was made under extreme provocation.[32] Further, there were other occasions when he had praised the work of various ISAs for the upliftment of the underprivileged Zulus. Traditionally the IFP had total support of the Zulus in The Kwazul Natal Province. Over the years the IFP has lost some of its support with the Urban Zulus inside Natal province particularly in Durban and Peitermaritzberg favouring the ANC.

Mbeki's criticism of the Indians

Mbeki's criticism of Indians can to some extent explain the ISA's swing away from ANC in the 1999 general elections and the 2000 local elections. Mbeki came under attack from the Indian community for describing it as having "ghetto psychology", "apathetic" etc. Addressing the Indian community before the elections in 1999 Mbeki had suggested that the Indian community needed to overcome its ghetto – psychology in order for South Africa to progress towards a fully integrated, non racial economy. Mbeki had urged Indians to identify themselves as part of the broader community and involve themselves in the development of a new South African society. He further emphasised that "we are all South Africans and either we swim together or sink together".[33]

He was more virulent in his disapproval of the ISA at a later date, where he raised the ire of the Indian community by describing them as "apathetic" and "supporters of former oppressors".[34] Addressing an election rally in November 2000, Mbeki had said that although Indians had participated in the struggle against apartheid they had now withdrawn into isolation, which implied that they had become 'racists'. To quote him, "Why does the Indian population in Durban which, for a century was very active in the struggle for liberation vote for the party of apartheid"?[35] His comments were a reaction to the media reports that the ISAs were disillusioned with the performance of the ANC and this could affect their voting pattern during the local government elections on December 5, 2000. Mbeki's observations had a negative impact on the traditional ANC activists and supporters among the ANC. Ms. Fatima Meer had openly expressed her disappointment and indicated that the President was wrong in his perceptions and that "the Indian community is only reacting to the ANC's failure."[36]

Nevertheless Mbeki's remarks were tame compared to the KwaZulu Natal Transport Minister S'bu Ndebele, also of the ANC. He had very categorically declared that those blacks, coloured and Indians who vote against the ANC would have problems as far as the delivery of services from the government were concerned.[37] This statement came under attack by the opposition parties as well as community at large. It shook the very foundations of a multi racial South Africa. The comments by Mbeki and later by S'bu Ndebele have tarred the image of the ANC. Right from its establishment ANC has portrayed itself as a multiracial party, representing the interests of all the communities in South Africa. These events indicated that there was a subtle change in its philosophy that had racial shades.

Conclusions

The Indian South Africans form a small though integral part of the democratic South Africa. In the past, a number of ISA had participated in the struggle against the apartheid regime with the African National Congress. A few of them form the part of the cabinet of the present elected government of South Africa. Nevertheless a study of the voting intentions of the Indian South African reveals that that they have not supported the ANC in large numbers. Here it is important to note that the ISA are not a monolith. There are differing opinions amongst the Indians in South Africa. In fact there is a pattern of cross - racial voting by the Indians in South Africa. Some Indians have supported the ANC while the others National party or the Democratic Party. This position has been influenced to some extent by the growing perceptions among the ISA of the ANC as an insular party and representing the African interests. It has also been fuelled by certain policies followed by the successive ANC governments – both under President Nelson Mandela and President Thabo Mbeki. In particular the policy of the affirmative action has put the lower income and less qualified ISA at a disadvantage. This in turn has led to their rebuff of the ANC. On the other hand, the more qualified and upper class Indians have hardly been affected by these policies and thus reaffirmed their support for the ANC.

The neo liberal economic policies of the ANC government have led to a rise in unemployment. This has affected the Africans and Indians equally. However, the rising unemployment and the relative economic divide between the Africans and the Indians have left the Indians open to hate crimes. The ineffectiveness of the ANC government to curb the rising crime and particularly the crime against the Indians has not endeared them any further. The parties such as the national party or the Democratic Party/Alliance have taken advantage of these insecurities of the Indian community. They have played the "racial card" to the hilt. Their election campaigns have focused on protecting the "Indian interests". Some of the Indians have succumbed to this logic and support the NP/DP combine. At the same time the criticism of their political position (support to NP/DA) by the ANC leaders i.e. calling them "traitors" and "supporters of the oppressors" has not helped. This environment has also led to some of the ISA becoming apathetic to the political and election process in South Africa. They feel voting has not got them any benefits and therefore their disenchantment is growing. For winning the support of Indians the ANC needs to understand their vulnerabilities and insecurities.

Notes

1. S.E. Dangor, "The myth of the 1860 settlers" *Africa Quarterly* Vol. 32, No.1-4, 1992-93 pp. 73-80
2. Ebrahim Ismail Ibrahim, "Contribution of Indians to the struggle against apartheid: 1948-1994" *Africa Quarterly* Vol. 39, No. 3, 1999 (special issue), pp. 119-134
3. Fatima Meer, " South African Indians: a historical perspective" *Africa Quarterly* Vol. 39, No. 3, 1999 (special issue), p. 104
4. Here we are not covering the latest general elections 2004 due to unavailability of data.
5. Reynold, Andrew, ed. Election '99 *South Africa: From Mandela to Mbeki.* (New york Saint Martins Press 1999) See also Karen E. Ferree. *The Micro foundations of Ethnic Voting: Evidence from South Africa.* Afrobarometer Working paper No. 40 June 2004; Cherrel Africa, Robert Mattes, Collette Herzenberg and Lerato Banda, *Political party support in South Africa: Trends Since 1994* Afrobarometer Briefing paper No. 6 2003; Karen Ferree, *Ethnicity and strategic behaviour: split Ticket Voting in Durban, 1994* Licep 'small ' project March 23, 2000; Institute for Democracy in south Africa, *Opinion 99* (Pretoria, Idasa, 1999) Human Science Research Council, *Public attitudes in Contemporary South Africa: insights from an HSRC Survey* (Pretoria, HSRC, 2002); Human Sciences Research Council, *South African social attitudes survey*, 2003. (Pretoria, HSRC, 2003).

6. Karen E. Ferree, *The Micro foundations of Ethinic Voting: Evidence from South Africa.* Afrobarometer Working paper No. 40 June 2004 pp.16-23. See also Idasa, *Election brief: Party Support in South Africa's third democratic election* (Pretoria, Idasa, 2004), p. 5.

7 *Ibid.*

8 *Ibid.*

9 Adam Habib and Sanusha Naidu, "Elections 99: was there a "Coloured" and "Indian" vote?" *Politikon* Vol. 26, No. 2, November 1999.

10 *Ibid.*

11 John S. Saul, " Cry for the beloved country: the post apartheid denouement" in Sean Jacobs and Richard Calland ed., *Thabo Mbeki's world: the politics and ideology of the South African President* (Pietermaritzburg, University of Natal Press, 2002), pp. 27-51.

12 Mohammed Allie, "As inequalities grow, South Africa's poor question the power of the ballot http:/www. globalpolicy.org/ socecon/develop/democracy/2003/11safrica.htm

13 Idasa, *Election brief: Party Support in South Africa's third democratic election* (Pretoria, Idasa, 2004), pp. 2-3.

14 *See* South African Police Service reports on crime statistics @ http//www.saps.gov.za

15 Ted Leggett, "The facts behind the figures: crime statistics 2002/ 3" *Crime Quarterly* No. 6 2003 at http://www.iss.co.za

16 Ibid see also 'South Africa Alarmed over violent crime' *Los Angeles Times* May 4, 2004.

17 National Victims Survey @http://www.iss.co.za/CJM/ SANVCSeminar02_03_04_files/frame.htm

18 *Ibid.*

19 'Ngema under fire for anti- Indian song' *Sunday Times* May 26 2002 @ http://www.suntimes.co.za/2002/05/26/news/durban/

20 *Ibid.*

21 Ajith Bridgeraj, " Inspiring the murder of Indians" a Rediff special on August 30,2002 at http:// www.rediff.com/news/2002/ aug/30spec.htm accessed on May 27, 2004.

22 *Ibid.*

23 *Ibid.*

24 *Ibid.*

25 Saul, n. 11. p. 32

26 Jagdish R . Hiremath, *Summering in South Africa: Diary of an Indian Indian* (New Delhi: Wiley Eastern Limited, 1993) p.51

27 Sèe Leonard Thompson, "The South African Indians: 'trapped in the middle "*Africa Quarterly* vol32. No.1-4 p.68

28 Ibrahim, n. 2 p. 122

29 Surendra Bhana, "Indianness reconfigured 1944-1960: The Natal Indian Congress in South Africa" *Comparative Studies in South Asia, Africa and Middle East* Vol. 17, No. 2, 1997 pp. 103-104 at http://www.cssaame.ilstu.edu/issues/V17-2/BHANA.pdf accessed on July 30, 2004.

30 *Ibid.*

31 M.K. Lokesh, "A profile of the Indian community in Kwazulu-Natal" *Africa Quarterly* Vol. 39, No. 3, 1999, pp. 61-65.

32 Jagdish Hiremath, "Indian South Africans: A contemporary portrait" *Africa Quarterly* Vol. 32, Nos.1-4, 1992-93, p. 43.

33 "Get behind new SA, Mbeki tells Indians" *Sunday Times* (Durban) March 21, 1999 at http:// www. suntimes.co.za/199/03/21/news/ Durban/nddn18.htm as accessed on March 22, 2004.

34 "Mbeki under fire for criticising Indians" *The Hindu* December 1, 2000 @ http:// www.hindunet.com/thehindu/2000/12/01/stories/ 0310007.htm

35 "South Africa Report of the High Level Committee on the Indian diaspora" p. 83.

36 "Mbeki under fire for criticising Indians" *The Hindu* December 1, 2000 @ http:// www.hindunet.com/thehindu/2000/12/01/stories/ 0310007.htm

37 Rajeni Munuswamy and others, "Silence of the ANC lambs" *Sunday Times* December 10, 2000 at http://www.suntimes.co.za/ 2000/12/10/news/news01.htm

List of Contributors

Anisur Rahman, Deputy Director, Academic Staff College, Jamia Milia Islamia University, Delhi.

Arshiya Sethi, Art activist / Scholar, Managing Trustee, Kri Foundation, New Delhi.

Md. Badrul Alam, Professor, Department of Political Science, Jamia Milia Islamia University, Delhi.

Prakash C. Jain, Professor, Centre for West Asian Studies, SIS, JNU.

Rahul Nath Choudhury, Research Fellow, IIFT, New Delhi.

Rajneesh Kumar Gupta, Ph.D Scholar, SIS/JNU.

Rakesh Kumar Patel, Ph.D Scholar, Department of Sociology, JNU.

Ruchi Tyagi, Associate Professor, Department of Political Science, Kalindi College, University of Delhi.

Ruchita Beri, Senior Research Assoiate, I.D.S.A., New Delhi.

S.K. Jain, Associate Professor, Department of Political Science, Saheed Bhagat Singh College, University of Delhi.

S.N. Sahu, Joint Secretary, Rajya Sabha Secretariat, Ministry of Parliamentary Affairs, Government of India.

Shivam, Ph.D Scholar, Department of Sociology, JNU.

Tenepalli Hari, Associate Professor, Department of Political Science, Assam University, Silchar, Assam-788011.

Tenepalli Hari, Associate Professor, Department of Political Science, Assam University, Silchar, Assam-788011.

Index

H

N

O

P

T

U